Understanding America's Gun Culture

Understanding America's Gun Culture

Second Edition

Edited by
Lisa Fisher and Craig Hovey

LEXINGTON BOOKS
Lanham • Boulder • New York • London

Published by Lexington Books
An imprint of The Rowman & Littlefield Publishing Group, Inc.
4501 Forbes Boulevard, Suite 200, Lanham, Maryland 20706
www.rowman.com

6 Tinworth Street, London SE11 5AL, United Kingdom

British Library Cataloguing in Publication Information Available

Library of Congress Cataloging-in-Publication Data

Names: Fisher, Lisa, 1972- editor. | Hovey, Craig, 1974- editor.
Title: Understanding America's gun culture / edited by Lisa Fisher and Craig Hovey.
Description: Second edition. | Lanham : Lexington Books, [2021] | Includes
    bibliographical references and index.
Identifiers: LCCN 2021025171 (print) | LCCN 2021025172 (ebook) |
        ISBN 9781793625151 (cloth) | ISBN 9781793625144 (ebook)
  Subjects: LCSH: Gun control—United States. | Firearms—Law and legislation—
    United States.
Classification: LCC HV7436 .U53 2021 (print) | LCC HV7436 (ebook) |
    DDC 363.330973—dc23
LC record available at https://lccn.loc.gov/2021025171
LC ebook record available at https://lccn.loc.gov/2021025172

Contents

Introduction to the Second Edition
Lisa Fisher and Craig Hovey

Most often, Americans who own guns say that they do so to protect themselves, their families, and their property; for hunting; and for other sports
and hobbies associated with the use and/or collection of guns (Pew Research
Center 2013). American gun culture is reflected and perpetuated in a number
of ways. Those include TV and movies as well as things like the concealed
carry movement, tremendous investments in and support for military strength,
and the enduring popularity of toy guns, including squirt guns, videogames
that provide virtual shooting experiences, and activities like paintball and
laser tag.

Although gun culture is alive and well in the U.S., the availability and use
of guns in American society remains a topic of much debate and concern.
Gun rights and gun control are generally considered contentious issues. The
Second Amendment to the U.S. Constitution, securing the right of the people
to keep and bear arms, is such a fundamental right deeply rooted in our colonial past and thriving in ideologies about individuality, personal freedom, and
personal responsibility that dramatic, sweeping policy changes are unlikely.
However, during the 2016 presidential election, it became clear that many
Americans believed that the election of Hillary Clinton would mean less
access to guns for law-abiding Americans. Indeed, the tremendous jump in
gun sales just prior to the election day and the record 27 million guns purchased in 2016 (Bedard 2017) provide evidence of that belief. We saw very
similar dynamics leading up to the 2020 presidential election, with estimates
of as many as 17 million guns purchased in 2020, and October 2020 sales
showing a 60 percent increase over October 2019 sales (Gibson 2020).

The gun culture narrative in the U.S. is complex but often focuses on gun
rights and gun violence. According to most estimates, not only are there more
guns than people in the U.S., but there are also far more gun deaths per capita

in the U.S. than in any other developed country. While almost everyone agrees that there is too much gun violence, there are serious disagreements about how to address it. It is for this reason that scholarship delving into the theoretical and practical complexities of this debate is needed.

Generally speaking, the debate on gun control and gun rights in the U.S. centers on belief in two different strategies for treating guns in society (Alters 2009). The first strategy is deterrence, advocated by organizations such as the National Rifle Association and Second Amendment Foundation. Deterrence advocates tend to support the enforcement of existing gun laws and the enactment of tougher penalties for criminal use of firearms, believing that if more citizens possess guns, criminal use of guns will be discouraged or deterred (Alters 2009). The second strategy is interdiction, advocated by organizations such as the Brady Campaign to prevent gun violence and the violence policy center. Interdiction advocates tend to support the enactment of measures to restrict access to guns, believing that doing so is the most effective means of controlling how they are used (Alters 2009).

Although these two strategies for treating guns may seem diametrically opposed, they are not. Even if people support the idea of controlling access to guns, they may be supportive of law-abiding citizens owning guns. Furthermore, if people support the deterrence strategy, they may be supportive of some measures which they believe limit access to guns in ways that provide public safety benefits, for example to children, without restricting the rights of law-abiding citizens who wish to own them (O'Neil 2016).

In fact, there are some areas of what seem to be fairly broad agreement among the American populace when it comes to guns. Gun owners and nongun owners often support policies that aim to keep guns out of the hands of people who have criminal intent (Webster 2014; Fingerhut 2016; Gallup 2017; O'Neil 2016; Pew Research Center 2018; Schaeffer 2019; Gramlich and Schaeffer 2019). Gallup found in a 2015 poll that 86 percent of Americans favor a law requiring universal background checks for all gun purchases across all fifty states (Gallup 2017). Studies by the Pew Research Center also suggest that there is widespread support for background checks and laws restricting gun access by the mentally ill among both Republicans and Democrats, with the level of support for both issues hovering just above 80 percent (Fingerhut 2016; Pew Research Center 2018).

The same Pew study found less agreement, however, when it comes to proposals to create a federal database to track gun sales or ban "assault-style" guns, with support from about 50 percent of Republicans in comparison to about 75 percent of Democrats (Fingerhut 2016).

This edited volume focuses on building understanding of some of the issues associated with U.S. gun culture and the contemporary debate about the availability and use of guns. The goal is to enrich debates that are too often entrenched, which was also the goal of 2017 Ashland Center for Nonviolence conference from which the volume arose.

This book is distinctive in that it draws on a wide variety of disciplines, presents perspectives on both sides of the debate, and delves into some of the less often discussed middle ground and nuances uncovered by recent scholarship. Contributors hail from the academic disciplines of history, social work, criminal justice, sociology, religion, and theological ethics as well as policy agencies.

Topics range from polarization in the debate to social violence to international perspectives and consideration of gun culture alongside topics like religion. Some chapters examine the issues social psychologically to help readers better understand dynamics within the debate as well as changes in gun culture over time. Others pose important ethical and philosophical questions about gun culture, even considering American gun culture alongside that of other nations. Still, other chapters address practical policy solutions for enhancing gun safety and minimizing gun violence.

This second edition of *Understanding American Gun Culture* includes literature published in the last two years, equipping us all to consider implications of those findings in an evolving American social context. The second edition also includes two new chapters, one focusing on gender within gun culture and another that features a conversation we, as editors, had with an ethnographic researcher with broad expertise in gun culture and research and policy trends.

The goal of this volume is to broaden the discussion. As editors, we did not attempt to modify the perspectives of the contributors but, rather, suggested means of refining chapters to highlight the strengths of their respective contributions as they relate to understanding American gun culture. For that reason, the volume represents a greater diversity of perspectives about guns and gun culture than Americans may be accustomed to hearing.

While it isn't possible to capture the full range of perspectives on America's gun culture within the scope of a single volume, these contributions collectively demonstrate that the issues they cover are not simple but stem from deep-seated cultural values about safety, protection, rights, family, and national identity that are rooted in our nation's history. Given these intricacies, the book also exemplifies the value that can come from stepping back from the situation to consider the complexities of gun culture and rejecting abridged, oversimplified point-counterpoint arguments that limit our ability to truly examine this important social issue. Our hope is that, taken together, the chapters collectively provide a thought-provoking compilation of articles that offer insightful findings, assist readers in considering novel theoretical and practical implications, and, most importantly, invite further exploration of the topic.

REFERENCES

Alters, Sandra. 2009. *Gun Control: Restricting Rights or Protecting People?* Gale: Gale Virtual Reference Library.

Bedard, Paul. 2017. "Boom: Record 27 Million Guns Bought in 2016." *Washington Examiner*, January 4. http://www.washingtonexaminer.com/boom-record-27-million-guns-bought-in-2016/.

Fingerhut, Hannah. 2016. "Pew Research Center Report: Five Facts About Guns in the United States." http://www.pewresearch.org/fact-tank/2016/01/05/5-facts-about guns-in-the-united-states/.

Gallup. 2017. "Guns: Historical Trends." http://www.gallup.com/poll/1645/Guns. aspx (citing data from as early as 1959 to 2016).

Gibson, Kate. 2020. "U.S. Gun Sales Surge to Record High in 2020." *CBS News Report*. https://www.cbsnews.com/news/gun-sales-record-high-2020/.

Gramlich, John, and Katherine Schaeffer. 2019. "Pew Research Center Report: 7 Facts About Guns in the U.S." https://www.pewresearch.org/fact-tank/2019/10/22 /facts-about-guns-in-united-states/.

O'Neil, Kathleen. 2016. "Research Shows Gun Owners Support Gun Violence Prevention." *Science* 352(6289): 1069.

Pew Research Center. 2013. "Why Own a Gun? Protection is Now Top Reason: Perspectives of Gun-Owners, Non-Owners." http://www.people-press.org/2013/03 /12/ why-own-a-gun-protection-is-now-top-reason/.

Pew Research Center. 2018. "Gun Policy Remains Divisive, But Proposals Still Draw Bipartisan Support." https://www.pewresearch.org/politics/2018/10/18/gun-policy -remains-divisive-but-several-proposals-still-draw-bipartisan-support/.

Schaeffer, Katherine. 2019. "Share of Americans Who Favor Stricter Gun Laws Has Increased Since 2017." https://www.pewresearch.org/fact-tank/2019/10/16/share-of-americans-who-favor-stricter-gun-laws-has-increased-since-2017/.

Webster, Daniel. 2014. "American Paths to Fewer Gun Deaths." *TEDMEDTalks*. http://www.jhsph.edu/research/centers-and-institutes/johns-hopkins-center-for-gu n -policy-and-research/daniel-webster-tedmed-talk.html.

Chapter 1

The Social Construction of Polarization in the Discourse of Gun Rights vs. Gun Control*

Lisa Fisher

Americans' perceptions and stances on guns appear to be highly polarized. Even the words "rights" and "control" lend to this polarization; however, recent studies also suggest some areas of rather significant agreement on gun issues among the American populace (Webster 2014; Gallup 2017; Fingerhut 2016; O'Neil 2016; Pew Research Center 2018; Schaeffer 2019; Gramlich and Schaeffer 2019) that are less often heard about in the discourse.

Applying the social psychological theory of Berger and Luckmann (1966) and Zerubavel (1991), the literary criticism theory of Kenneth Burke (1969), and the method of qualitative content analysis, I analyzed a sample of 726 pages of publicly available online information pertaining to "gun control" and "gun rights." I argue that the rhetorical strategies employed by advocates on both sides of the issue socially construct the polarization by advancing arguments about being under siege, seeking to identify and magnify the sources of threat as they see them, cleanly demarcating their position relative to the other, and seeking to simplify and essentialize their messages down to key talking points. Areas of agreement are seemingly ignored or downplayed, which results in them being less visible to the American public, perpetuates polarization, and seemingly strengthens the resolve of those at the poles to remain there.

BACKGROUND

There is a plethora of publicly available information about each side of the gun debate. Much of the information is easily accessible online and

---

* Margaret Clark provided research assistance for this study.

focuses on delineating perspectives; providing background on the laws and legislative actions in different states and at the federal level; and citing statistics on crime, injuries, and deaths due to homicide, suicide, and accidental death, particularly that of children, relating to gun use (e.g. Alters 2009; MacKay 2013; Merino 2013). In addition, the long-standing debate about the interpretation of the Second Amendment's reference to a "well-regulated militia" and whether that indicates an individual right to bear arms or something akin to today's National Guard has been a frequent topic (ex. Williams 2003; Hal-brook 2008; Cornell and Kozuskanich 2013; Waldman 2014).

Social science scholars have also dug deeper to understand cultural factors underlying the commonly cited outcome measures and debates about guns in American society. Studies have reexamined the long-studied origins of American gun culture (McGrath 2018) as well as regional gun subcultures in the U.S. (Boine et al. 2020) and changes in those cultures over time (Yamane 2017; Boine et al. 2020).

In addition to investigating these foundational ideas, scholars have examined how the ideas within the gun debate are shared and understood. Studies examining social media posts to understand the construction of policy narratives that those on both sides of the gun rights vs. gun control debate use storytelling to identify victims, assert blame, recognize "heroes," and offer policy solutions (Merry 2016). Relatedly, when mass shootings are discussed, studies suggest a shift in the framing of accounts from individual-level events to much broader societal-level concerns with increased focus on mental health (DeFoster and Swalve 2018). Scholars have also examined ways that research on guns in American society is approached and understood, tracing a shift from a focus on scientific evidence to the processes of interpretation and meaning-making (Carlson 2020).

The construction of gun debate narratives has also been examined in relation to gender. Studies have largely focused on associations between guns, masculinity, and heroism (Connell 2005; Carlson 2013; Joyce 2018), romanticized notions of masculine frontier heroism (Atlas 2019; Melzer 2009), and ways that predominant ideas about guns and masculinity emphasize white hegemonic masculinity (Burbick 2006; Carlson 2013; Stroud 2012) which is set in contrast to stereotypical notions of black hyper-masculine criminality (Harris 1999; Harcourt 2006; Simon 2007). More recent studies have examined the relationship between gun culture and women's experiences. These studies delve into socially constructed ideas about crime being perpetuated by dangerous strangers and women's vulnerability to those circumstances (Carlson 2013) as well as messages of women's empowerment through participation in gun culture, as found in the narrative of the National Rifle Association (NRA) (Schwartz 2019).

Although gendered notions about women's vulnerability are present in the discourse, recent Pew Research Center poll data suggest that men and women are about equally likely (65 percent and 71 percent, respectively) to cite protection as a major reason for owning a gun (Gramlich and Schaeffer 2019). Attending to the construction of these narratives provides useful insights into the issues, but it is also important to consider the quality of the information woven into the narratives.

Some have questioned the level of accuracy and objectivity of this information, particularly when it comes to presenting public sentiment. Given the reliance on polls, it can be difficult to gauge the importance of issues to respondents, for example, do people really care about these issues or are they just making a forced choice between alternatives that do not matter all that much to them minutes after they are polled (Alters 2009)? There are also questions as to whether polls may underreport the number of guns in American households, as some people may be hesitant to reveal that information in surveys (Ikeda 1994; Wellford et al. 2005).

The wording of questions can also make a difference in how people respond. For example, if people are asked to indicate whether gun rights or gun control is more important to them and are provided with only a dichotomous choice, those respondents are not able to indicate any type of hybrid or middle ground stance. Polling practices employed by even the most reputable organizations, such as Gallup, attempt to distill the issue down to a single percentage point based on a simplified framing of very complex issues. Although this has become a hallmark of the practices of quantifying and simplifying data points in the information and knowledge society, it does not lend to capturing and understanding the full complexity of Americans' stances on issues.

Wording choices in academic studies also reveal impactful subtleties of framing. For example, Merry's (2016) statement, "While one side emphasizes the importance of sensible 'gun reform,' the other decries 'gun control' and emphasizes the right of individuals to own firearms for self-defense" (377), implicitly presents those who argue for "gun reform" as "sensible" and those who argue against "gun control" as complaining and criticizing.

Studies suggest that those who feel strongest about issues and are most informed about them do tend to show attitude bias, or what Taber and Lodge (2006) dubbed "motivated skepticism," toward arguments that run counter to their beliefs. Findings suggest that people may even demonstrate stronger beliefs after being exposed to counter arguments and increased resolve to defend their beliefs (Taber and Lodge 2006; Abelson and Prentice 1989). A more recent study also found that when neutral information is lacking, as we often find in the gun debate in the U.S., motivated skepticism is more likely to occur (Montpetit and Lachapelle 2017). Further, findings shed light on the process of policy learning and key dynamics behind opinion shifting, opinion softening, opinion hardening, and position-taking (Montpetit and Lachapelle 2017). Also of significance to the gun debate is the notion that when at least one side of a debate demonstrates openness to considering the other side's perspective and evidence, policy learning and movement toward opinion convergence are more likely to occur (Montpetit and Lachapelle 2017).

Looking specifically at areas of known convergence in the gun debate, poll data suggest strong across-the-board support for background checks for private gun sales and gun show sales, barring gun purchases by those known to have mental illness (Schaeffer 2019), and restrictions on gun purchases by those on federal watch lists (Pew Research Center 2018). Polling organizations are also tracking what appear to be small increases in support for stricter gun laws and banning of high-capacity ammunition magazines in the U.S. in the last few years (Schaeffer 2019). Although this research suggests how and where processes of convergence might be possible or beneficial in the gun debate, a great deal of attention is still paid to understanding the divide.

When it comes to support for gun rights vs. gun control, the divide often falls along political party lines (Dimock 2017; Pew Research Center 2018; Schaeffer 2019). Although recent studies have found within-party differences based on whether or not people are gun owners themselves (Joslyn 2020; Pew Research Center 2018), the primary focus in the debate is the fact that many who identify as politically conservative tend to align with the "gun rights" side of the debate, whereas those who identify as politically liberal are more likely to align with the "gun control" side. The widest gap appears when pollsters delve into questions of whether or not teachers should be armed and concealed carry rights expanded (Pew Research Center 2018). When it comes to opinions on gun laws, 86 percent of those who identify as Democrat/leaning Democrat say stricter gun laws are needed vs. 31 percent who identify as Republican/leaning Republican (Gramlich and Schaeffer 2019). These trends have maintained for at least the past twenty years (Gramlich and Schaeffer 2019). The biggest change in that time period has been that Republicans have grown dramatically more committed to gun rights and less supportive of measures of gun control (Pew Research Center 2018). Independents also indicate greater support for gun rights and less support for gun control. Democrats, while more likely to support gun control, have changed little in their support for either cause over the 20-year period (Gramlich and Schaeffer 2019).

Relatedly, there is evidence that party lines influence Americans' choices of media outlets, which impacts the sources of information consumed about gun rights and gun control. According to a 2014 report from the Pew Research Center entitled "Political Polarization and Media Habits," Americans often choose media outlets that mesh with their ideological beliefs, particularly those who identify as consistently conservative or consistently liberal (Mitchell et al. 2014). The study also found that those at both the left and right ends of the spectrum, who together comprise about 20% of the public overall, have a greater impact on the political process than do those with more mixed ideological views. They are the most likely to vote, donate to campaigns and participate directly in politics. (Mitchell et al. 2014)

Clearly, there is a division between the most politically active liberals and the most politically active conservatives, and this division is likely to carry implications for how the narratives in this debate are constructed as well as whether and the degree to which narratives are presented as polarized.

Looking across this literature, there is a tremendous amount of information circulating about the issue of gun rights vs. gun control, and much of the information focuses on differences between the two perspectives. Studies suggest a fairly high degree of public agreement on some of the key issues within the larger debate, yet given the likelihood that ideological differences about guns fall along party lines and the likelihood that people are choosing media outlets that mesh with those ideological notions, much of what the general public hears about gun rights vs. gun control appears highly polarized without much middle ground.

Although scholars have examined processes of social construction and narrative building in this debate, little attention has been paid to the processes of social construction that maintain the focus on polarization. Instead, most assume that the polarization is real and objectively defined as such, increasing focus on the divide itself. Studies are needed to examine the language and meaning construction employed on both sides of the debate to understand more about how it is that areas of agreement are downplayed and areas of disagreement are emphasized, as these social processes lend to continued perceptions of divisiveness and detract from the ability of those on both sides of the issue to engage in meaningful dialogue about guns in American society.

THEORETICAL FRAMEWORK

Berger and Luckmann's (1966) Social Construction of Reality, Zerubavel's (1991) "Islands of Meaning," and Burke's (1969) literary theory provide a useful lens with which to view the processes of social construction at work in the discourse on gun rights vs. gun control in the U.S.

Berger and Luckmann (1966) argue that social order and thus definitions of reality are produced by human beings through complex means. In this view, people create and come to understand reality through a dialectical process involving externalization, objectivation, and internalization. People first create social order through their actions (externalization), then experience the created reality as objective (objectivation), and then, through that experience, come to internalize and understand it through the lens of subjective experience. Thus, "(s)ociety is a human product. Society is an objective reality. Man (sic) is a social product" (Berger and Luckmann 1966, 6).

This process of the social construction of reality is largely transparent to those who participate in it. As Berger and Luckmann (1966) state, "[S] ince (people) themselves have shaped this world in the course of a shared biography which they can remember, the world thus shaped appears fully transparent to them" (Berger and Luckmann 1966, 4). In social psychology, this is sometimes referred to as the "fish in water" effect; everything the fish does occurs within and depends on the water, but the fish does not recognize the water as providing that context. For humans engaging in social construction of reality then, the social world appears historically based and objective as it congeals into an internally logical conceptual universe and symbolic world. When older members of the social world (or, in this case, advocates on either side of the gun debate) attempt to teach their ways and beliefs to the younger members (those seeking more information about the gun debate), the transmission renders these processes partially visible, which also reveals mechanisms of institutionalization.

During the transmission process, the ways and beliefs of the social world take on greater significance. Berger and Luckmann (1966) state

> The objectivity of the institutional world "thickens" and "hardens" not only for the children, but (by a mirror effect) for the parents as well. The "There we go again" (of routine actions) now becomes "This is how these things are done." A world so regarded attains a firmness in consciousness; it becomes real in an ever more massive way and it can no longer be changed so readily. For the children, especially in the early phase of their socialization into it, it becomes the world. For the parents, it loses its playful quality and becomes "serious." For the children, the parentally transmitted world is not fully transparent. (Berger and Luckmann 1966, 4–5)

In order for objectivation and internalization to occur then, there must be clear delineation of the ways and beliefs, which must include direction and teaching about the nature of the social reality. To the individuals who inhabit the social world, the facts are undeniable and powerful not only by the nature of their "facticity" but because of the control mechanisms at work to maintain the social world.

Once a social world is created, its objectivity and "facticity" are often threatened, either through variations in the processes of socialization or direct threats to legitimacy. These threats are problematic and require inhabitants of the social world to work to maintain their conceptual universe. Berger and Luckmann (1966) discuss two "conceptual machineries of universe-maintenance": therapy and nihilation. When threats to the conceptual world are encountered, one of these strategies must be employed to address the deviant views.

According to the theory, therapy is enacted as a tool to change minds. Using this machinery, those who adhere to the ways and beliefs of the conceptual universe identify the deviant(s) and, using knowledge from their conceptual universe, attempt to help them to see the error of their ways. Therapy is successful when it achieves resocialization into the symbolic universe and the deviant(s) can be brought back into the fold. Whereas therapy is enacted to bring deviants back into the conceptual universe, nihilation is used to shut them out entirely.

Nihilation is enacted to deny the view of reality set forth by the deviant(s) and discredit their ways and beliefs to neutralize the threat of the alternative perspectives by presenting them as inferior, nonsensical, and unworthy of attention. As this happens, nihilation also functions to affirm the reasonableness and validity of the conceptual universe being defended. Any arguments made by the deviant(s) are translated, within the machinery of nihilation, as defensive and indicative that, deep down, the deviant(s) know(s) the "truth" (Berger and Luckmann 1966). The successful employment of these machineries and the perpetuation of the symbolic universe as a whole rely on complex processes of meaning-making.

A symbolic universe is constructed through processes of naming and defining. Zerubavel (1991) states, citing earlier work by Burke (1969)

(T)he word define derives from the Latin word for boundary . . . To define something is to mark its boundaries, to surround it with a mental fence that separates it from everything else . . . These lines play a critical role in the construction of social reality . . . Examining how we draw them is therefore critical to any effort to understand our social order. (12)

While categorizing is a fundamental human activity (Zerubavel 1991), just like the construction of reality within social worlds, the activity of categorizing is a social process. Words are important indicators of meaning, values, and assumptions in the society. In this way, the words employed in the perpetuation and maintenance of a social world act as "mental fences," to use Burke's words that indicate values and assumptions. These words and the dividing lines that they signify are neither objective nor remarkable but hail from different definitions of reality in the debate on gun rights vs. gun control.

The two camps appear to inhabit different social worlds garnered by very different definitions of reality when it comes to the possession and value of guns in American society. These worlds are conceptual universes largely defined by the mental fences erected around "rights" and "control." The ways that those in the debate use these terms signify how they define and name circumstances and experiences within their respective socially constructed conceptual universes. Whereas "rights" focus on those things which are imbued upon people as citizens and may be described as "inalienable," "control" focuses on regulation, tightening up, and perhaps even domination. Even though many gun control advocates have eschewed the term "gun control" in favor of "violence prevention," the word "control" still weighs heavily in the debate as it remains, to gun rights advocates, a salient descriptor for interpreting the actions of those seeking to place more restrictions on gun ownership in American society.

Viewing "gun rights" and "gun control" as opposing camps, arguments made by each side make visible very different trajectories of thought stemming from different definitions of reality based on different naming and categorizing within their respective symbolic universes and social worlds. If a person feels particularly strongly in one way or another about the issue of guns in American society, they enter the conceptual universe of the respective camp. It is also possible that those who are undecided on the issue could be the targets of therapy from either camp. Once entering or telegraphing possible entrance to a camp, they are socialized using the naming and definitions in that conceptual universe and learn acceptable and "normal" ways to think and feel about the issue of gun rights vs. gun control within that camp. Those meanings then shape perceptions and influence all future meaning interpretation and interaction (Sandstrom et al. 2014) within the camps and between them.

Both camps engage in case building to legitimize their views and present those views as wholly internally logical. Their arguments make visible very different trajectories of thought stemming from different definitions of reality based on different naming and categorizing within their respective symbolic universes and social worlds.

Therapy may be enacted to change the minds of wavering or dissenting deviants or those seeking information to understand differences between the two camps. We see some evidence of this conceptual machinery at work with the tremendous amount of information available online as to the primary arguments on both sides of the debate, delineating perspectives and providing background on the laws and legislative actions being taken in different states and at the federal level. However, given the focus on the two polarized camps and discursive emphasis on opposition between those camps, therapy may be perceived as ineffectual and futile.

This would then support reliance on nihilation as a conceptual machinery to dismiss and discredit opponents, which could help to explain the increasingly contentious nature of gun debate discourse in the U.S. The prevalent use of nihilation in the larger arenas of American politics and media may also reinforce and perpetuate reliance on that conceptual machinery as a rational, valued discursive strategy. The normalization of nihilation in the larger social context also likely obscures limitations imposed by that conceptual machinery, which means that both camps accept the "facticity" (Berger and Luckmann 1966) of the diametrical opposition between their social worlds, assume convergence is no longer possible, and, driven by motivated skepticism (Tabor and Lodge 2006), become increasingly committed to entrenched polarized positions, which further shapes the discursive strategies they employ.

METHOD

To collect data, I asked my research assistant, Margaret Clark, to conduct a Google search for publicly available online information. Between January 23 and January 26, 2017, she conducted two separate searches, using the terms "gun rights" and then "gun control," and pulled the first thirty results that came up for each search. The goal was to capture the most frequently accessed information on those topics, excluding paid sites and content farms.

Working with each set of results, Clark clicked on each of the sixty links to locate articles and other content behind the links. In some cases, one result would yield a series of links, which was a collection of articles either referenced together or linked separately by the article title. When that happened, Clark followed each link to locate the content behind it, to capture all the data that came up in those first sixty results. Content included articles written by media sources or advocacy groups, government documents, ads, and posted comments by readers. Clark compiled all the content that came up under each search, saving the links and printing hard copies.

As I began reviewing the data, I excluded pages that were completely or mostly blank or unrelated to guns, for example, pages at the end of an article that only provided a list of links to other articles in a publication. When I came across a duplicate article that identically matched one I had already analyzed, I removed it. This was not duplicate content but identical duplicate pages that came up under both searches because the words "gun rights" and "gun control" appeared together in the content. Altogether, I removed 198 duplicate pages. I also excluded one six-page article that came up under "gun control," which addressed ways to resist Trump during the presidential inauguration, because there were no mentions of gun rights or gun control policy or perspectives in the article.

Not counting the pages excluded during data analysis, the total data capture was 726 unique pages of content. Of that total, 356 primarily addressed "gun rights," and 370 primarily addressed "gun control."

To analyze the data, I conducted conventional qualitative content analysis (Hsieh and Shannon 2005). Qualitative content analysis is the "interpretation of the content of text data through the systematic classification process of coding and identifying themes or patterns" (Hsieh and Shannon 2005, 1278). This method was particularly useful because it allowed me to examine varied presentations of content (quantitative, qualitative, or a mixture of the two) across the body of data. Most of the data qualified as what I would call "web-friendly" content, shorter in page and paragraph length with simpler phrasing for consumption by the general public; however, there were also research center reports and some professional white papers that cited many references.

As I read all the data, I noted main ideas in each section. I paid particular attention to the language employed and noted that there were tremendous consistencies in the types of words that were employed by the respective "camps." Employing the constant comparative method (Glaser and Strauss 1967), I engaged in open coding to inductively derive themes and patterns indicative of both explicit and implicit meaning in the text. As I moved through the body of data, I compared segments of text that appeared to evidence a theme with other segments of text already assigned to that thematic category. I then reevaluated and adjusted the categories as I moved through the process of coding and constant comparison. I kept a journal to catalog the incidence of each theme and the page number on which it was found, which allowed me to easily locate the major themes. My goals were to identify the major themes, dimensions of the thematic categories, relationships between categories, and any patterns that were evidenced when I looked across the body of data (Bradley 1993).

FINDINGS

I found that rhetorical tactics employed by those on both sides of the gun rights vs. gun control issue socially construct the polarization and divisiveness known to characterize this debate. Each side presents themselves as being under siege from threats to their rights, safety, and well-being. Both sides identify and magnify, or draw attention to and provide evidence of the sources of threat as they see them, which also allows each to relay and affirm their own vision for how guns should be viewed and used in American society.

Gun Rights under Siege

Gun rights advocates presented gun rights as essential rights under threat, for example:

> "The right to keep and bear arms is a vital element of the liberal order that our Founding Fathers handed down to us." (151, www.freedomsphoenix.com/s ubjects/00050-LAST-gun-rights.htm)

> "Gun Owners Civil Rights Alliance has fought for Minnesota gun rights since 1989. Our members contribute and participate because they believe that SELF DEFENSE IS A HUMAN RIGHT." (282: https://www.gocra.org/)

By invoking imagery of founding fathers and presenting gun rights as a central feature of American life entrusted to citizens to protect, gun rights activists appealed to notions of patriotism and duty. The essentiality of these rights was underscored by words like "vital" and the implication of a continuing need to protect these rights as the legacy of a proud national past.

There were also many references to gun owners stepping forward and using their guns for protection of themselves or others. Example headlines read:

> "Former Felon with Restored Gun Rights Saved Trooper in Arizona Ambush." (42: www.bearingarms.com/bob-o/201701/25/hero-saved-arizona-trooper-felon -restored-gun-rights/)

> "Pizza Hut Worker Kills Robber With Own Personal Handgun." (23: www.n ewsmax.com/PrintTemplate.aspx/?nodeid=770060)

Content that came up from the NRA website also featured these types of stories, for example:

> "Clerk shoots at crook during robbery." (288: https://www.nraila.org/gun-laws/)

> "Man who fired shot that killed Penbrook robbery suspect won't be charged." (288: https://www.nraila.org/gun-laws/)

These stories emphasized the righteous and benevolent behavior of gun owners who, at their own peril, exercise their Second Amendment rights and stop violent acts. Sometimes these stories contained religious references, for example:

"A man with a concealed handgun shot an armed robber . . . . The good
Samaritan with the (concealed handgun) license could have been injured." (23:
Reyner 2017, www.newsmax.com/PrintTemplate.aspx/?nodeid=770060)

A good Samaritan is a reference to an admirable person who steps in to do
good for others' sake. The person who shot the robber was referred to as a
good Samaritan. Just like other law-abiding gun owners, the person with the
concealed handgun stood up for good.

Another example of a religious reference described the right to bear arms
as:

"(C)onferred . . . by our Creator to safeguard life, liberty, and property, as well
as to help preserve the independence of the nation." (131: https://www.constitu
tionparty.com/gun-control-1/)

To describe the right to bear arms as God given elevates the cause and the
calling of those who support gun rights and own guns, positioning them as
playing a special and honorable role in society as they act to protect life,
liberty, and property. These narratives also reflected rhetorical subthemes
about heroes and villains, as Merry (2016) found. The telling and retelling of
these stories provided a means of redemption, purification of intentions, and,
despite the challenges of being under siege, a call to stay the course. For gun
rights advocates, protecting this divinely bestowed right hinged on protecting
the Second Amendment.

Many gun rights advocates invoked the Second Amendment in their arguments. For example, readers commented on stories, charging that government
officials

"(W)ork(ed) tirelessly to nullify the 2nd amendment because their system will
not work with an armed populous." (686: http://www.breitbart.com/big-gove
rnment/2017/01/26/six-gun-controls-president-trump-can-undo/)

A statement on Trump's campaign website argued:

"The right of the people to keep and bear Arms shall not be infringed upon.
Period." (27: https://www.donaldjtrump.com/policies/constitution-and-second
-amendment)

Anyone or anything that threatened gun ownership was treated as a serious
threat that required vigilant action to take a stand for gun rights. For example,
a Minnesota gun rights advocacy group's website stated:

"Anti-rights legislators didn't waste a moment exploiting the tragedy (of the gun deaths in Newtown, CT), and introduced almost a dozen gun control bills . . . including universal registration . . . Their goal was universal gun registration, which they called universal background checks." (283: https://www.gocra.org)

The site went on to say:

"We flooded the Minnesota State Capitol . . . and rallied thousands . . . to contact their representatives and tell them to say NO to infringing our civil rights." (283: https://www.gocra.org)

A report from Reuters cited a statement in a lawsuit:

"Massachusetts prohibits firearms it pejoratively defines as 'assault weapons,' which is a non-technical, entirely fabricated, and political term of uncertain definition and scope." (191: Malone 2017, http://www.reuters.com/article/us-m assachusetts-guns-idUSKBN15821V)

These statements not only presented the gun control laws as unfair and requiring vigilant action but also reflecting the misinformed nature of judgmental lawmakers who did not even know technical specifics about which they were legislating but rather just sloppily referred to them in ways that met their political goals to restrict gun rights. The latter article went on to say:

"We are drawing a line in the sand where Massachusetts' gun control agenda tramples the fundamental individual right to defend oneself and family in the home." (191: Malone 2017, http://www.reuters.com/article/us-massachusetts -guns-idUSKBN15821V)

Drawing a line in the sand implied outlining territory, mobilizing for action, and making clear that when the line was crossed, action would ensue. Referring to the state's gun control agenda as "trampling" individual rights demonstrated a belief that the state had brashly and unapologetically ignored the rights of people seeking to protect themselves, their families, and their homes, which suggests a belief that gun rights were indeed under siege.

In relation to the same lawsuit, another article said:

"If there's anything positive about AG Healey's unprecedented and unilateral politically motivated attack on lawful citizens, it is that our plight has been pushed onto the national civil rights stage." (193: http://www.foxnews.com/ politics/2017/01/24/gun-rights-activists-sue-over-massachusetss-firearms-laws .print.html)

Referring to gun rights activism as a "plight" and the activities of this politician to restrict gun rights as an "attack" presented gun rights as being under
continuing siege.

Gun rights advocates believed the Massachusetts lawsuit was just one of
many to come in what was described as a targeted campaign against gun
rights. As one article stated:

> "In addition to the anti-gun groups, such as Brady Campaign to Prevent Gun
> Violence and the Michael Bloomberg-backed Everytown for Gun Safety,
> there's a new, organized effort by groups of attorneys nationwide committed
> to rolling back gun rights through targeted lawsuits." (290: Taft 2016, http://ijr
> .com/2016/12/765876-new-gun-laws-coming-in-2017-tell-you-all-you-need-to
> -know-about-who-states-view-as-the-real-threats/)

By listing the gun control entities alongside the mention of the organized
movement of attorneys desiring to take away gun rights, the threat was
described as real, present, and mounting.

Skepticism of President Obama's motives was particularly prevalent.
Many writers discussed how they believed President Obama kept gun rights
and gun rights advocates under siege. For example, one article asked:

> "Will UN-style gun control be rammed down our throats? . . . . Gun ban imports
> . . . Microstamping of firearms . . . Ammunition bans . . . This anti-gun wish list
> could be part of a secret trade agreement that President Obama is getting ready
> to spring on the Congress . . . . This trade pact is called 'fast track,' and what it
> means is that Obama can write any form of gun control he chooses into a trade
> agreement . . . It can't be filibustered . . . It can't be amended . . . and the GOP
> can't refuse to consider it." (303: https://www.infowars.com/secret-deal-could
> -contain-a-myriad-of-gun-restrictions-ammo-bans/)

The statement invoked imagery of the use of force against gun owners. It was
accentuated by the mentions of bans as part of an "anti-gun wish list," which
the author argued was not only a threat to gun rights but the larger congressional processes.

As a result of this distrust, the undoing of President Obama's actions was
celebrated as a victory over injustice and evidence that, even though gun
rights were under siege, there could be victories along the way in the continuing fight, for example:

> "Congress is poised to unravel one of the Obama administration's midnight
> regulations that could prevent Social Security disability beneficiaries from buy-
> ing guns." (24: Lucas 2017, http://dailysignal.com/print?post_id=310941)

"Protecting Americans' fundamental rights is a top priority. . . and that includes undoing this Obama-era power grab against our Second Amendment rights." (25: Lucas 2017, http://dailysignal.com/print?post_id=310941)

The word "unravel" implied there was a need to not only undo the regulations but come in to responsibly clean up the mess made by them. Describing these as "midnight regulations" also implied that Obama tried to "sneak them in" prior to the end of his presidency. These statements suggest perceptions of ill-intent, distrust, and the need to be vigilant against messy, confusing, under-handed tactics perpetuated by government officials against gun owners.

Although Obama was highly criticized as impeding gun rights, Hillary Clinton was described as a potentially larger threat, for example:

"Clinton has proven she holds no respect for the rule of law and the Constitution of the United States . . . (she) will appoint radical Supreme Court justices that will virtually abolish the Second Amendment . . . NRA CEO Wayne LaPierre explained, 'If she could, Hillary would ban every gun, destroy every magazine, run an entire national security industry right into the ground' and put gun-own-ers' names on a government registration list.'" (NBC News, May 20, 2016) (28: https://www.donaldjtrump.com/policies/constitution-and-second-amendment)

This was a damning array of ways that Clinton was expected to not only keep gun rights under siege but take actions to severely cripple the Second Amendment. LaPierre's quote then punctuated the threat with references to banning, destroying, ruining, and further monitoring gun owners, all of which demonstrated the condition of being under siege.

A statement by Trump during a 2016 presidential debate, in response to what he would prioritize when selecting a Supreme Court Justice confirmed these beliefs, even used the words *under siege*:

"People that will respect the U.S. Constitution. Also, the Second Amendment, which is totally under siege by people like Clinton." (http://www.ontheissues.o rg/2016/Hillary_Clinton_Gun_Control.htm)

Clinton's responses were dismissed as elusive talk from an untrustworthy politician keeping gun rights under siege. Exemplifying this idea, a website defined gun control as:

"(L)eftist doublespeak and a term used when advocating unconstitutional laws designed to disarm the American people by restricting the lawful purchase, ownership or carrying of guns under the guise of 'public safety'." (161: http:// www.conservapedia.com/Gun_control)

The description went on to state:

> "The emasculation of the citizenry by gun control also arguably reduces the
> resistance of a society to intimidation." (163: http://www.conservapedia.com/
> Gun_control)

The focus remained on the need to be vigilant and aware of the tricks that
could be used to enact gun control and disarmament, which were not only
threatening but symbolically placed alongside castration, a means of removing one's very virility.

There were continuing conversations mirroring "this is what they say, but
this is what they mean," demonstrating a belief that gun control advocates
were deceitful in their efforts. For example, after President Obama voiced
praise for Australia's gun control efforts, an article stated:

> "You simply cannot praise Australia's gun-laws without praising the country's
> mass confiscation program. That is Australia's law."

The article continued:

> "When gun control advocates say they want Australian gun control laws in the
> United States, what they are really saying is that they want gun confiscation in
> the United States." (310: http://thefederalist.com/2015/06/25/the-australia-gun
> -control-fallacy/)

> "(T)hey keep speaking in code and talk about 'Australia' and not 'wholesale
> confiscation'." (313: http://thefederalist.com/2015/06/25/the-australia-gun-cont
> rol-fallacy/)

Seeing through the "leftist doublespeak" and "code" was presented as highly
important in the continuing fight for gun rights because gun control was
viewed as a dangerous, slippery slope that could easily lead to confiscation
and disarmament, along with other risks:

> "(L)eftists and liberals alike push gun control because it increases the de-pendency
> of voters on government for protection while disarming citizens capable of fight-
> ing back against tyranny." (161: http://www.conservapedia.com/Gun_control)

These messages appeared to be intended as warnings and proof of the need to
continue to defend and fight for gun rights.

Historical evidence was also proffered. There were several books listed
relating to the dangers of gun control. One entitled *Death by Gun Control:*

The Human Cost of Victim Disarmament, by Aaron Zelman and Richard Stevens, featured cover art depicting a crime scene outline of a dead body with a puddle of blood near the head of the figure. The descriptive text about the book read:

> "The message is simple: Disarmed people are neither free nor safe—they become the criminals' prey and the tyrants' playthings. When the civilians are defenseless and their government goes bad, however, thousands and millions of innocents die. Professor R.J. Rummel, author of the monumental book Death by Government, said: 'Concentrated political power is the most dangerous thing on earth.' For power to concentrate and become dangerous, the citizens must be disarmed. What disarms the citizens? The idea of 'gun control.' . . . It comes in many forms, but in every form it enables the evildoers and works against righteous defense." (31: http://jpfo.org/filegen-a-m/deathgc.htm)

The overarching idea presented was that gun control and disarmament lead to death because, when people are disarmed, they are unable to "righteously" defend themselves.

A similar argument was presented in the promotional copy of Stephen Holbrook's book *Gun Control in the Third Reich: Disarming the Jews and "Enemies of the State,"* featured on the Independent Institute's website, which read, in part:

> "(R)estricting firearms membership . . . rendered political opponents and the Jews defenseless. A skeptic could surmise that a better-armed populace might have made no difference, but the National Socialist regime . . . ruthlessly suppressed firearm ownership." (614: http://www.independent.org/guncontrol/)

Conservapedia also mentioned this historical reference along with an example of gun control enacted by Josef Stalin:

> "The Nazis . . . forbade Jews from owning guns or any other weapon . . . Josef Stalin, . . . a murderer of over 20 million people, infamously supported gun control in the fear that his evil regime might be torn down." (168: http://www .conservapedia.com/Gun_control)

Citing examples of Hitler and Stalin, two of the most notorious dictators in world history, as gun control politicians suggested that gun control was not only emasculating, it was life-threatening. This information painted the picture that disarmament was only one step away from genocide.

JPFO also provides "The Genocide Chart," which links gun control laws in various nations in the twentieth century to genocidal actions of government.

One of the events included was Rwanda's 1994 genocide, which the chart states resulted in the deaths of 800,000 people, justified by an "overall 'gun control' scheme of register(ing) guns, owners, (and) ammunition; (requiring that) owners must justify need; (making) concealable guns illegal; (and exercising) confiscating powers" (31–32: http://jpfo.org/filegen-a-m/deathgc .htm). The evidence elevated the import of the fight for gun rights by intensifying the level of threat faced if people passively failed to act while under siege. In short, maintaining gun rights was essential to fighting back, which gun rights advocates presented as a guaranteed response to any attempted confiscation. As one publication said:

> "Let there be no doubt. Gun confiscation would have to be administered by a force of arms. I do not expect that those who dismissed their fellow citizens for clinging bitterly to their guns are so naïve that they imagine these people will suddenly cease their bitter clinging when some nice young man knocks on their door and says, 'Hello, I'm from the government and I'm here to take your guns.'" (313: http://thefederalist.com/2015/06/25/the-australia-gun-control-fal lacy/)

This statement called to mind the worst fears of gun owners by painting a picture of someone "from the government" coming to their house to seize their guns. It appeared to be a way to rally the troops, so to speak, by issuing a contemptuous warning that gun rights advocates would fight back in the face of such a threat, supporting their central argument about the essentiality of gun rights as a deterrent. The contrary yet confident tenor of this argument also seemed to define the parameters of the debate and construct the space within which gun control advocates could make their case.

Gun Control under Siege

Using parallel tactics but relying on a different definition of the situation and different content, gun control advocates also presented themselves as being under siege as they strove to argue the essentiality of control against seemingly mounting support for gun rights. Whereas the definition of threat for gun rights advocates hinged on a generalized threat and the need to be responsive and always-vigilant, the definition of threat for gun control advocates centered on the guns themselves and the broad access to them in American society, for example:

> "Year after year, we see a powerful correlation—states with stronger laws have fewer gun deaths per capita while states with weak laws have more gun deaths. When you drill down into specific issues, like domestic violence, mental health,

and gun trafficking, the results are even clearer: gun laws work." (244: Law Center to Prevent Gun Violence, http://smartgunlaws.org/)

"Weak gun laws" that provided unfettered access were presented as introducing risk, increasing the number of deaths, and reducing the safety of the populace. However, gun control advocates often eschewed the language of "gun control" in favor of "violence prevention." For example:

> "We can—and must—end the epidemic of gun violence." (196: https://www.hil laryclinton.com/issues/gun-violence-prevention/)

The same site described related actions that Clinton said she would take if elected president:

> "Take on the gun lobby by removing the industry's sweeping legal protection for illegal and irresponsible actions, which makes it almost impossible for people to hold them accountable." (197: https://www.hillaryclinton.com/is-sues /gun-violence-prevention/)

Clinton also spoke about this during a 2015 Democratic primary debate in Las Vegas, saying:

> "This has gone on too long, and it's time the entire country stood up against the NRA." (230: http://www.ontheissues.org/2016/Hillary_Clinton_Gun_Con -trol.htm)

The campaign statements present the gun lobby and, in particular, the NRA as threats that Clinton was poised to meet with what were often described as "sensible, reasonable" approaches to gun regulation. Demonstrating this, Clinton's campaign website stated:

> "Hillary has a record of advocating for commonsense approaches to reduce gun violence." (196: https://www.hillaryclinton.com/issues/gun-violence-preventio n/)

"Commonsense approaches" were described as stemming from the actions of benevolent politicians to protect the greater good, which suggested that these matters were best handled by rational government. But because gun rights advocates were generally skeptical and distrustful of the motives of government to control guns and viewed them as wholesale infringements on their Second Amendment rights, "commonsense approaches" were often perceived as just further evidence of "leftist doublespeak."

Gun control advocates seemed to desire to move away from engaging on the issue of the Second Amendment as it appeared to be a losing battle, for example:

> "I'm happy to consider the debate on the Second Amendment closed. Reopening that debate is not what we should be doing." (322: Goldberg 2012, http://www .theatlantic.com/magazine/achive/2012/12/the-case-for-more-guns-and-more -gun-control/309161/)

Yet, the amendment remained an issue at the center of the debate due to the insistence of gun rights advocates. During a 2016 presidential debate, Clinton was asked about it. Her reply was:

> "I'm not looking to repeal the second amendment. I'm not looking to take people's guns away, but I am looking for more support for the reasonable efforts that need to be undertaken to keep guns out of the wrong hands." (111: Hains 2016, www.realclearpolitics.com/video/2016/07/31/Clinton_every_right_that _we_have_is_open_to_and_subject_to_reasonable_regulations.htm)

The gun rights side was able to force Clinton to engage on it. Clinton framed her statement as a defensive position focused on what she was "not looking" to do. She was attempting to defend her stance under siege of gun rights advocates who alleged her desire to repeal the Second Amendment, but, given the difficulty of arguing that "reasonable efforts" would not infringe on Second Amendment rights, Clinton shifted to keeping guns "out of the wrong hands," to move the conversation away from rights infringements and toward violence prevention.

I found many sources that provided statistics on gun violence and deaths, for example:

> "Gun violence is a crisis. 117,000 Americans are shot every year, a rate that outpaces our peers by orders of magnitude. Horrific mass shootings dominate the headlines. Firearms amplify domestic violence . . . Underserved urban communities are pervaded by shootings . . . Over 20,000 Americans kill themselves with guns every year, and news stories regularly report episodes of toddlers shooting themselves or their parents with poorly stored firearms." (244: Law Center to Prevent Gun Violence, http://smartgunlaws.org/)

> "Every year, about 33,000 Americans die from gun violence. Americans are nearly 20 times more likely to be murdered with a gun than people [in] other high-income peer countries." (339: Kelly 2017, http://www.huffingtonpost. com/entry/the-fight-for-common-sense-gun-safety-policies-are-far-from-over_ us_58861924e4b096b4a232ffe7)

The statistics were presented to demonstrate that the American people were under siege by guns. Death statistics tended to focus on homicides, suicides, and gun accident deaths, especially the accidental deaths of children, which functioned to bring the conversation back to the central focus of protection against guns. Of this, Clinton said:

> "We have to do everything possible to keep guns out of the hands of children . . . It does not make sense for us at this point in our history to turn our backs on the reality that there are too many guns and too many children have access to those guns—and we have to act to prevent that." (231: http://www.ontheissu es.org/2016/Hillary_Clinton_Gun_Control.htm)

The need for prevention and protection was heightened when it came to the threat of mass shootings, as revealed in the following sample headlines:

> "Charleston: Dylann Roof Unrepentant for Emanuel AME Church Massacre." (18: www.democracynow.org/2017/1/5/headlines/charleston_dylann_roof_un -repentant_for_emanuel_ame_church_massacre)

> "Alaskan Veteran Is Indicted in Fort Lauderdale Airport Rampage." (586: https ://www.nytimes.com/2017/01/26/us/esteban-santiago-ft-lauderdale-air-port-sh ooting.html)

Mass shootings were discussed frequently by gun control advocates as they identified and magnified threat. This stood in stark contrast to the gun rights advocates, who did not often discuss mass shootings or indicated that mass shootings could be countered through deterrence or more effective mental health intervention. Gun control advocates presented the situation as emergent, calling for politicians to:

> "(W)rite laws that (could) protect our families and communities from the scourge of gun violence." (245: Law Center to Prevent Gun Violence, http:// smartgunlaws.org/)

Describing gun violence as a "scourge" was an attempt to magnify the problem and position it as a plague or curse. Although guns were constructed as the primary threat, the power and reach of the NRA were also viewed as threats. As one article said:

> "(I)f lawmakers seem to tiptoe around gun issues, its likely at least in part because the NRA and other gun rights groups are loaded for bear with a seemingly limitless stash of cash ammunition." (157: https://www.opensecrets.org/ news/issues/guns)

The friendly relationship between the NRA and the Trump administration seemed to exacerbate this threat in the minds of gun control advocates. Shannon Watts, founder of Moms Demand Action, put it this way:

"Trump owes an enormous political debt to his most potent 2016 backer: the NRA, which spent more than $30 million to get him elected." (662: Dickinson 2017, http://www.rollingstone.com/politics/features/meet-the-leaders-of-the-trump-resistance-w460844)

Watts went on to say:

"With the NRA's champion in office, we see ourselves playing a lot of defense." (663: Dickinson 2017, http://www.rollingstone.com/politics/features/meet-the-leaders-of-the-trump-resistance-w460844)

Against the formidable opponents, gun control advocates seemed to believe they would remain under siege in the foreseeable future, but they indicated that they were ready for it:

"(W)e will be prepared to fight the new administration and the new Congress on policies that threaten our communities. The gun lobby is seeking to allow guns in schools . . . They're also pushing to ignore states' rights by mandating the unrestricted 'concealed carry' of firearms and allow free access to dangerous silencers . . . These policies are a public safety threat." (339: Kelly 2017, http://www.huffingtonpost.com/entry/the-fight-for-common-sense-gun-safety-polici es-are-far-from-over_us_58861924e4b096b4a232ffe7)

In addition to facing the primary threats introduced by what they viewed as unfettered access to guns in American society and the violence that they argued stemmed from that access, gun control advocates faced the threat of gun rights advocates and their legislative agenda. This description of the agenda demonstrated gun control advocates' perceptions of the power and force behind gun rights advocacy. By listing all the different gun rights goals, the excerpt above rhetorically compounds the notion of threat as coming from many different angles in the course of civic life and perpetuates the "us vs. them" polarization between gun rights and gun control.

Simplifying, Translating, and Summarizing

Looking across all the data, there seemed to be a tremendous amount of focus on simplifying, translating, and summarizing the issues as advocates on both sides made the case that they were under siege and identified and magnified the threats they saw. The simplifying, translating, and summarizing were clearly undertaken as a means of creating content judged to be easier to navigate and more reader-friendly, which is often expected in the information age, but they also served a rhetorical function that only furthered the perception of polarization between the two sides.

Although most of the content fell cleanly on one side of the debate or the other, some sources attempted to present summarized versions of the debate as a whole, for example:

"The 'gimme all the guns' side says it's about being able to defend yourself and your family. But the 'keep those away from me' side points out that tens of thousands of people are killed by guns each year, and since Americans don't wear colonial clothes anymore, it's time to stop making guns so accessible . . . . WHAT THE GOP SAYS . . . Guns don't kill people, people kill people. We need more guns in the hands of those who could fight back . . . WHAT DEMOCRATS SAY . . . We don't want to ban guns altogether. But the Second Amendment was written hundreds of years ago. It doesn't make sense in today's world to have military assault weapons on the streets."(1: www.theskimm.com /2016-election/issues/gun_control)

The paragraph above offered an overview of the "GOP vs. DEMOCRATS" stance on guns, which would likely draw readers in its capacity to simplify and interpret the complexities of the issue; however, a latent effect was that the issue was presented in a way that focused only on the points of diametrical opposition between the two sides. Although this may have been unintentional, there did appear to be cases where it was intentional, for example:

"This issue really can be boiled down to one point: No American should be denied their constitutional rights." (24: Lucas 2017, http://dailysignal.com/print ?post_id=310941)

"(If people are) barred from acquiring firearms . . . (I)t deprives them of their civil rights without due process of law." (588: Crane, Baldwin and Blackman 2017, http://thehill.com/blogs/congress-blog/civil-rights/316139-congress-sh ould-rescind-social-security-regulation-that)

These simplified interpretations functioned like "closing arguments" and presented issues as open-and-shut cases in support of one position or the other. Another characteristic example came from a statement by Gwen Patton of the Pink Pistols in her criticism of California's response to the San Bernardino shootings:

"California has responded . . . by blaming the gun. Ohio's response to the Ohio State terror attack was to blame the terrorist. We don't see any efforts in Ohio to ban motor vehicles or sharp implements." (293: Taft 2016, http://ijr.com/ 2016/12/765876-new-gun-laws-coming-in-2017-tell-you-all-you-need-to-know -about-who-states-view-as-the-real-threats/)

The quote continued:

"The contrast . . . is as stark as night and day. While California is making it more difficult to buy ammunition with draconian rules requiring background checks and limits on how many rounds you can buy, Ohio is increasing the number of places where concealed carriers can legally carry." (299: Taft 2016, http://ijr .com/2016/12/765876-new-gun-laws-coming-in-2017-tell-you-all-you-need-to -know-about-who-states-view-as-the-real-threats/)

The statement summarized the issue by contrasting the approaches of the two states, elevating one as "reasonable" and vilifying the other as "draconian" and evidencing that gun rights were indeed under siege. By distilling the argument down to simple "sides" without acknowledging any possible middle ground, this type of summarizing and simplifying further lent to the social construction of polarization between the sides.

Some of the statements offered in this regard were very brief, for example:

"We emphasize that when guns are outlawed, only outlaws will have them." (131: https://www.constitutionparty.com/gun-control-1/)

"The only thing that stops a bad buy with a gun is a good guy with a gun" (http:/ /www.npr.org/2012/12/21/167824766/nra-only-thing-that-stops-a-bad-guy-wit h-a-gun-is-a-good-guy-with-a-gun)

The statements above focus on the generalized threat of harm in American society and the need for gun owners to remain at the ready to address those threats. The "good guy, bad guy" contrast, stated by Wayne LaPierre of the NRA, was widely shared and quoted. These statements were presented in a very straightforward fashion, which seemed to match the perception among gun rights advocates that the issue itself was very simple: Guns are good. Gun control is bad. In addition to being effective rhetorically, these statements lent to being remembered and repeated.

It seemed that the summaries, interpretations, and simplifications offered by those on the gun rights side of the issue were much more common and generally more adversarial, polarizing, and pathologizing of those on the other side, for example:

"Oddly enough, many politicians who support gun control, in addition to making terrible arguments for it, are surrounded by armed security guards . . . Naturally, their calls for more gun-free zones while being constantly protected by men with guns make them total hypocrites. If they truly believe that gun control works and that civilians should be disarmed, they should first give up their own armed security. Of course, nobody expects them to do this, because everybody knows that they'd be easy targets if they did." (417: Tartt 2016, http://thelib-ertarianrepublic.com)

This statement criticized and mocked gun control advocates, issuing a challenge to act in line with their words and arguing the ultimate "truth" and rationality of the gun rights stance.

At times, challenges were directed at specific people. For example, NRATV's Grant Stinchfield challenged Illinois Congressman Luis Gutierrez, even offering $500 to a charity if the congressman accepted the challenge, with the following statement:

"You have the guts to go on MSNBC . . . I dare you to come on NRATV and defend your lies." (307: http://www.ammoland.com/2017/01/328652/#axzz4 WvpcUO6K)

These challenges not only demonstrated the confidence that gun rights advocates had in their views and the surety they felt about being on the side of justice and lawfulness, but they also upped the aggression level of ill-will and distrust for the other side, which lent to even greater appearance of polarization between the sides.

Even if face-to-face debate did not happen often, gun rights advocates displayed a great deal of frustration and cynicism about continued calls for gun control, which they acted to discredit, for example:

"Gun control doesn't work, so let's stop pretending that it does . . . Let's try something that allows good people to fight back against bad people who are bigger and stronger that they are. Let's try something that respects natural and Constitutional rights. Let's try something that prevents people from being dependent on the police who likely won't get there until its too late. Let's try freedom." (417: Tartt 2016, http://thelibertarianrepublic.com)

"Calls for stronger background checks . . . or a new ban on "assault weapons" have become formulaic. They're like winding a Victrola: The record resumes spinning but it plays the same old song . . . (H)owever, it is worth listening to . . . (It) shows the chorus of the media and gun-control advocates . . . at their most disingenuous if not dishonest." (308: http://thefederalist.com/2015/06/25/the-australia-gun-control-fallacy/)

These statements were very common and offered summary interpretations of gun control arguments and proposals as downright foolish. The statements were dismissive, combative, demonstrating continued distrust, and underscoring polarization between the two sides. There was a clear tenor indicating that gun rights advocates "had heard it all before" but were not falling for it. This suggested the rationality and righteousness of the gun rights cause, which stood in contrast to the "disingenuous" gun control cause. There were also continued references to being under siege, for example presenting bad people as "bigger and stronger" and arguing that guns were necessary in the fight, especially since people being threatened by others often must wait at least a few minutes for police to respond. In short, gun rights advocates argued that gun owners could rely only on themselves and rhetorically positioned freedom as premised on gun rights.

Sentiments reflecting this same tenor were present in many forms, for example appearing as reader comments to gun control articles:

"Support gun control—Win elections—Choose one." (625: http://www.dailykos.com/story/2017/01/22/1623335/-Guns-vs-People)

The use of short phrases was a particularly effective tool for presenting a simplified and memorable argument. In this case, the writer seemed to argue that the will of the people was against gun control, and if politicians or people chose to pursue it, they would lose, suggesting that the gun rights cause represented both might and right. Generally, these short phrases were used by those on the gun rights side of the debate.

On the gun control side, efforts to simplify were uncommon, which could parallel the apparent belief among gun control advocates that the issue was actually quite complex given the need, as they saw it, to create new laws to address specific problems in American society.

That being said, though, those on the gun rights side of the issue just seemed more apt to engage in this type of "straight shooting" argument construction, and it appeared to be quite effective for them. Not only did it reflect gun rights advocates' seeming desire to tell it "like it was," but it also directly countered the perceived artificial complexity of "leftist doublespeak."

The data and analysis offered here demonstrate that this debate is an ongoing social process that largely takes the form of point–counterpoint. Both sides present themselves as threatened, but they are not on equal footing. The gun rights side seems to exercise more power in defining the situation and dictating the terms of the discourse such that the gun control side is more often responding to statements and allegations levied by the gun rights side than proactively relaying their own stance.

As the gun control side responds, they attempt to clearly demarcate their position in relation to that of gun rights advocates. Because of the commonality of comparing perspectives on political issues, the points of opposition between the two camps become the focus as they themselves and the general public seek to delineate clean differences between them. Given the focus on points of opposition, the two sides are only understood in opposition to each other, which draws attention to them as two separate, entrenched, warring, polarized positions.

Furthermore, the conversation is dominated by the most vocal advocates on both sides of the issue, who are most committed to their positions, most likely to step forward to argue and advance their respective cause and less likely than more moderate voices to concede ground in the debate, which only underscores the polarization.

As they make their respective cases, both also attempt to simplify, interpret, and summarize the issues for readers, which results in messages being essentialized to streamlined arguments punctuated by keywords and phrases that leave virtually no middle ground between the two positions. Thus, the absence of moderate voices, magnified definitions of threat, and essentialized arguments with a lack of middle ground between them lend to a socially and rhetorically constructed polarization between the two sides.

CONCLUSION

Given the method of sampling data for this study, the data analyzed likely represent some of the most frequently accessed online content about the gun rights vs. gun control debate. The critical mass of Americans with online access who wish to learn about these issues and read content on the most popular gun rights or gun control sites are likely accessing some of these very pages.

Most of the content analyzed in this project came down rather cleanly on one side of the issue or the other and therefore proved very useful for examining the social and rhetorical construction of polarization. Alters' (2009) distinction between the strategies of deterrence and interdiction was also useful in that it provided an organizing framework for me to consider the tactics enacted by those on both sides of the issue.

Given the polarization constructed between perspectives, there did not appear to be any gray area or middle ground; however, this is reflective of the processes of social and rhetorical construction as the most vocal advocates on both sides of the issue duked it out online. In the process, differences between the two sides were magnified in order to cleanly delineate who stood for what, and these differences become even more pronounced as both sides engaged in efforts to simplify, interpret, and summarize the issue and questions at hand for their readers. Together, these social and rhetorical processes lent to the appearance of impassable polarization between those on either side of the debate, despite the presence of data showing that Americans are not necessarily sharply divided on all sub-issues within the gun rights vs. gun control debate (Webster 2014; Gallup 2017; Fingerhut 2016; O'Neil 2016; Pew Research Center 2018; Schaeffer 2019; Gramlich and Schaeffer 2019). In short, the middle ground simply "fell out" of the discussion in favor of orderly side-by-side checkboxes that allow a point–counterpoint comparison of the views and the ways that they differ.

Berger and Luckmann's (1966) theoretical constructs of the symbolic universe and strategies for dealing with information incongruent with a universe of meaning were particularly helpful. Given the different definitions of the situation present on opposing sides of this debate, it was useful to consider the opposing factions as inhabiting different symbolic worlds.

It seemed that the gun control side, while they did at times demonstrate the use of nihilation as a means of discounting and discrediting counter arguments, most often relied on strategies akin to therapy. This suggests that those on the gun control side may view it as essential to win converts, which could also explain why the gun control side has been found to offer more evidence in building their case (Smith-Walter et al. 2013). It could be that the strategy of therapy, which, as Berger and Luckmann (1966) state, lends to a focus on mind-changing, requires more information. My findings also suggest another possible explanation for why arguments on the gun control side may be longer.

I found that online content authors on the gun rights side seemed to consistently, strategically seek means of simplifying and interpreting arguments such that arguments were just generally shorter. I also found that, given the power that the gun rights side exercised over defining the agenda of the gun control side, the gun control side may feel generally compelled to offer more information in the interest of defending their stance.

Those on the gun rights side seemed more inclined to rely on nihilation as a strategy for not only discrediting but obliterating counter arguments. It may be that therapy is enacted in some contexts wherein it is strategic and practical for gun rights advocates to win converts and socialize them within the symbolic universe of gun rights. However, based on the findings here, these strategies do not appear to be enacted by gun rights advocates when they are "separated by a line in the sand" from the most committed, diametrically opposed gun control advocates, as it may be perceived as futile. For gun rights advocates, it is also a very open-and-shut case.

Allport and Postman's (1947) classic experiment about the social psychological processes involved in the transmission of rumors may also be useful here to understand how social construction of meaning is shaped by humans' selective attention to, interpretation, and sharing of information. Allport and Postman said that, as information is shared, three processes occur: leveling, sharpening, and assimilation. Leveling occurs when some details are dropped from the story being told. Sharpening occurs when other details are highlighted, and assimilation occurs when details are altered to fit the teller's preconceived notions and biases and assist them in making sense of information and situations (Sandstrom et al. 2014). By selectively dropping some information, attending closely to other information, and altering or reframing some information in the service of one's perspective, information is tacitly distilled.

In addition to these processes, scholars should further examine Tabor and Lodge's (2006) motivated skepticism theory and Montpetit and Lachapelle's (2017) findings on opinion shifting, opinion softening and hardening, and position-taking in relation to the gun debate discourse. Researchers should apply these fruitful concepts to studies of groups actively engaged in polarized positions (Mitchell et al. 2014) as well as those occupying less known middle ground stances. Lastly, given my findings about both sides of the debate presenting themselves as being under siege and magnifying sources of threat as they saw them suggests that Gerbner's (1995) mean-world syndrome theory may also prove insightful in future studies.

Given the understanding of gun rights vs. gun control as a very divisive issue in American society and the likelihood that the most vocal advocates on both sides of the debate seek out information that meshes with what they already think about the issue, the information they read is likely to be distilled and simplified accordingly, further supporting the appearance of polarization between diametrically opposed camps.

Although distillation and simplification may appear to be effective strategies for presenting an argument in a way that encourages people to "take a side," there are major downsides to effectively cutting out the middle ground. Not only does it limit the capacity for people to consider complexities and nuances of issues that may lend to better understanding of the problems and possible solutions, but it also lends to ignoring information and considerations that do not neatly fit in the point–counterpoint debate. In addition, there may be a risk that opposing sides stop seeking means of productive engagement and convergence, becoming ever more comfortable in their entrenched positions as they seek to recruit and socialize newcomers and vigilantly defend their social world.

Critically overshadowed in this long-standing, entrenched debate between the most vocal advocates on both sides is the fact that African American men are disproportionately negatively affected by gun violence. They are dramatically more likely to be shot and killed by a gun, yet discussions of this problem are exceedingly rare in the discourse, as policy solutions are more likely to favor the protection of socioeconomically privileged White Americans, for example suburban school children. I found very little mention of the dangers to African American men in the data I analyzed. Future research should examine this issue in relation to the larger discourse of gun rights vs. gun control as well as on its own, outside of the limiting framework of the polarized debate, to consider means of addressing this issue of social justice.

The social construction of polarization requires the interaction of those on both sides of the gun rights vs. gun control debate; however, of all the actors involved, the NRA clearly drives the processes of social and rhetorical construction and exercises a great deal of influence over the argument construction of those on both sides of the debate. Future research should consider how this impacts the ability of people on both sides of the issue to engage in meaningful debate. Future studies should also dig deeper into citizens' perspectives about guns in ways that do not require forced-choice dichotomies in the interest of simplifying public sentiment but instead effectively engage with the complexities and nuances of this important issue and encourage meaningful dialogue about guns in American society.

REFERENCES

Abelson, Robert P., and D. A. Prentice. 1989. "Beliefs as Possessions: A Functional Perspective." In *Attitude Structure and Function*, edited by Anthony R. Pratkanis, Steven James Breckler, and Anthony G. Greenwald, 361–381. Hillsdale, NJ: Erlbaum.

Allport, G., and L. Postman. 1947. *The Psychology of Rumor*. New York: Holt, Rinehart and Winston.

Alters, Sandra. 2009. *Gun Control: Restricting Rights or Protecting People?* Gale: Gale Virtual Reference Library.

Atlas, Pierre. 2019. "Of Peaceable Kingdoms and Lawless Frontiers: Exploring the Relationship Between History, Mythology, and Gun Culture in the North American West." *The American Review of Canadian Studies*, 49(1): 25–49.

Bedard, Paul. 2017. "Boom: Record 27 Million Guns Bought in 2016." *Washington Examiner*, January 4. http://www.washingtonexaminer.com/boom-record-27-million-guns-bought-in-2016/.

Berger, P., and T. Luckmann. 1966. *The Social Construction of Reality*. New York: Random House.

Boine, Claire, Michal Siegel, Craig Ross, Eric Fleegler, and Ted Alcorn. 2020. "What is Gun Culture? Cultural Variation and Trends Across the United States." *Humanities and Social Sciences Communications*, 7(21): 1–12.

Bradley, Jana. 1993. "Methodological Issues and Practices in Qualitative Research." *Library Quarterly*, 63: 431–449.

Burbick, J. 2006. *Gun Show Nation: Gun Culture and American Democracy.* New York: W.W. Norton.

Burke, K. 1969 [1945]. *A Grammar of Motives.* Berkeley, CA: University of California Press.

Carlson, Jennifer. 2013. "The Equalizer? Crime, Vulnerability and Gender in Pro-Gun Discourse." *Feminist Criminology*, 9(1): 59–83.

Carlson, Jennifer. 2020. "Gun Studies and the Politics of Evidence." *Annual Review of Law and Social Science*, 16: 183–202.

Connell, R. 2005. *Masculinities.* Berkeley, CA: University of California Press.

Cornell, Saul, and Nathan Kozuskanich. 2013. *The Second Amendment on Trial: Critical Essays on District of Columbia vs. Heller.* Massachusetts: University of Massachusetts Press.

DeFoster, Ruth, and Natashia Swalve. 2018. "Guns, Culture, or Mental Health? Framing Mass Shootings as a Public Health Crisis." *Health Communication*, 33(10): 1211–1222.

Dimock, Michael. 2017. "How America Changed During Barack Obama's Presidency." *Pew Research Center.* http://www.pewresearch.org/2017/01/10/how -amer-ica-changed-during-barach-obamas-presidency/.

Fingerhut, Hannah. 2016. "Pew Research Center Report: Five Facts About Guns in the United States." http://www.pewresearch.org/fact-tank/2016/01/05/5-facts-abou t-guns-in-the-united-states/.

Gallup. 2017. "Guns: Historical Trends." http://www.gallup.com/poll/1645/Guns.asp x (citing data from as early as 1959 to 2016).

Glaser, Barney, and Anselm Strauss. 1967. *The Discovery of Grounded Theory: Strategies for Qualitative Research.* Chicago: Aldine.

Gramlich, John, and Katherine Schaeffer. 2019. "Pew Research Center Report: 7 Facts About Guns in the U.S." https://www.pewresearch.org/fact-tank/2019/10/22/facts-about-guns-in-united-states/#:~:text=7%20facts%20about%20guns%20in%20the%20 U.S.%201,gun%20laws%20should%20be%20stricter.%20More%20items...%20.

Hains, Tim. 2016. "Clinton: Every Right That We Have Is Open to and Subject to Reasonable Regulations." *Real Clear Politics.* http://www.realclearpolitics.com/ video/2016/07/31/clinton_every_right_that_we_have_is_open_to_and_subject_to _reasonable_regulations.html.

Halbrook, Stephen. 2008. *The Founders' Second Amendment: Origins of the Right to Bear Arms.* Chicago: Ivan R. Dee.

Harcourt, B. 2006. *Against Prediction.* Chicago, IL: University of Chicago Press.

Harris, D. 1999. "The Stories, the Statistics, and the Law: Why 'Driving While Black' Matters." *Minnesota Law Review*, 84: 265–326.

Hsieh, Hsiu-Fang, and Sarah Shannon. 2005. "Three Approaches to Qualitative Content Analysis." *Qualitative Health Research*, 15(9): 1277–1288.

Ikeda, Robin. 1994. "Estimated Intruder-Related Firearm Retrievals in U.S. Households, 1994." *U.S. Centers for Disease Control and Prevention.*

Joslyn, Mark. 2020. *The Gun Gap: The Influence of Gun Ownership on Political Behavior and Attitudes*. New York: Oxford University Press.

Joyce, Justin. 2018. *Gunslinging Justice: The American Culture of Gun Violence in Westerns and the Law*. Manchester: Manchester University Press.

Mayring, Phillipp. 2000. "Qualitative Content Analysis." *Qualitative Social Research*, 1(2). Last accessed March 18, 2017. http://www.qualitative-research.net/index.php/fqs/article/view/1089.

McBeth, Mark K., Elizabeth A. Shanahan, and Michael D. Jones. 2005. "The Science of Storytelling: Measuring Policy Beliefs in Greater Yellowstone." *Society and Natural Resources*, 18: 413–429.

McGrath, Roger. 2018. "The American Gun Culture (Michael Bellesiles and the Historical Inaccuracies of 'Arming America: The Origins of National Gun Culture')." *New American*, 34(1): 17–21.

Melzer, S. 2009. *Gun Crusaders: The NRA's Culture War*. New York: New York University Press.

Merino, Noel. 2013. *Gun Control*. Detroit: Greenhaven Press.

Merry, Melissa. 2016. "Constructing Policy Narratives in 140 Characters or Less: The Case of Gun Policy Organizations." *The Policy Studies Journal*, 44(4): 373–395.

Mitchell, Amy, Jeffrey Gottfried, Jocelyn Kiley, and Katerina Eva Matsa. 2014. "Political Polarization and Media Habits." *Pew Research Center, Media and Journalism*. http://www.journalism.org/2014/10/21/political-polarization-media-habits/.

Monpetit, Eric, and Erick Lachapelle. 2017. "Policy Learning, Motivated Skepticism, and the Politics of Shale Gas Development in British Columbia and Quebec." *Policy and Society*, 36(2): 195–214.

O'Neil, Kathleen. 2016. "Research Shows Gun Owners Support Gun Violence Prevention." *Science*, 352(6289): 1069.

Pew Research Center. 2016. "Opinions on Gun Policy and the 2016 Campaign." *August 16 Report*. http://www.people-press.org/2016/08/26/opinions-on-gun-policy-and-the-2016-campaign/.

Pew Research Center. 2018. "Gun Policy Remains Divisive, But Proposals Still Draw Bipartisan Support." https://www.pewresearch.org/politics/2018/10/18/gun-policy-remains-divisive-but-several-proposals-still-draw-bipartisan-support/.

Sandstrom, Kent, Kathryn Lively, Daniel Martin, and Gary Alan Fine. 2014. *Symbols, Selves and Social Reality: A Symbolic Interactionist Approach to Social Psychology and Sociology*. New York: Oxford University Press.

Schaeffer, Katherine. 2019. "Share of Americans Who Favor Stricter Gun Laws Has Increased Since 2017." https://www.pewresearch.org/fact-tank/2019/10/16/share-of-americans-who-favor-stricter-gun-laws-has-increased-since-2017/.

Schwartz, Noah. 2019. "Called to Arms: The NRA, The Gun Culture, and Women." *Critical Policy Studies*, December.

Simon, J. 2007. *Governing Through Crime: How the War on Crime Transformed American Democracy and Created a Culture of Fear*. New York: Oxford University Press.

Smith-Walter, Aaron, Holly L. Peterson, Ashley Reynolds, and Michael D. Jones. 2013. "Gun Stories: How Evidence Shapes Firearm Policy in the United States." Paper presented at the Fall Research Conference of the Association for Public Policy and Analysis Management (APPAM), Washington, D.C.

Stroud, A. (2012). "Good Guys with Guns: Hegemonic Masculinity and Concealed Handguns." *Gender & Society*, 26: 216–238.

Taber, Charles, and Milton Lodge. 2006. "Motivated Skepticism in the Evaluation of Political Beliefs." *American Journal of Political Science*, 50(3): 755–769.

Waldman, Michael. 2014. *The Second Amendment: A Biography*. Simon & Schuster.

Webster, Daniel. 2014. "American Paths to Fewer Gun Deaths." *TEDMEDTalks*. http://www.jhsph.edu/research/centers-and-institutes/johns-hopkins-center-for-gun-policy-and-research/daniel-webster-tedmed-talk.html.

Wellford, Charles, John Pepper, and Carol Petrie (eds). 2005. *Firearms and Violence: A Critical Review*. By the Committee to Improve Research and Data on Firearms and the Committee on Law and Justice, National Research Council of the National Academies. National Academies Press.

Williams, David. 2003. *The Mythic Meaning of the Second Amendment: Taming Political Violence in a Constitutional Republic*. Ebook. New Haven: Yale University Press.

Yamane, David. 2017. "The Sociology of U.S. Gun Culture." *Sociology Compass*, 11(7). https://onlinelibrary.wiley.com/doi/full/10.1111/soc4.12497 2017.

Zerubavel, Eviatar. 1991. "Islands of Meaning." In *The Production of Reality: Essays and Readings on Social Interaction*, edited by J. O'Brien, 5th ed., 11–27. Thousand Oaks: Pine Forge Press.

Chapter 2

American Gun Culture Encounters Christian Ethics

A Clash of Narratives

Mark Ryan

THE "THEO-ETHICS" OF THE GUN

The ethical debate about guns in America is permeated by political individualism. Public arguments for greater gun control or more extensive gun liberty both assume the government faces its citizens fundamentally as individuals who bear rights and suffer benefits and harms. No substantive account of the common good underlies this relationship. Because of the atomistic nature of our political discourse, it is little wonder the debate does not take us very far.

In this chapter, I will interpret some central rhetorical and behavioral practices regarding guns in America as manifestations of distinct "theo-ethical visions" in contention. By a "theo-ethical vision," I intend in part the underlying vision of persons-in-society on which these practices rest, though often in inchoate form. The current debate, for example, rests on a vision where society exists to serve the interests of the private individual, or to curtail said interests when the question is interference with the rights of other individuals. The nature of the concept is brought out by comparison to Charles Taylor's use of the notion of "social imaginaries" to distinguish worlds of human significance, or ontological landscapes for meaningful action toward and among others (Taylor 2007, 171–176). These are, Taylor argues, always articulated in narratives that orient human agents to their world. I choose instead the term theo-ethical vision to highlight that, as Taylor also argues, the orientation to reality is also an orientation to something ultimate (Taylor 1989, 25–52). Further, many of those under consideration here will be religious persons who call this ultimate "God."

In the first section, I describe two ways that guns become involved in generating a theo-ethical vision of social relationships in America. While they differ in appearance, my aim is to unearth the deeper commonalities among them. That discussion serves the further aim of examining how Christians are contributing to a theo-ethics of guns in America. While, as a Christian theologian, I contend this theo-ethics is mistaken—indeed, I will argue that Christians should be offering an alternative to the theo-ethical vision inherent in American gun culture—, it is by no means clear that Christians themselves are living in step with their story. Rather, a better case can be made for the contrary.

To see what an alternative, Christian theo-ethical vision might look like requires moving beyond modern individualism. For this, I turn to Aristotle and especially his account of friendship found in the *Nichomachean Ethics*, an account that was taken up by later Christian authors. Aristotle's notion of friendship, in contrast to individualism, assumes that a certain kind of social participation precedes and provides the condition for mature human action. Yet to display the Christian alternative means taking this account deeper into the Christian narrative, and I turn to Thomas Aquinas's adaptation of Aristotelian friendship to do this. Through this description, my hope is to display the incoherence of much Christian participation in American gun culture.

Throughout the chapter, I will make reference to Abigail Disney's 2015 film *The Armor of Light* which tells the story of conservative, Christian lobbyist Rev. Rob Schenck, alongside that of gun control spokeswoman and activist Lucy McBath. Whereas Schenck approaches the issue of gun violence from an establishment position in the political arm of conservative Evangelicalism, McBath is propelled into activism when a National Rifle Association (NRA) member, seemingly emboldeneed by Florida's "Stand Your Ground" law, shot down her unarmed son at a gas station. The film documents Schenck's process of falling out with the agenda of Conservative Christian lobbyists, at least with regard to gun rights, alongside McBath's rise to a position of public prominence in the effort to reform American gun laws away from "Stand Your Ground."

HOW "AMERICA" SHAPES A "THEO-ETHICS OF THE GUN"

In this section, I suggest that what we are confronting in contemporary American gun culture are theo-ethical visions that project a social reality within which human agents may orient themselves to others. In particular, I call attention to two ways in which guns play a shaping role in the imagining of social relations in America. While one has been rhetorically honed as the position of a powerful lobby and thus more recognizable than the other, neither contradicts the basic premises of individualism, wherein fear and violence are normalized, as other people can readily be configured as threats to one's own person.

The first vision begins with the notion of America as a sacred polity wherein guns operate as a symbol of the American ethos of freedom. Within this frame, guns, their ownership, and use have become powerful symbols of what constitutes America as a unique nation. For instance, in a speech delivered to a large gathering of members of the NRA, spokesman Wayne LaPierre proclaims that the right of private citizens to own and operate guns encapsualates all of the freedoms that mark out what it means to be an American. Indeed, the freedom to own guns, not to mention guns themselves, act as a condition for securing the others. To infringe on gun rights, then, is to infrigne all of the rights that together constitute the freedom of an American citizen. In this way, any effort to impose even moderate limits on citizens' gun rights can be quickly painted as the work of America's enemy par excellence—i.e., the overbearing government that wishes to rob us of all our rights. Note here the structuring presence of the dichotomy, government vs. individual, typical of modern political individualism.

LaPierre further situates these claims about the foundational status of guns rights within a narrative that depicts an ongoing battle in which a true, Authentic America is depicted as the insurgent force, locked in combat with a more powerful, "false" America. While the former is symbolized by recalcitrant citizens claiming their liberties, the latter are insinuated to be those sleepily permitting the progressive encroachment of the already oversized government. True and false make up part of the dichotomy, but morally good vs. slovenly play a complementary role. LaPierre's audience, naturally, are among the "more than 100 million *good* Americans" who own guns (Disney 2015). He exhorts them, moreover, to remain vigilant for ongoing, albeit subtle, attacks from their powerful opponents. LaPierre reinscribes ordinary efforts through the law to make it more difficult to get the weapons required to carry out mass shootings within an apocalyptic vision of Washington bureaucrats barging into private homes to confiscate the guns of responsible Americans.

Along with the strong rhetorical contrast of bad Americans vs. good Americans, LaPierre portrays a society where everyone is "on his own" to stave off attack (Disney 2015). He thus pairs the image of a society composed of atomistic individuals who must secure their own right to live against government overreach with an ethos of gun ownership. Gun rights set the stage for good guys to express virtues by being ready to defend what is their own. Yet, the narrative generates ironic tension as well. For instance, how, one wants to ask, does the idea of constant suspicion of one's neighbors comport with the idea of America as a virtuous and free people?

In LaPierre's pitting of good vs. evil in a grand battle, it is easy to see a theological vision at work. Since the theology entails an account of virtuous behavior—namely, that of the good gun owner—it is rightly called a "theo-*ethics*." From here on, I will refer to this vision as "Authentic America" because it is sustained by the narrative of reinstating and purifying America from corruptive forces. Yet, the very different, and usually mundane, reasons that actually drive many Americans to purchase and prepare themselves to use guns indicate weaknesses in the story this theology tells. Its reflection of our actual gun habits is at best incomplete. To demonstrate some of Authentic America's shortcomings, I will present a more mundane example of Americans arming themselves.

The first such portrait comes from *The Armor of Light*, where we are brought to the living room of a young, middle-class couple and their toddler. The man is a lawyer and the woman is currently staying home with their child. They recount for the camera how one day she came home, groceries in arms and child at her side, to a house ransacked by thieves. The culprits, they deduce, had departed only minutes before they arrived. The event seemed to bring home to them a truth that could be simply put: "the world is a dangerous place."

Not long after this experience the lawyer bought a gun, which he identifies as a Glock 9-millimeter as he demonstrates how to hold it for the camera. Anticipating his later role as the lawyer who represents Lucy McBath against her son's killer, he recounts how easy it was to lawfully acquire it in the state of Florida where he lives. The couple reports the decision to arm themselves as automatic. "We didn't really discuss it," one of them says. Rather, the necessity of getting the gun seemed so natural that it required no deliberation. "We weren't going to be victims," they report thinking at the time.

In other words, rather than a vision of dramatically reclaiming the authenticity of one's country through virtue, the theo-ethics of gun ownership found in this typical American family stems from a jarring encounter with the truth of one's vulnerability, combined with the ready philosophy that in this dangerous society one is on one's own. The drive to empower oneself against this truth by owning a gun emerges as if driven by natural law. This sequence too reflects an underlying social vision, the second form in which guns shape a theo-ethical vision for Americans, that I will here call "the politics of strangers" (or simply "Strangers" for short). It mirrors the vision of early modern political thinkers who imagined society in the form of the state as a conglomeration of individuals whose "interests" are essentially private and individual. Society, an artificial imposition on these individuals, exists essentially to be a hedge against the potential aggression of the other person. Fellow "citizens" are defined against the background of potential threats to ourselves. The prevalence of the politics of strangers within American gun culture gives the lie to the Authentic America narrative by hinting that its roots lie not in a glorified freedom but rather desperate survival.

The normalization of violence that accompanies the politics of strangers is dramatically illustrated in the scene of an altercation between two sets of young middle-class males described in a *New Yorker* piece that showcases the business of gun manufacture and retail in America. As author Evan Osnos tells it, the protagonist Gerald Ung's initiation into gun culture began with regular viewing of the nightly news and its disproportionate reporting of violent crime within or near the neighborhood of his residence. The cumulative effect of this media diet was a heightened fear of becoming the next victim. The marketing employees of gun companies, as though working in tandem with the news, helped him toward the decision to arm himself, the next stage of his journey.

Ung's indoctrination came to a climax outside a Philadelphia night club. What began as the posturing of two groups of males in their twenties, progressed into shoving, before culminating with Ung firing six bullets into the torso of one of the other young men, recent Villanova graduate Edward DiDonato. DiDonato would be crippled for life as a result.

Fear in response to the truth of vulnerability signals the presence of the politics of strangers. It may seem from the examples that this politics fails to raise big picture questions of the sort invoked by Authentic America. Osnos, however, provides a window into a deeper dimension of the politics of strangers when he describes the encounter between Ung and DiDonato immediately after the bullets were fired. On the tape of the 911 call, Ung could be heard talking further to DiDonato—"Why did you make me do it?" The tragic nature of the question is worth pausing over. On one hand, it gives voice to what are taken to be law-like rules of the politics of strangers; if I use deadly violence, it is because I will be forced to do so by the hostility of the other. These sorts of things are inevitable. Thus, what might seem to be ordinary fear has theo-ethical dimensions.

On the other hand, we hear in Ung's question an ambivalence which haunts the politics of strangers. Deep down he has a desire, perhaps as we'll see later a desire for friendship, at war with his construal of the other as threat to his well-being.

Above, I described the theological vision or narrative that supports the vision of an Authentic America, symbolized by the freedom to own guns. And I have juxtaposed the politics of Authentic America, with a more ordinary and even banal society of strangers, where guns become necessary for isolated individuals to protect themselves against fellow citizens they have learned to see as threatening—i.e., the politics of strangers. The examples of the politics of strangers indicate that Authentic America does not offer a complete picture of why Americans seek to own guns. Indeed, neither politics does.

On inspection, there are some deep similarities between these two visions despite their superficial differences. Both, at bottom, trade on a negative account of human freedom as freedom *from* interference by others. And both imply a habit of seeing the other first and foremost as a potential threat to what I value (my own well-being in the case of the stranger's model, and myself as true patriot or virtuous citizen, or an "innocent" third party in the case of Authentic America). Authentic America comes to look like a highly dramatic disguising of the politics of strangers. Fear for survival is dressed up in the garb of moral heroism. Ironically, reliance on moral heroism is a natural complement for a society lacking in genuine common goods.

We may at least say that the theological vision articulated by LaPierre of an Authentic America neither adequately distinguishes itself from the politics of strangers nor provides a truthful account of why Americans have been arming themselves at alarming speeds. But what is more important for my purposes is the adoption of the Authentic America narrative, together with its sacred symbol of the gun, by many American Christians. *The Armor of Light*, referred to above, reveals and explores the tension created within American Christianity by this arrangement.

Finally, the theo-ethical visions described above shed some light on the stalemate between proponents and opponents of gun control in the U.S. At least we now see that both positions rely on atomistic individualism, from which starting point we ought to expect it to be difficult to discover common ground.

THEO-ETHICS OF FRIENDSHIP

In describing one sort of theo-ethics of guns in America above, I have begun to make conceptual room for an alternative. The sources of this theo-ethical vision are in the accounts of friendship found in Aristotle and Thomas Aquinas. Aristotle's view that the purpose of politics is friendship (*philia*) makes it crucially different from the politics of strangers described above. As a result, presenting the Aristotelian perspective will allow me to reframe the debate about guns in America. Yet because Aristotle's account of friendship assumes the inevitability of violence, it needs to be supplemented in order to adequately confront America's theo-ethics of guns. The necessary addition is found in Aquinas's conception of friendship as *caritas*, a love that participates in the character of God. Again, this groundwork is necessary to establish the alternative on a footing distinct from individualism and the normalization of violence.

Aristotle envisioned societies (or *poleis*) in relation to an essential function or purpose. He assumed that belonging to a community was basic to human life as such. He had no idea of being human, nor of human agency, that was prior to, and thus could be abstracted from, belonging and participation within a society. For Aristotle, the question of authentic human life and that of a rightly ordered community were of a piece and impossible to separate. Thus, the function of societies was to make people good.

Further, in light of his essentially social understanding of society's function, Aristotle named friendship as the point and purpose of politics. Participating in friendship is how human beings grow in virtue, thus becoming capable of being members of a good society. Society (politics) is *for* friendship.

Although it is difficult for us as moderns, accustomed to thinking of friendship as a private matter, to comprehend, Aristotle's elevation of friendship shows his clear difference from the individualistic understanding of society familiar to the politics of strangers. Whereas the latter sees politics as a neutral means to gain what is desired by the private individual, for Aristotle participating in political friendship is partly constitutive of one's well-being.

How does this difference impact ethical judgments about guns? At one point in *The Armor of Light*, Rev, Rob Schenck, who has been gradually becoming aware of the pervasiveness of the mythology of guns among American Christians, remarks, "I hadn't realized how deeply guns figured in their thinking" (Disney 2015). Far from being mere tools, he saw, guns had migrated to the center of American Christians' vison of reality, and especially their vision of society. In light of Aristotle's focus on the common good, the basic ethical question concerns neither rights nor duties, but whether owning and using guns promote the conditions for a society's growth in friendship. How, in other words, do the meanings guns have for us shape our vision of common life, of friendship? Does our possession and use hinder or help our society to carry out its essential function—namely, to nurture the kind of relationships, the ethical friendships, in which alone human agents individually and corporately achieve the flourishing proper to us? Having identified the importance of trust and solidarity, theologian Lyndon Shakespeare argues in Aristotelian fashion that assault weapons "fail to fit within a definition of human well-being [because] the use of such weapons is a piece of human activity that destabilizes the kind of human relations necessary for a political arrangement of friendship" (Shakespeare, 617).

What happens to the rights that individuals assert to promote their liberty from coercive force, together with the duties preventing infringement on the rights of others in an Aristotelian frame? An ethics of rights soon becomes a morality centered around explicit rules, a sort of formal contract among strangers. Rules continue to play some role with an Aristotelian framework, but appeal to rules only becomes intelligible within a broader ethical frame generated by focusing on the need to articulate as best we may a conception of the good. Human cooperation provides the setting for a conception of human fulfillment, itself the governing measure of attributes of human excellence or the virtues. Herbert McCabe suggests seeing moral rules as something like the rulebook for a game or sport. Breaking the rules of a game regularly—for example, using your hands to direct the ball in a soccer game—signals that you are not really playing *this* game at all. Yet rules don't tell you what playing well looks like; that is a matter of training and habituation (McCabe 2017).

While it is true that it would be difficult to square Aristotle's claim about the centrality of friendship to a good society with our contemporary practices of private gun ownership in America, Aristotelian friendship alone cannot subvert the theo-ethical assumptions of Authentic America and the politics of strangers. For American gun culture is rooted not only in the assumption of individualism but also that violence is to be taken for granted as a means of maintaining order. To disrupt this assumption, we must go beyond Aristotle to Aquinas's account of friendship as "caritas."

Aristotle's friendships are at bottom exclusive and the societies of friends he imagines have definite boundaries. Those outside the polis—the society of virtuous friends—were to be seen as potential threats to virtue and to the good of the friendship enjoyed by those within. Aristotle's friendship thus pushes violence to the borders, but does not entirely subvert its role in shaping a theo-ethical vision. Christian ethicists Charles Pinches and Stanley Hauerwas argue that we can see the exclusiveness of Aristotle's friendship reflected in the fact that, for him, the paradigmatic act of courage was to die on the battle-field while fighting on behalf of one's city state (Hauerwas and Pinches 1997, 151–162). Violence in defense of one's shared identity was thus an inevitable part of reality. In this sense, friendship in Aristotle resembles the theo-ethical vision of Authentic America, though the latter's conception of human agency and freedom are more rooted in the content-less liberty described above.

Thirteenth century theologian Thomas Aquinas adopted Aristotle's conception of friendship in expounding the Christian moral life and also adapted it to the theological vision flowing from the narrative of Christian faith. In place of *philia*, Aquinas used the term *caritas*, whose primary reference is to the love Christians claim God has shown toward creation. Aquinas held friendship, caritas, to be the point and purpose of Christian life in community. He uses the term caritas because, he avers, Christians must recognize their friendship as fundamentally a *gift*. It is because God first befriended us that we in turn can learn to befriend one another (Aquinas, ST, II-II, Q. 23, Art. 1).

What difference does *caritas* make for a theo-ethics of guns? Shakespeare points out that the key to the Christian account of God's friendship is that its decisive embodiment revolves around the violence done to a human being. God's friendship is revealed in its finality in the life of Jesus of Nazareth, who was crucified at the hands of the religious and political powers of his place and time. So, one point of intersection with our topic is Jesus' violent death.

But, the story of Jesus as told in Christian scripture does not end with the crucifixion but continues to narrate God's resurrection of Jesus. The resurrection expresses God's affirmation of Jesus and his life. It renders credible the identification of the life of Jesus with the character of God. Jesus's story contains the paradigmatic display of what God's love, *caritas*, looks like.

Hebert McCabe argues that the story of Jesus opens up new ethical possibilities for those of faith. While Jesus's death displays what must happen to someone whose friendship refuses to honor the necessities of exclusion and violence, the resurrection signals the outbreak of a new way of life, the frienship of *caritas*, that transcends these necessities (McCabe 1968, 132–133). Shakespeare describes this dynamic eloquently, when he writes, "For Christians, the possibility of *caritas* is grounded in a violent act, but one that reorients the necessity of further violence through the creation and maintaining of a particular community *of philia* and *caritas,* the community of the church" (Shakespeare, 617). The reality of human violence is made real to us in the image of the crucified savior, but its inevitability is undermined by Christ's ongoing work in and through the community shaped by *caritas*.

My overarching point is that, in distinction from both Aristotelian friendship and the project of Authentic America, Christian friendship refuses to accept violence as inevitable. The theo-ethical vision of *caritas* generates a community both called and empowered to transform the predilection for violence through the practices of forgiveness and reconciliation. These ethical responses are made both possible and fitting or virtuous by the Christian's living into friendship with God.

An implication is that Christian Americans who have adapted themselves to the theo-ethics of Authentic America will find themselves caught in a contradiction that ought to produce cognitive dissonance. The Christian theo-ethical vision inevitably conflicts with that of LaPierre and the NRA. While fear is at times appropriate for Christians, who rightly value their lives and relationships, something has gone awry when violence comes to be seen by them as a fact of life and one they ought to feel little troubled by. Because it is always open to human agents to try to transform enmity and hatred into union and love, an outlook which presumes violence is necessary must be unsatisfactory in the light of Christian revelation.

INCOMMENSURABLE VISIONS: CARITAS AND THE POLITICS OF STRANGERS/AUTHENTIC AMERICA

The friendship of caritas offers a substantial alternative to American gun culture's politics of strangers, a politics that normalizes violence. It further makes a strong claim to be itself an authentic expression of the Christian theo-ethical vision. Yet it strikingly is not the conceptual background against which the response of the majority of American Christians to American gun culture makes evident sense. That response is largely one of complicity with, or creative adaptation of, the Authentic America story.

In this final section, then, I offer further support for the claim that the politics of caritas constitutes a rival and incommensurable theo-ethical vision to the politics of strangers and of Authentic America. We see this in the tensions experienced by American Christians as they seek to wed a pro-gun stance to their ongoing commitment to the sanctity of human life. Again, my examples are drawn from the film *The Armor of Light*, and especially its chronicle of the journey of Rev. Rob Schenck from mainstream conservative activist to gadfly to his community for its complacency about gun violence. Schenck's story illustrates the normative status of *caritas* in the Christian tradition both negatively and positively. We see in it both the doomed compromise of Authentic America, but also a hope generated by the lingering virtue of truthfulness about the compromise. A hope that in Schenck's case ultimately issues in repentance.

Schenck's story as minister-lobbyist, as portrayed in the film, reflects a Christianity standing at arm's length from Aquinas's account of caritas, or friendship with God in Christ. One source of the conflict stems from the widespread adoption by American Christian conservatives of the individualistic assumptions of modern politics. Schenck is deeply indebted to Christian efforts to "outsource" politics to the state, a strategy that construes power as a mere means or mechanism for advancing individual/group interests. Schenck's high-profile positions of power include chaplain to the Capital Forum Club (Described on Schenck's Wikipedia page as the "only private association to meet regularly within the U.S. Capitol"), President of the National Clergy Council, and President of the conservative religious lobbying institute, "Faith and Action in the Nation's Capital." Further, the institute occupies elegant accommodations in a brownstone opposite the Supreme Court. Photos around the office show him leading a prayer with a group of politicians that includes Senator Ted Cruz, hobnobbing with members of the Supreme Court, as well as with Sarah Palin, who also appears in the film as a celebrity speaker at an NRA rally.

He is institutionally positioned to influence the directions of state power on behalf of a large and well-funded interest group. For someone so situated, "wise decision making" always begins by taking the pulse of opinion within the constituency. Thus, he confesses with regard to "taking on the issue of gun violence" that a good friend and adviser has warned him solemnly to go slow with the issue, given the strong personal sentiments in favor of guns and second amendment rights of most conservative Christians in America. It is, in other words, a "hot button" issue in American politics, and he must be guided by the preferences of the people on whose financial support he counts.

The assumption behind this strategy of outsourcing politics is that the church must move beyond its own life as a social entity before it becomes properly speaking "political." It needs a special instrument to become political. Thus, "friendship" for Schenck has become a means to power, rather than a way of embodying the telos of love. These assumptions are at the heart of modern individualism, which habituates us to fear the other. They result in participating unreflectively in the mechanisms of fear and violence.

Indeed, even as the movie documents Schenck's increasing awareness (and vexation) by the incoherence of the outsourcing arrangement, and the insupportable compromises of this strategy, he proves unable to rid himself of its key assumptions. So, when it comes to raising the issue of Christians' relationship to guns in America, he finds he must frame the question as a "moral" and "theological" one *rather than* a political issue. The private (moral/theological) and public (political) distinction of modern individualism continues to inhabit his thinking, even as he tries to break free of it. Thus, a key consequence of the Christian strategy that involves "outsourcing" politics to the state of is that the arrangement comes to seem natural.

In addition to displaying the American Christian adaptation to the politics of strangers and its individualist assumptions, Schenck's story reflects the dynamics of the theo-ethical vision of Authentic America. The vision of an Authentic America is perhaps an even more potent attraction to conservative Christians in America, and to his credit Schenck grows increasingly aware that it is a temptation. To review, the LaPierre narrative of an Authentic America struggling to renew itself while under attack presupposes a cosmic struggle between clearly demarcated good guys and bad guys. Freedom and virtue are expressed in successfully battling—taking up arms—against the enemy. As a result, LaPierre's narrative projects violence as inevitable, and indeed as ennobling insofar as it expresses the will to renew America.

Schenck confronts the vision of Authentic America in his Washington colleagues who argue that being pro-gun flows automatically from being pro-life. The argument, made by Troy Normand (President of Operation Rescue), in a scene in a restaurant where Schenck has called together three associates to discuss "Christians and guns," is that a common goal is found in the defense of innocent life from an aggressor. But this kind of reference to innocence, it should be noted, relies on the LaPierre narrative depicting a world clearly divided between good guys and bad guys. Normand reveals his captivity to this narrative when he leads in with LaPierre's signature line: "The only thing that can stop a bad guy with a gun is a good guy with a gun." He goes on to paint a scene where an "unbalanced individual" enters a church and opens fire. That guy will be limited in the damage he can cause, if an armed person like himself is ready to respond. At this point, another colleague raises the question whether the government should at least require that those who wish to own guns first receive minimal training. Normand replies testily that he for one does not wish to aid the country's transformation into a "nanny state."

Picking up on his example, Schenck enters the fray by questioning whether Normand's confidence doesn't rest on a false view about how these events actually go down. Is this a world in which good guys are always easily picked out from bad guys? Indeed, are good and bad so easily demarcated in real people? And do would be heroes always find themselves possessed of the calm required to act well in crisis situations, rather than make matters worse?

Yet, Schenk's story also reflects an increasing awareness of the tension engendered by the Christian adoption of the theo-ethics of strangers and the myth of Authentic America. An exchange in another of his gatherings to discuss the alliance of Christians with the pro-gun agenda reveals this awareness. One of the leaders present articulates the view that, "If you took away guns, people would just find some other way of killing each other." The problem, she explains, is with the human will and laws cannot change that. Schenck pounces on this comment, seeing rightly that it is not merely hers but an argument that underwrites the bargain a large proportion of American Christians have made with the strangers/Authentic America vision. What's more it is a theological proposition. "So," he says, "what we needed is Jesus . . . *plus*, a sidearm." He continues probing the argument's theo-logic, "we need Jesus for the healing part, and if that fails, we need a gun to protect ourselves from the sinner" (Disney 2015). In other words, under the guise of placing Christian convictions at the center, Christians have actually tightly circumscribed the role they can play. The narrative of what God has done in Jesus, defeating violence by submitting to it, no longer retains its normative force.

In sum, Normand's argument for an easy extension of pro-life principles to a pro-gun position expresses the compelling attraction of the theo-ethics of Authentic America for many American Christians. His reference to the good guys/bad guys schema shows his adoption of the narrative of a strug-gle for patriotic authenticity, while his reference to a "nanny state" reflects his political individualism, echoing LaPierre's portrayal of the enemy as governing elites. He goes on to normalize violence, stating that "an armed society is a polite society." In other words, even should the society pro-jected here reach its fulfillment, ceasing to be an insurgent force, violence would remain a normal part of social life. Similarly, his second interlocutor relies on the narrative of Authentic America with its positing of clearly dis-tinguishable good guys and bad guys, saved and damned. She thus accepts, or reinstates, violence as a normal part of reality—i.e., a reality unaffected by Jesus' death and resurrection. As her comment shows, the myth of

Authentic America has enabled many Christians to keep the requirements of caritas at arm's length.

Schenck's story, then, at its self-questioning best, indicates where many Christians (himself included) have gone awry. That is, it begins to name the problem of Christianity's adoption of the incommensurable visions of Authentic America and the politics of strangers. At the same time, Schenck's saga provides evidence of caritas's normative status within Christianity, even when its refusal of the inevitability of violence is suppressed by Christians themselves.

Schenck's story is not without hope because of its implication that it is never too late to renounce one's complicity in a theo-ethical vision that proclaims violence to be necessary—that is, a story at odds with one in which Christ invites his followers to join him. It is indeed fitting that personal repentance lies at the center of this theo-ethical vision, for the Christian theo-ethical vision claims not to be neutral but self-involving.

CONCLUSION

This essay has argued that the American gun culture is sustained by a politics of strangers, rooted in fear, together with the myth of an Authentic America. I have suggested reading these as theo-ethical visions—that is, as visions that orient human agents to a conception of the good through world-shaping narratives. Christians are deeply enmeshed in these theo-ethical visions. This theo-ethical vision gives rise to the debate over guns whose center of gravity is individual rights. Aristotelian philosophy breaks the stranglehold of individualism by imagining politics as ordered to friendship. To excel in community is to seek together the good life for human beings. Yet, Aristotle's account of friendship presupposes the inevitability of violence toward those outside the circle of friendship.

Christians in America live in a false peace with the theo-ethics of Authentic America and its individualism. But this ought to generate a profound tension with their ethical tradition, for I argued that Christian friendship purports to break the cycle of fear and violence by proclaiming caritas, or a love whose character is to overcome enmities. As a form of friendship, caritas proclaims that violence is not inevitable. To display the incommensurability of a theo-ethical vision rooted in caritas with that of both the politics of strangers and Authentic America, I turned to Disney's depiction of the story of Rob Schenck. The tensions and contradictions displayed in Schenck's life, I claimed, reveal that the strategy of American Christians to make peace with a politics rooted in fear must ultimately fail.

REFERENCES

Disney, Abigail E. 2015. *The Armor of Light*. DVD. Directed by Abigail E. Disney. New York: Purple Mickey Productions, 2015.

Hauerwas, Stanley, and Charles Pinches. 1997. *Christians Among the Virtues: Theological Conversations with Ancient and Modern Ethics*. South Bend: University of Notre Dame Press.

McCabe, Herbert O. P. 1968. *Law, Love and Language*. London: Continuum.

McCabe, Herbert O. P. n.d. "Veritatis Splendor in Focus: Manuals and Rulebooks." Accessed August 25, 2017. http://www.natural-law-and-conscience.org/readings/mccabe.asp.

Osnos, Evan. 2016. "Making a Killing: The Business and Politics of Selling Guns." *New Yorker*, June 26, 2016.

Shakespeare, Lyndon. 2013. "Friendship, Love, and Mass Shootings: Toward a Theological Response for Gun Control." *Anglican Theological Review*, 95(4): 614–615.

Taylor, Charles. 1989. *Sources of the Self: The Making of the Modern Identity*. Cambridge, MA: Harvard University Press.

Taylor, Charles. 2007. *A Secular Age*. Cambridge, MA: The Belknap Press of Harvard University Press.

Thomas Aquinas, *Summa Theologica* II-II, Q. 23, Art. 1.

Chapter 3

Social Violence

The Role of Gun Culture

Binod Kumar

The roots of violence are many because they sprout from diverse sources. Often the sources interact and confound to make violence a complex societal phenomenon. In the context of this chapter, violence is defined as intents and/ or acts of doing harm to an individual or a group of people under a pretext of a real or imaginary conflict. Violence is thus a very broad term and encompasses numerous social and political acts of a typical citizen, social groups, leaders, rulers, and governments. The sources of violence can be broadly classified as natural, social, political, commercial, and technological. The classification of the sources, their respective roots, and associated impacts are presented in table 3.1. Each of the sources of violence possesses its own traits, social impacts, and long-term consequences. Except for the natural source, all other sources originate from human activity. Even some of the so-called natural causes such as global warming or the COVID-19 pandemic were mediated by human activities. Therefore, their elimination also depends upon human action and resolve. The differentiation among various forms of violence created by humans can be often murky. In fact, a certain class of violence can feed into another to distort its traits and character. Some business practices (commercial violence) can lead to income inequality and social stratification (social violence). Justification of social justice by certain political actions ("set-asides" and "equal opportunity") and propagating political and religious goals using digital tools and methods by terrorist groups are other noteworthy examples. In the context of the classification, it would be appropriate to refer to Gandhi's vision on diffusion of societal functions and activities: "I claim that human mind or human society is not divided into watertight compartments called social, political and religious. All act and react upon one another" (Attenborough 1982, 63). The proposed classification of violence is not very far from Gandhi's vision of social discourse and it does not imply

Table 3.1   Source/Root and Impacts of Violence

Natural	Climate change, drought, famine, earthquake, pandemic, etc.
Social	Racism, apartheid, gangs, fire arms, mental health, human trafficking, drugs and inequality
Political	Dictatorships, weak governments and hybrid (religious and political) states
Commercial	Environmentally questionable products, processes and waste disposals; excessive production of goods and services, and unsustainable consumption
Technological	Internal combustion engines (greenhouse gas emission and climate change) and digital revolution (a tool to propagate religious fundamentalism, terrorism, and bullying)

rigid boundaries among the five forms resulting from human activity. Thus, the forms of violence are not mutually exclusive.

However, delineating sources of violence is an exercise of paramount importance for developing an effective set of priorities, solutions, and social policies aimed at their rectification.

Perhaps, the most troublesome and long-lasting form of violence emanates from social traditions, beliefs, and practices. They have existed since the very beginning of human civilization, often modulated by religious traditions, generally distorted by colonization. Such violence has been reincarnated in different forms over centuries. Some of the important forms of social violence include the institutions of slavery, racism, apartheid, human trafficking, drug culture, inequality, and gangs. In general, the social violence is legitimized through the perceived needs of the society, prevailing social practices, religious beliefs, and corrupt, misguided political power. It is a long-lasting social stigma, and extremely detrimental to the objectives of just and fair civil society. Social violence can be carried on for generations and centuries. It is also extremely difficult to uproot, and often attempts to uproot them lead to a different form of violence.

Social violence can be further aggravated by economic factors such as poverty, broken families, drug and substance abuse, dysfunctional mental health policies, and technological advances. Technological advances may include the violent television programs under a broad umbrella of games and entertainment, a flow of hateful campaigns coupled with religious extremism, and access to powerful semiautomatic and automatic firearms. All of these factors generally shift the social equilibrium from a relatively peaceful (civil) to a violent society. A social discourse with civility (polite, reasonable, and respectful behavior) is fundamental to the existence and sustainment of the civil society. A term "civility index" is often used to assess social behavior of students in classroom situations (Clark 2013; Kaslow and Watson 2016).

If the term "civility index" can be used to assess the state of social equilibrium, many of us would conclude that a decline of the index has taken place in recent times, in spite of the progress in democratizing world governments, technological advancements, and eradicating hunger worldwide. Recent examples of worldwide political events in major democracies of the world further illustrate the decline in the state of "civility index," almost intruding the domain of civil unrest and violence.

Widespread access to powerful weapons, such as semiautomatic and automatic guns in the U.S., introduces a lethal dimension to social violence. A small but significant percentage of a population with a mindset to harm lives and institutions, and equipped with lethal weapons (a fatal combination), is a threat to the survival of the civil social structure. Such a fatal combination challenges long-term sustenance of a civil society. In recent times, the U.S. has witnessed mass shootings in schools and university campuses, places of worship, shopping malls, athletic arenas, nightclubs, and movie theaters. After the mass shootings in Newtown, Aurora, Orlando, and Columbine High School, voices of activists and reform-minded politicians raising voices on gun violence have been drowned out. For example, in spite of the sincere effort by former president Obama and like-minded politicians, little has been accomplished. The antigun violence activists and reform-minded politicians remain ineffective. Regrettably, mass shootings have continued since the publication of the first edition. A gunman opened fire with a semiautomatic rifle at Marjory Stoneman Douglas High School in Parkland, Florida, on February 14, 2018, killing 17 people and injuring 17 others. These shootings are the symptoms of the damaging influence and power of the gun culture. The proponents of the culture, such as the National Rifle Association (NRA), have managed to deflect real issues encountered by the society.

The gun culture sprouted from the societal need for security of an emerging nation and it was nurtured by the basic tenets of democracy, capitalism, and the desire for security against perceived threats. The aforementioned shootings point to an alarming trend and await resolute societal and political actions. Admittedly, underlying causes of social violence in general and gun violence in particular is complex, which make them challenging social issues to address and resolve. The complexity of the gun culture in the U.S. arises from the fact that (a) it has been a part of the American history for centuries, (b) a large proportion of the population believe that they need guns for their way of life and security, (c) the gun industry contributes over thirty billion dollars to the economy and employs about quarter of a million people, and (d) the Second Amendment ensures the right of most citizen to bear arms. But, the complexity of the issue need not be a pretext for indifference toward the victims of gun violence.

SOCIAL ACTION AND REACTION

The roots of violence emerge from various human endeavors resulting from social, religious, cultural, economic, environmental, and military aspirations of a society. An analysis of these societal aspirations leads one to surmise that mass violence possesses a common feature which originates from counteracting forces of social action and reaction. An action required to satisfy a societal function precedes a specific form of violence. For example, to grow crops and provide food to masses, the social groups discovered an action plan in the form of a profession of agriculture. The action plan provided employment to people and business activity to entrepreneurs and traders. It can neither be stopped nor postponed (unless forced by natural causes) because that will lead to famine and starvation. The violence in the form of slavery resulted from this societal requirement. Subsequently, the society needed to figure out a solution to deal with the violence embedded in the plan of action for agriculture. The emerging solution is called a reaction.

The coupling of social action and violence often takes a long time to understand and delineate. The practice of slavery illustrates this argument. The coupling was initially ignored, even justified because the action was required to satisfy the need of the society. The bigger purpose (although grossly oppressive) of the society prevailed. Once effects and impacts of the social action became evident and proved to be harmful to the society, remedial measures were sought, deliberated, and implemented. After deliberations and consent of the political power, some of the remedial measures (societal reactions/policies) were executed. The processes of identifying and correcting social actions and reactions have taken centuries.

The social reactions are generally well-intended. However, their impact on the welfare of the society may depend upon their constituent elements. For example, a number of considerations proposed by genuine and/or vested interests may be considered and incorporated in the formulation of the social reaction. Some of the considerations are likely to yield desired effects that can sustain civil and law-abiding society for a long time, while others may sow seeds of perpetual violence. Present day racism is the remnant of the slavery. The overall outcome of an executed reaction could lead to a spectrum of societal impacts ranging from a fair and equitable to extremely unjust living conditions for the people. The execution of the societal reaction completes a cycle of social action and reaction which can be collectively called a social practice. An ill-conceived social reaction plants a seed of perpetual violence and initiates a societal conflict. An uninterrupted social practice may continue for a long time. An ordinary social practice may be transformed into a major, long-lasting violent conflict. The conflict could become perpetual and may last for generations and centuries! Slavery, racial injustice, and caste systems are typical examples of flawed and repressive social reactions.

Figure 3.1 schematically shows the relationship among societal actions, reactions, and violence. As stated earlier, the survival and sustenance of the human race require social actions. Social institutions needed to be developed and sustained. Military establishments provided security to people, their wealth, and institutions. These actions also led to some tensions in the society. To address the violence emerging from the tension, certain rules, regulations, and laws (collectively called social reactions) were conceived and enforced. The motivations for the social reactions were driven by the need to bring order, peace, and prosperity to the society. Commitments to the rules, regulations, and laws were expected. But, unintended consequences of the social reactions emerged: one of them was the violence. Thus, it can be surmised that the violence is rooted within the counteractive forces of action and reaction which are components of a given social practice. The practice of slavery has lasted for centuries and in spite of protests and reforms for over centuries it exists even today in the form of racism.

It may be conjectured that a violent root sprouts from the flawed social reaction, but not social action. This is because a social action is required for the survival of the human race; the action is intrinsic to the existence of the race. If there is any violent component embedded in the social action, it needs to be removed by the societal reaction. If a given reaction does not work, then other reactions need to be devised until one with the least harmful and broadly accepted outcome is discovered. Subsequently, the least harmful reaction needs to be implemented. It is required for the well-being and

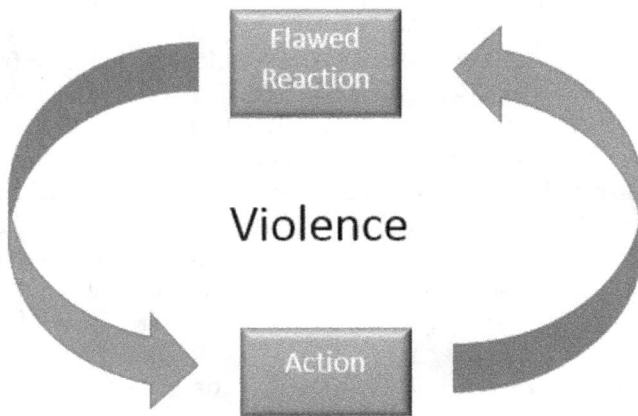

Figure 3.1 Violence results from a continuous cycle of action and flawed reaction. The cycle may become perpetual, transforming an ordinary societal issue into a chronic, violent conflict.

long-term sustenance of the society. A sustained, long-term public policy reflects an ultimate societal reaction in response to the violence embedded in the original action or flawed reaction.

It takes a long time to establish equilibrium between social action and reaction for a civil society. The equilibrium can be perturbed by technological and commercial advances that accelerate deterioration of a cohesive social discourse. It is also broadly accepted that societal needs and human activities strive for scientific, technological, and commercial advances. Thus, these needs and activities are bound to shift the equilibrium toward violence with time if no corrective measures are taken to counterbalance the technological and commercial advances.

The gun culture and associated issues can be analyzed in the context of technology-driven violence. The gun culture in the U.S. emerged from the social need of hunting (outdoor sports) and militia (frontier and revolutionary) ethos. But, the technological and commercial advances have shifted the equilibrium of the culture toward disproportionate, unacceptable social violence. After nurturing gun culture for centuries while aggressively providing space for technological advances, the society has come to recognize some of their antisocial and lethal impacts. Unfortunately, public and government responses have been inadequate to alleviate the impacts. Because of the inadequate measures, the social practice of the gun culture and violence emanating from it have remained unabated, if not with greater force and lethality. Now, guns are available to the general public which allow loading of multiple rounds. These guns are capable of inflicting serious, large-scale harm to the public.

The tradition of gun ownership precedes the history of the U.S. as a sovereign and democratic nation. The phrase "gun culture" was coined by a historian (Hofstadter 1970) to describe the long-held desire of U.S. for owning guns. The American mindset of gun ownership dates back to days even earlier than the American Revolutionary War. During that time, it was a necessity to possess shooting skills for rural American men and it was considered to be a rite of passage for males entering adulthood. Thus, many American citizens embrace and celebrate gun ownership and consider it to be a part of their heritage. Hunting (a method to control animal population and an outdoor activity for food) and security against external threats remain central justifications for gun ownership. The militia spirit remained an important element of the gun culture.

Modern community settlements drift away from the need for rural living. Most of the American population resides in urban communities. The 2020 census reports that 82.7 percent of the American population lives in urban areas. The urban communities are in no need to pursue subsistence hunting (food) for living and survival. Furthermore, the military protects the security of the state and civilian law enforcement personnel secure rural and urban communities. Thus, the attitude of the public toward gun culture perplexes people from other parts of the world (for examples, Europeans and Asians) who wonder why the American public has not demanded stricter gun control measures in the face of mass shootings. Fatalities from gun crimes outnumber the deaths inflicted by terrorism (guns also as weapons) or automobile accidents, yet the public and policymakers remain indifferent to enact stricter laws for gun control.

After reviewing the gun culture in a historical context of the U.S., one needs to have an objective assessment of the Second Amendment of the U.S. Constitution ("A well-regulated Militia, being necessary to the security of a Free State, the right of the people to keep and bear arms, shall not be infringed"). The Second Amendment provides a constitutional protection for gun ownership. The Amendment was adopted on December 15, 1791, and is the subject of varied interpretations with regard to the definitions of "a well-regulated Militia" and also "security of a Free State." In addition, social needs are markedly different today than what they were over 230 years ago when the Second Amendment was drafted and adopted. The argument to protect the rights of armed people against the government raises questions about the survival of democracy. The recent U.S. presidential election (2020) and the insurrection at the Capitol that followed has brought us to a crossroad, requiring us to assess the threat of gun culture to the future of the U.S. democracy. Nonviolent actions such as boycotts and noncooperation are powerful and proven methods of "Satyagraha" to counter unjust policies and tyranny of governments in a democratic system. Why do we need a "well-regulated Militia" when we possess the most powerful armed forces in the world? Of course, the elements of the Second Amendment are the topics of constitutional arguments, and a fairly large number of opinions already exist about them.

HUMAN RIGHTS, VIOLENCE, AND NONVIOLENCE

The central theme of this chapter is to analyze social violence in the context of gun culture. The social violence infringes on, if not it takes away, human rights. They are closely linked, but in an antagonistic manner. This section will explore the relationship and arrive at a qualitative conclusion with respect to the impact of the gun-culture-driven social violence on human rights.

Moral traditions of different civilizations, cultures, and religious practices of the world enlighten us about their intentions for and relevance in safeguarding basic human dignity (rights). However, a formal recognition and broader acceptance of human rights began with a document prepared and released by the United Nations (UN) on December 10, 1948, titled "Universal Declaration of Human Rights." The declaration was prepared and published after several years of deliberations among prominent intellectuals from the major countries of the world at the time. The foundation of human rights advocacy and its implications for governance are contained in this document.

There are thirty articles in the Declaration of Human Rights. Each article specifies rights of human beings which are essential for their survival and prosperity. None of the articles specifies root causes that infringe upon the rights. Perhaps, the nonspecificity was justifiable because an attempt to correlate causes and infringements may have taken the UN and governments of most countries into uncharted territory of the world order at the time of the declaration. The uncharted territory consisted of the mode of and accountability in governance in different parts of the world. Article 3 of the Declaration is relevant to gun culture; it specifies the right to life ("Everyone has the right to life, liberty and security of a person").

The most chronic, damaging, and long-lasting forms of violence emerge from social traditions, beliefs, and practices. Some of the practices that have led to gun violence are the basic elements of the gun culture. They include liberal firearms licenses and availability of guns to armed criminals and gangs in some neighborhoods and social groups. These combined with governmental negligence of mental health issues, ubiquitous supply of drugs, and human trafficking further aggravate the fault lines of the social structure. The gun culture has been justified by the perceived human needs (tools for hunting and security) and social practices (gun ownership). This culture has been carried on for generations and centuries. The longer it has been practiced, the more arduous it has become to uproot in spite of the fact that the gun control advocates are even better organized today than they were over two hundred years ago. Social needs justify and sustain the gun culture. A major segment of the society has been persuaded to defend and propagate the culture. However, the gruesome violence occurring in some cities and institutions of learning, worship, and hospitals can't be explained and justified by the traditional arguments. Simply, with all intellectual honesty, it needs to be stated that gun violence is the legacy of gun culture and defenders of the culture must own the legacy.

A review of gun violence in the context of global advocacy of human rights by the UN takes us toward the central theme of this chapter. It is accepted that the guns by themselves do not take away life, liberty, and security of a person and, therefore, guns do not infringe upon human rights. But, guns are made to function according to the wishes of the owner or operator. Therefore, a gun and the user should be treated as a single entity, while the sole responsibility for the damage to a person or a group of people rests on the individual human being using it. The harm caused or to be caused by guns need not be countered by supplying additional guns under the pretext of defensive measures in the prevailing social environment ("an eye for an eye leaves the whole world blind"). Easy access of guns to people with questionable mindsets and backgrounds does infringe upon the right to life, liberty, and security of a large number of victims in the society, as illustrated by homicides directly attributed to gun violence in recent years (>39,000 in US/yr.). The gun culture of today includes a major fraction of the U.S. population: law-abiding gun owners, criminal elements, and a small mentally troubled group of people. The human right is violated by the last two groups. We as a society need to understand and accept that the violence emanating from the gun culture does infringe upon basic human rights (Article 3). The violence can be mitigated without harming the rights of law-abiding gun owners by legislating appropriate laws and control mechanisms.

After the first edition of this book was published, Amnesty International has issued a statement on its website: "Gun violence is a contemporary human rights issue. Gun related violence threatens our most fundamental human rights, the right to life" (Amnesty International 2021). It is heartening to learn that institutions of repute such as the Amnesty International are raising awareness on gun violence and right to life. The violence kills over 100 people every day. Those near and dear ones to the victims would greatly appreciate every help they can muster.

The severity, frequency, and lethality of the violent incidents emanating from the gun culture intensify with technological innovations and advancements. Some recent examples include widespread use of social media, fake news, and internet videos propagating hate and religious extremism. These innovations in conjunction with gun culture inflict spontaneous and large-scale damage to civil society irrespective of geographical boundaries.

It should be appreciated that technological innovations and advancements have unintended consequences and they could constitute major threats. This is another example of the social action and reaction catalyzing new forms of violence for which the society was not prepared for before the technological innovations were introduced in the social space. To alleviate these new forms of violence (mediated by technology), numerous ideas and suggestions are being discussed and debated (with respect to the content, use, and software of the internet) and hopefully appropriate solutions/reactions will emerge. Censorship and bans on the electronic media are not an answer. Most of us appreciate that the media has also improved the quality of our lives by bringing people of the world closer. But, the recognition of the conjoined problem and finding moral solutions are needs of our time.

A social reaction, now let it be called as a public policy, is shaped by a number of considerations as it is the public policy which is implemented with a due constitutional process. The social reaction is a concept of abstract

nature, whereas public policy is a term devised and executed by the adminis-
trative hierarchy. Some of the policies (such as to reward interests of a select
group or enhance revenue of the state) may have damaging influences on
the outcome of the executed policies. For example, the internal combustion
engine (ICE) and related products were developed for the benefit of a select
group of commercial enterprises. From the very beginning it was known that
the ICEs will emit enormous amounts of carbon dioxide in the atmosphere
which will lead to global warming and climate change. Yet, for over a century, commercialization and widespread use of the ICE were promoted by
implementing policies to satisfy interests of a select group. These policies
may be identified as flawed because they are primarily devoid of the just or
moral forces and hence they become sources of distress, protests, violence,
and social conflict. It is only in recent years that some automobile companies have begun phasing out ICEs by electric vehicles. The gun culture is
the result of the flawed social policies; and like the ICEs, the time has come
to phase out toxic elements of the culture. It is interesting to note that some
political groups in the U.S. oppose both phasing out of ICEs and gun culture.

To deal with gun violence, the American people require the development
of just policies. A social consciousness needs to be developed and nurtured
to allow manifestation of moral forces in the formulation and enforcement of
just policies, while simultaneously discarding elements of immoral forces.
The policy elements with repressive influences, even to a very small group
of people, need to be rejected. In the context of gun culture, the moral forces
should emanate from the lives of victims (who may or may not be gun
owners) and children in schools and universities who are likely to become
potential victims, rather than from the interests of business establishments
promoting the gun sales and the profit motivation of firearms industries.

Furthermore, gun ownership should be limited to only those who are eli-
gible, competent, and with a need to must have them. Those who own guns
must be thoroughly screened, educated, trained, and held accountable for
their safety and lawful deployment. It is apparent that too many people in the
U.S. possess them in spite of the fact that they don't need them and are even
likely to misuse them.

The aforementioned narratives on violence and gun culture leads one to
reconstruct the schematic for the societal action and reaction as presented earlier in figure 3.1. The "flawed reaction" is replaced by "just reaction" such as
depicted in figure 3.2. The social practice employing just reactions (policies)
will lead to a societal order expected to be civil (nonviolent) and law abiding.
The social actions and reactions are centered on the principles of nonviolence.
In such a civil society, there will be compatibility between the aspirations of
the people, development, human rights, and rule of law. In an unstable social
environment (with elements of violence), the human rights become matters of

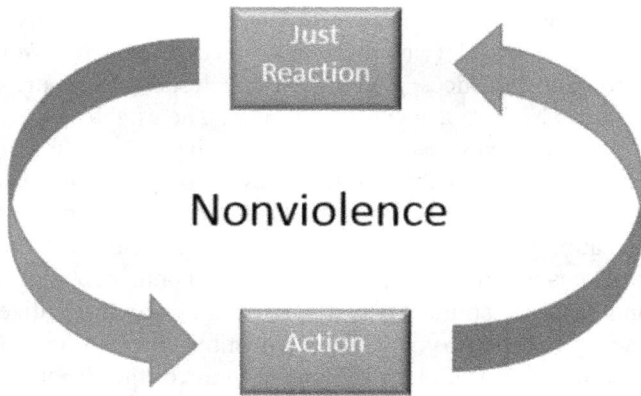

Figure 3.2 For a culture of nonviolence to be initiated and sustained, the nature of reactions needs to be carefully chosen. The reaction must not be based on negative emotions (anger, greed, vindictiveness, etc.). They need to be derived from positive emotions (love, sympathy, generosity, etc.), and therefore termed as just reaction.

secondary importance, if not totally abandoned. Such a violent society may survive, but eventually it heads toward its rapid decline and extinction.

Figure 3.3 qualitatively shows interrelationships and interactions among human rights, violence, and nonviolence. It is inclusive of Gandhi's vision of social discourse referenced earlier with regard to the interplay among

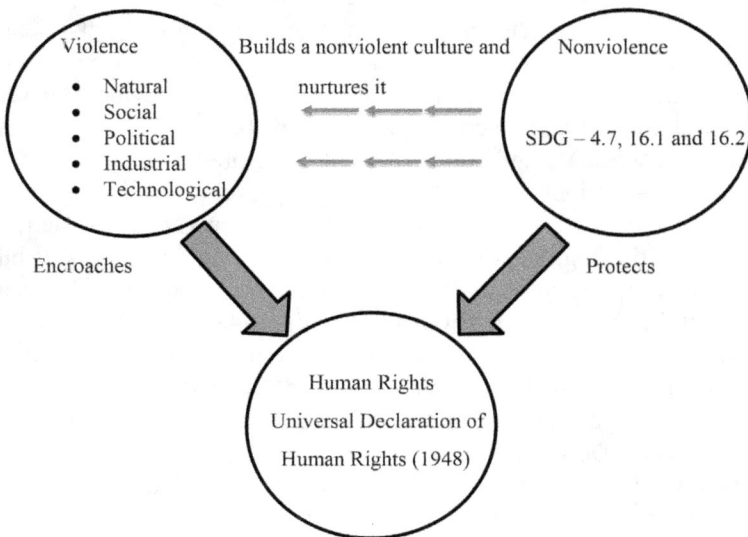

Figure 3.3 Interrelationships between human rights, violence, and nonviolence.

political, social, and religious endeavors. A constant interplay between moral (nonviolent) and immoral (violent) social forces emanating from human aspirations, religious practices, government policies, economic disparity, and business practices leads to a social equilibrium. The established equilibrium defines acceptable, perhaps tolerable limits of social violence at a given time. It is apparent that these tolerable limits are results of long-term social experiments. It should also be noted that the limits of tolerable violence are not rigid social demarcation boundaries, but are subject to displacements and adjustments with the change in climate, population migration, technological developments, and nature of political power. Civil and law-abiding citizens would welcome, accept, and honor socially compatible and enforceable human rights policies which are within the tolerable limits of the social distress.

It is also noted from figure 3.3 that violence of any kind encroaches on human rights. The violence may be rooted in social practices (reactions or policies) which could be results of diverse causes confounded into a given form. The violence is inflicted on individuals or a significant segment of the society, denying their dignity and just expectations.

The violence emanating from gun culture denies human rights. The gun culture empowers a group of people to harm persons of their choosing and even take away their lives. Such a decision and action are beyond the natural intellect and wisdom of humans as endowed by God (Cortright 2009, 14–20). The argument highlights that there are inherent limits of human knowledge and judgment, thus, it is not possible for humans to grasp and execute absolute, moral truth. Life and death is such a moral truth.

For the sake of completeness, a relationship between the nonviolent philosophy and organized advocacy of human rights needs to be discussed. An appreciation and enforcements of human values are evident in various cultural traditions, moral practices, and religious beliefs. But, they remained only intuitive wisdoms and were subject to interpretations and distortions. Such misinterpretations and distortions could justify and legalize slavery and apartheid for centuries. With respect to the progress of nonviolence philosophy since the beginning of human civilization and awareness of human rights in recent times, three major events in the last century may be recalled. First was the Declaration of Human Rights in 1948, and over more than a half century later the second event was an announcement of the millennium development goals (MDGs) (United Nations MDGs 2000). Subsequently, the third event was a declaration of the sustainable development goals (SDGs) (United Nations SDGs 2015). The topics of nonviolence and human rights are much broader, but the UN documents endorse them globally with a purpose and focus on human values.

The MDGs initiative was mute with respect to nonviolent methods and actions for the advocacy of human rights in achieving global peace; however, the initiative was considered to be successful. Subsequently, the UN recognized the role of nonviolence and civil culture in the global arena for advocacy of human rights, and later some nonviolent goals and actions were articulated as SDG subgoals 4.7, 16.1, and 16.2. Table 3.2 presents the SDGs 4.7, 16.1, and 16.2.

The SDG 4.7 states that all students acquire skills to honor human rights, gender equality, and promotion of a culture for embracing nonviolence and peace, global citizenship, and cultural diversity. Admittedly, at the global level, this is an enormous task that requires commitments of all governments around the world. Furthermore, achieving the goal by 2030 is undoubtedly a major challenge considering the fact that many parts of the world even today lack educational infrastructure. The SDG 16.1 is a qualitative goal for reducing all forms of violence and related death rates. The subgoal again requires massive commitments of all governments for developing a reliable statistical database including crimes from all kinds of violence. The governments must also commit to the objective of the subgoal that progress will be made toward an agreed upon target on a yearly basis. The SDG 16.2 is a children-centric goal to end abuse, exploitation, torture, and trafficking. The subgoal is extremely important to defend and protect the young population and future generations of global citizens, but again the subgoal is qualitative and would be difficult to monitor and quantify without any clearly identified target.

The SDG subgoals, related tasks to be performed, and the timeline to achieve them were prepared and shared with noble intents. However, they seem to be more like stretch-goals. One can imagine the magnitude of social, economic, and political capital that need to be invested into reforming just one form of violence—the prevailing American gun culture. The documentation of the subgoals is certainly a positive development. Because, it is for the first time a global institution, the UN has recognized the role of nonviolent culture for protecting and promoting human rights. The initiatives can conceivably steer the global community toward peace, prosperity, and security. But, just the recognition of nonviolent culture for the good of society at the global level will not be enough. Their implementation and accountability will require

Table 3.2 Sustainable Developmental Goals for Developing Nonviolent Culture

SDG # 4.7	By 2030 ensure all students acquire knowledge and skills through education to honor human rights, gender equality, promotion of a culture embracing peace and nonviolence, global citizenship and an appreciation for cultural diversity
SDG # 16.1	Significantly reduce all forms of violence and related death rates everywhere
SDG # 16.2	End abuse, exploitation, trafficking, and all forms of violence and torture against children

substantial effort and resources which the global community must provide because the root causes that initiate and perpetuate violence are many and they emerge from diverse origins. Furthermore, the confounding effect distorts the original violent roots, often requiring a long time to understand and define the social malady to formulate proper corrective measures. Developing a social policy to address chronic violence thus becomes a difficult task.

It should be understood that an uninterrupted, continuing escalation of violence is like a fuel to the fire that can irreversibly damage the social fabric and even threaten its existence. An objective analysis of the roots and causes of each form of violence is essential before appropriate, corrective measures can be developed and implemented for a sustainable civil society. At the same time, a sustainable and progressive society must be intellectually and economically capable of protecting human rights, as these rights are universally acceptable irrespective of time and place.

Smaller arrows from nonviolence to violence in figure 3.3 point out that the sphere of influence of violence should be constrained by implementing and practicing principles of nonviolence. Furthermore, it is apparent from the schematic that there is a need for social institutions to promote nonviolent culture and enforce compliance with human rights. These institutions ought to be conceived, developed, and sustained. Furthermore, they need to be endorsed and secured by the political power so that they become integral parts of the social structure. The objectives of these institutions would be centered on the development of a nonviolent culture, the elimination of violent policies sowing seeds of long-term conflict, and the promotion of human rights. Such institutions would ensure that a nonviolent culture prospers and human rights are honored to the fullest.

GUN-CULTURE-INSPIRED EVENTS

Chicago, Illinois

For a while, the crime rates in a few suburbs of Chicago have been a subject of extensive media coverage and remain a matter of major concern from the law and order points of view. In the context of the gun culture, it is illustrative to have a brief assessment of the chronic crime situation. In 2015 and 2016, the number of homicides in Chicago was 528 and 812, respectively. It showed a gradual but slight reduction down to 516 through 2019. Subsequently, it increased to 769 in 2020 (ABC News 2021). It may be argued that little has changed since the first edition of this book was published in 2018. Apparently, whatever policies and actions were taken by the federal and local governments have remained ineffective.

To address the violent crime problem in 2017, the city of Chicago flooded the streets with one thousand extra police officers on the Fourth of July weekend. But, they could not make a dent in the frequency of the continuing gun violence. In fact, the city experienced it as one of the most violent Independence Day weekends in recent years. At least 102 people were shot between late Friday afternoon and early Wednesday. Among the people shot, fifteen were killed and the remaining eighty-seven were wounded. In spite of the deployment of a new technology, "ShotSpotter," law enforcement was unable to bring the violence under control. The trigger points for the violence were petty disputes that escalated into a situation when someone pulled out a gun. The violent and organized groups in the city of Chicago absorbed illegal guns coming from external sources. These external guns added fuel to the fire already ignited by existing guns, poverty, unstable families, gangs, and drugs. A total of 159 guns were seized during the Fourth of July weekend of 2017. It is apparent that modern technology and law enforcement resources are not enough and unlikely to succeed in getting Chicago gun violence under control.

A transformation of the gun-violence-infested neighborhoods to a civil community which is nonviolent, caring, and supportive needs to take place. Such a transformation is the call of the city of Chicago neighborhoods. The transformation requires inculcation of moral forces within the family, neighborhood, law enforcement, and the governments at all levels. The process of inculcation of moral forces is slow, for which patience and sustained resources are basic needs. As presented earlier, the process can be implemented by embracing and practicing socially compatible moral reactions and policies.

The civil society and justice system in Chicago appear to be under criminal assaults. In spite of sufficient law enforcement resources the situation continues to deteriorate. Yet, a major segment of the society—primarily, proponents of the gun culture in the country—appears to be ambivalent. The American public would like to know plans of the gun culture proponents to curb perpetuation of the violence, for example, the NRA. Their denials and narratives have even created an uncertainty about the causes of the violence in the city and, for that matter, in other cities and institutions of the U.S. as well.

One can imagine the state of social behavior and power of the criminal enterprise of the same crime-infested neighborhoods in Chicago if there were no guns. Significantly, fewer people would be hurt and there would be a drastic reduction in life-threatening injuries. The gun violence is the result of social reactions burdened with flawed policies such as portability and access of powerful guns as they are crafted by vested interests representing the gun and ammunition industries. Remedial measures based on just social reactions and appropriate policies are necessary to alleviate the crime aggravated by an uncontrolled supply of the powerful semiautomatic and automatic guns. The governments are empowered to develop a policy and enforce the supply limits. An objective assessment of the situation in Chicago leads one to believe that the gun culture is the prime contributor to the criminal enterprise perpetuating violence. However, it is not the only contributor. Social ills such as gangs, drugs, poverty, and race relations along with guns have collectively led to the deterioration of the city neighborhoods to the present deplorable state.

An effective solution to the problem needs to consider and study the lifestyles and values at the individual, family, and neighborhood levels. The transformation toward a nonviolent lifestyle and culture must begin with individuals and then extend to groups, neighborhoods, and communities. Parents need to be informed, educated, and involved to shape the future of their offspring. The adolescents with violent background and history must go through rigorous rehabilitation and education programs before they become a part of the society. And families must take responsibility for making communities and neighborhoods peaceful. The law enforcement should complement the efforts made by the families, neighborhoods, and communities. The law enforcement alone can't be disproportionately burdened and held accountable for the deteriorating crime situation of the troubled neighborhoods and city.

Alexandria, Virginia

The shooting of the Republican Congressman Steve Scalise at a congressional baseball practice in Alexandria, Virginia, on June 14, 2017, is an important episode in the long history of gun violence in the U.S.. The shooting was a horrific act of a lone shooter, James T. Hodgkinson, perhaps a mentally troubled person. During the encounter, he was shot by the Capitol police and died.

The shooting of the lawmaker, known for his support of gun culture energized his colleagues with a similar political background and philosophy. For a considerable period, some members of Congress have been making persistent calls for more relaxed gun control laws. Their voices became even louder after the shooting. Some of them were suggesting that lawmakers should carry guns wherever they go. The justification is that the proximity of a gun to a potential victim ensures protection of her or his life against threats from guns of attackers. These lawmakers are proponents of the idea that the law-abiding citizens should be able to defend for themselves anywhere and everywhere. Bills were introduced in the House to allow lawmakers to almost always carry a concealed weapon, eliminate federal control on silencers, and recognize concealed carry permits of other states to be legal in Washington

DC. These developments illustrate the attitude, thought process, and power of gun culture. The initiatives undertaken by the congressmen are examples of flawed policies under development. One wonders about and searches for lawmakers defending the rights (Article 3 of the Declaration) of potential victims of all ages.

Perhaps, the most disturbing outcome of the tragic shooting of Congressman Scalise and three others is the motivation for some lawmakers to justify laws to arm people with more guns in the names of "self-defense" and "good guys with guns." It is now personal for these lawmakers. Several of them have cited a list that was found in the possession of the gunman with names of six members of the Congress. The justification for the proposed relaxation of gun laws was coming from the political leadership, and therefore it should be taken seriously. It is my view that if this justification had any merit, by now the U.S. should be a gun-violence-free country since "good guys" have owned guns for "self-defense" and also for defense of others attacked by the guns of bad guys. Congressman Scalise, an avid supporter of the second amendment, remains an ardent opponent of gun restriction proposals as of this writing. He believes that the shooting of 2017 has affirmed his views on gun ownerships.

More recently, pro-Trump protesters stormed the U.S. Capitol building on January 6, 2021 in response to claims of election fraud, leading Trump to lose. Some of the protesters were armed with guns and other deadly weapons. The Capitol building was placed on lockdown, with members of Congress locked inside safe places. Five U.S. citizens were killed; the first one was shot on the neck and succumbed to the injury, three others died because of "medical emergencies," and the fifth person was a police officer beaten to death with a fire extinguisher.

The mayhem took place during a session of Congress within a period of what is usually celebrated for being a peaceful transfer of power in a country globally known as the beacon of democracy. Collectively, we need to do some soul searching to understand the ramifications of the gun culture and the harm it can inflict to the civil society and governance of the country. Admittedly, the mayhem is a case of political violence, but we were fortunate that the gun violence in its known form and lethality did not emerge in this case. One can easily imagine the outcome of a synchronized political and gun violence. An uncontrolled gun culture coupled with a false political narrative would not spare the most powerful of lawmakers, let alone be the average citizens. Fortunately, the country was spared large-scale mayhem by wise and timely intervention of the law enforcement.

Gandhi's protest movement "Satyagraha," based on the practice of nonviolence, has withstood the test of time. The concept of the movement emerged from the Eastern Philosophy and it has been universally practiced for over a century now. The name of the movement was derived from two root words of Sanskrit; "Sat" (God/truth) and "Agraha" (hold on/humble request). The narratives of progun proponents are coupled with false information. The campaign to institutionalize the culture with American way of life is doomed to failure because it is coupled with falsehood, itself a form of violence. It is also antinature.

Pillars of Support for Gun Culture

Social violence of any kind is often conjoined with the power structure that may have originated from societal needs, racial distinctions, religious beliefs, business practices, and ethical norms of the political power. The gun culture of the U.S. is sustained by a power structure embedded in the social traditions and the U.S. Constitution. Earlier discussions on the social requirements for guns, constitutional protection, and current practice of the gun culture have already shed some light on the probable pillars of support for the culture.

According to a political theory of hierarchy (Sharp 2013), power is inherent in practically all social and political relationships. The power resides on social and political support pillars. Therefore, the violence emanating from the power must also rest on support pillars erected by the social and political establishments. The support pillars of violence are generally multifaceted. To address a social issue emerging from the gun culture, one needs to identify these pillars. Subsequently, nonviolent actions need to be conceived, designed, developed, and executed sequentially in order of their effectiveness to dismantle the pillars.

The power of gun culture rests on the support pillars of a large number of indifferent citizens, heavily endowed and politically powerful gun lobby, lawmakers financially sponsored by the gun lobby, and the Second Amendment. Through these pillars (representing a large proportion of the population), the gun culture dictates its wishes onto even those who vehemently oppose their beliefs and practices. A nonviolent plan of actions needs to objectively assess the strength of these pillars and develop strategic initiatives with the priority of bringing them down one by one. Obviously, all these pillars of support need to be removed if one wishes to uproot the menace of gun violence in its entirety.

CONCLUSION

The ramifications of the gun culture on violent social crimes, specifically in the context of human rights encroachments, have been discussed and analyzed. A historical perspective of gun culture reveals that it has been an integral part of the American heritage for almost three centuries. The social tradition justified legal protection of gun ownership through the Second Amendment to the Constitution. An analysis of the gun culture through a conceptual framework of social action and reaction (applicable to all kinds of violence) and the nature of societal response emerging from them have been conducted. The culture was a result of the social action designed to satisfy the societal needs well before the independence of the U.S.. Centuries later, an analysis of the culture leads one to believe that the interests of the society are not served by its perpetuation. The time has come to accept that technology has made guns more lethal and social needs are now very different from what they were almost three centuries ago. Such an acceptance is essential if we are to move forward with reforms of the gun culture to minimize continuing damage to the society.

An organized and focused advocacy for the advancement of human rights began in 1948 under the auspices of the UN. A number of initiatives were undertaken by the UN to protect, preserve, and promote human rights in all of its member countries. Some countries protested specific contents of the rights, and even today these countries are defiant to a few specific articles of the declaration. For example, Saudi Arabia had reservations on religious freedom and the former Soviet Union, now Russia, disagreed with the right related to employment. The encroachments on human rights by social violence emanating from the gun culture are an expected but worrisome reality that needs to be dealt with. Two events of the last decade representing the current state of affairs, the first in Chicago and the second in

Washington DC (including recent insurrection of the Capitol building) highlight violations of the rights of people comprising social strata from ordinary citizens in Chicago to very powerful and privileged lawmakers in Washington DC. The SDGs of the UN announced in 2015 duly recognizes the role of nonviolent culture for global peace. The SDG has set three subgoals for the member countries to adopt, implement, and monitor.

This chapter infers that there are inherent elements of incompatibility between the gun culture and advocacy of human rights in the U.S. that arise from the lethality and abundance of automatic and semiautomatic guns. To address and rectify the social ills associated with the gun culture, reconciliation needs to be made between the Second Amendment of the U.S. Constitution and Article 3 of the UN Declaration of Human Rights. The number of lives lost to gun violence in the country is inordinately high. It could be minimized through bans on assault weapons, and tougher controls on gun shows and the online firearms business. Furthermore, even greater benefits could be accomplished if availability of guns is restricted to only those who must have them. An enforcement of the UN's SDGs for the development of a culture embracing nonviolence as the cohesive force in communities of the world is a step in the right direction. Social practices with moral actions and reactions are the guiding lights for nurturing and sustaining nonviolent cultures.

Technological developments and progressive societal activities tend to drive the social discourse toward an unjust and unfair culture. It needs to be understood and recognized that development, progress, prosperity, and higher standard of living are coupled with some detrimental consequences. A proactive approach to investigate emerging scientific and technological innovations with potential for detrimental outcomes needs to be pursued by the government and corporate establishments. Appropriate actions to maintain societal harmony and peace should be communicated to the concerned segments of the population.

REFERENCES

ABC News. 2021. http.www.abcnews.go.com/US/wire story/Chicago-ends-2020-7 69homicides-gun-violence-surges-75005949 (citing data from January 1 report).

Amnesty International. 2021. http.www.amnesty.org/en/what-we-do/arms-control/gun-violence/.

Attenborough, Richard. 1982. *The Words of Gandhi.* New York: HarperCollins Publishers.

Clark, Cynthia. 2013. *Creating and Sustaining Civility in Nursing Education.* Indianapolis: Sigma Theta Tau International Publishing.

Cortright, David. 2009. *Gandhi and Beyond: Nonviolence for a New Political Age.* Boulder: Paradigm Publishers.

Hofstadter, Richard. 1970. *America as a Gun Culture.* Chicago: American Heritage Publishing.

Kaslow, Nadine J., and Natalie N. Watson. 2016. "Civility: A Core Component of Professionalism." *Psychology Teacher Network* (September).

Sharp, Gene. 2013. *How Nonviolent Struggle Works.* East Boston: Albert Einstein Institution.

United Nations Organizations MDG. 2000. "Millennium Development Goals." *Millennium Summit,* September.

United Nations Resolutions A/RES/70/1. 2015. "Sustainable Development Goals."

Chapter 4

Gender Differences in Youth Gun Culture

A Discussion of Caribbean Findings Using the Lens of U.S. Gun Culture

Carolyn Gentle-Genitty, Jangmin Kim, and Corinne C. Renguette

In the last decade, we have seen many studies touting the associations with gun access and increased risks to persons using those guns (Ruback et al. 2011; Schroeder and Mowen 2014). New studies are expanding discussions of access to guns (Caputi et al. 2020; Choi 2017; Everytown for Gun Safety 2019; National Center for Education Statistics 2017; Stroope 2017). Yet, other budding studies are expanding discussions of gun access influencing parenting, parenting styles, discipline, and supervision quality. Many of these activities have gained national and international attention. The national attention brought with it questions of whether U.S. gun culture and the underlying factors related to it are fully understood.

As we grapple with these issues in the U.S., there is a benefit to examining what we can learn from other nations' experiences with these same issues. In this chapter, we discuss the findings from a Caribbean study and examine them using a U.S. gun culture lens with a focus on underlying risk and protective factors. Both U.S. and Caribbean youth have increasingly committed gun-related crime and violence. Much of the crime and violence have been correlated with a wide range of both risk and protective factors at individual, family, and school levels. Furthermore, gender inequality and male dominance in general violence are of primary concern in Caribbean contexts. Previous studies' findings warrant an in-depth investigation of the gender differences in youth gun culture.

This study used self-reported data collected from 512 youth in five Caribbean countries: Jamaica, Antigua and Barbuda, Trinidad and Tobago, Saint Lucia, and Saint Kitts. The surveys were administered to youth during the summer of 2014. In November 2013, the Caribbean Community (CARICOM) Secretariat (with funding from the Kingdom of Spain) embarked on a pilot project to reduce youth-on-youth violence in schools and communities in these five CARICOM member states. The project was developed out of the concern for the escalation of gang violence and other related forms of violence in schools and the surrounding communities. Antigua and Barbuda, St. Kitts and Nevis, Saint Lucia, Jamaica, and Trinidad and Tobago were identified as the five member states in which to pilot the project. Using a set of criteria, each country was asked to identify one high school perceived to be at-risk. This study found that when male and female perceptions of access to guns were compared, males responded more favorably to stating that access to guns was easy. Secondary research on U.S. gun culture shows that cross-culturally, both the U.S. and the Caribbean can benefit by recognizing the gender differences in these cultures in relationship to gun culture. This chapter concludes with a discussion of the implications for effectively addressing gender issues around gun culture.

RESEARCH QUESTIONS

In the U.S., gun culture has been studied extensively, and social gun culture is prolific in addition to the gun culture of crime and violence. The cross-cultural relationship to gun culture in both the U.S. and the Caribbean will be explored in the literature. A dearth of research exists on Caribbean gun culture, however, and this study shows the results of primary research examining two research questions:

1. Do youth in Caribbean countries have different perceptions of gun culture by gender?
2. How do the different aspects of youth gun culture—community norms against gun carrying, access to guns, and peer involvement in gun carrying to school—correlate with risk and protective factors at family and school levels, and do these correlations differ by gender?

In addition to discussing what this research found, this chapter will examine parallels between what has been found in the U.S. research surrounding gun culture, especially as it relates to age and gender.

LITERATURE REVIEW

Gun culture in the U.S. continues to be pervasive (Bindu et al. 2016; Coker et al. 2017; Kocsis 2015; Parker et al. 2017; Utter and True 2000). There is enough variation in the literature about Caribbean gun culture that to date, current findings do not provide clear insight into the research questions in this chapter. The United Nations Office on Drugs and Crime has begun shedding light on global efforts through their 2020 Global study on firearms trafficking building on their 2015 study on firearms. The study tracked the flow of guns to the black or illicit market. (See figure 4.1)

Outside of New York Times (August 25, 2019) reports showing links to guns in U.S. showing up Jamaica, comparisons are not common between U.S. and Caribbean nations. However, an attempt is made here, using access to the current literature, to present ideas being

discussed from this most current study of the Caribbean gun culture in relationship to what has been studied in the U.S. The U.S. gun culture is extremely complicated and divisive and cannot be fully explored in the context of this chapter; however, some elements of these issues might be useful to include when looking at the study herein.

Guns. They have been a staple of our culture. Today, they are no longer hidden for its use and access, and its role has changed. Moving from social and recreational roles in some cultures, to power, fear, and violence in others,

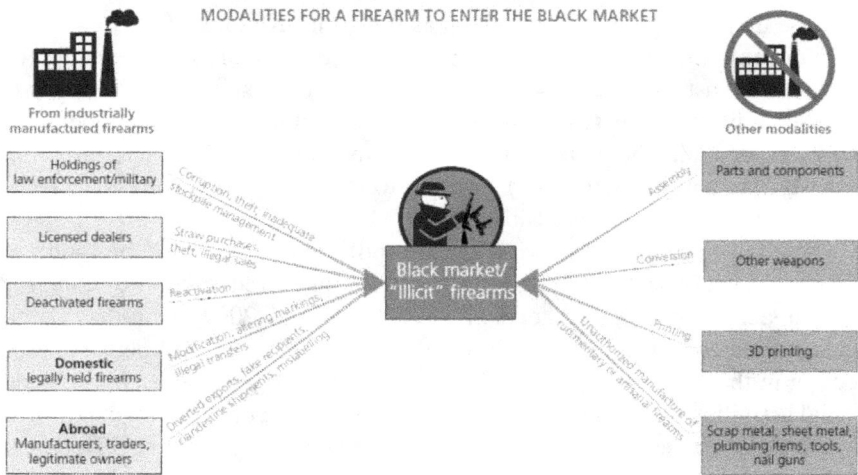

Figure 4.1 Modalities for a firearm to enter the black market. UNODC, 2020, p. 38 | Used with permission: Global Study on Firearms Trafficking, 2020.

and still a symbol of work and income for other groups. During the pandemic, U.S. scholars Caputi et al. (2020) reported Google search data showed a rise in gun presence. Their concern centered on use in unintentional shootings, domestic violence, suicides, and city violence. Their results showed, from March 8 through April 11, 2020, 2.1 million searches were for cleaning or preparing and buying guns, a 40 percent spike compared to times following the mass shootings of Sandy Hook and Parkland. Because of such shootings, gunfire on school grounds continues to fuel the National Center for Education Statistics (NCES) to collect data on school crime and safety recording violent deaths, nonfatal student and teacher victimization, fights, weapons, fear and avoidance, discipline, safety, security, and more. 2017 NCES reported that "about 16 percent of students in grades 9-12 shared that they carried a weapon anywhere, at least once during the last 30 days, 4% of whom reported carrying it on school property." A nonprofit research group, Everytown for Gun Safety (everytownresearch.org) has also flagged the lack of consistent data of gun incidents involving schools and students. In 2019, the group reported alarming data of over 16K students shot or injured with over 3K children and teens shot and killed, while countless others suffered trauma from exposure, violence, and abuse. In 2020, the group reports that even during a pandemic, injuries climbed, deaths were recorded, and incidents of gunfire reported in the schools made the news. Many continue to explore the real influence of guns and its hidden power.

We know that norms and practices of gun culture support a recursive practice. Recursive practice is that the belief that individuals, in their own right, create and perpetuate practices that carry on from generation to generation because that family has adopted them as the norm (Kondrat 2002).

The idea of recursive practice assumes a cyclical nature in the creation of culture. For instance, when examining gun culture, it may be safe to say that there is a difference between the U.S. culture and that of the Caribbean. In the U.S., guns may be perceived, largely in social and professional (policing, security, law enforcement, etc.) settings, to be more prominently displayed, more visible, and more accessible.

The citizens of the U.S. own over 200-million guns, they can be found in 30–35 percent of homes, and getting a gun is considered to be easy, even for those under 18 (see, e.g., Coker et al. 2017; Feder et al. 2007). Guns have been and continue to be owned for both recreational activities and for personal protection in the U.S. (Bindu et al. 2016). Both types of gun ownership include social activities that continue to perpetuate the culture of gun ownership. In a survey of 4000 people, about 29 percent owned a gun, and about 27 percent felt that their family life or social life (or both) involved or should involve guns or they would be looked down upon for not owning a gun (Bindu et al. 2016). Peer and family behaviors strongly influence gun culture. Nearly 80 percent of gun owners have peers who are also gun owners, and having peers who own guns are more common for males than females (Parker et al. 2017). Guns are often purchased as gifts or for personal use in recreational and sport activities such as hunting, recreational target practice, sport shooting (e.g., specialty gun associations, reenactment groups, cowboy shooting societies, etc.), collections (specialty, historical, art, and rare guns), and of course for protection and self-defense. One study showed that about 13.4 percent of gun owners in the U.S. were given their guns as a gift (Bindu et al. 2016).

Those who lived in a house that had guns growing up are more likely to be gun owners when they are adults (Parker et al. 2017). In addition, gun ownership often starts at a young age. Of those who had guns in the home growing up, 47 percent got their first gun when they were under 18 years of age, although that is more common for males than for females (Parker et al. 2017). Gun owners often see gun ownership as a right to protect their freedom based on the Second Amendment of the U.S. Constitution (Parker et al. 2017).

Cross-culturally, those holding strong views about gun ownership may have experienced the perception of gun carrying and purpose growing up and may pass this view down from previous generations. As such they may see continuing that perception through recursive practice as tradition. Thus, gun carrying is not seen as bad or unusual, but relevant to who they are and how they see themselves as a person and, as such, those who carry guns may advocate for more of such. In the U.S., one example of this is the strong membership of the National Rifle Association, which advocates for Second Amendment rights and continuing gun ownership, sport shooting, and gun culture in the U.S. (National Rifle Association 2017).

Therefore, many people in the U.S. see the acts of crime and terror from an adolescent getting access to guns at home, from a display case, or from other locations in the home as isolated incidents. The fear among this group is not the gun and what it can do or the culture and what it perpetuates, but the person and what that person does with the gun. With this view, the person must be fixed and medicated, not the community, culture, or practices. Of course not everyone in the U.S. agrees, as is evidenced by the polarized debates over these issues (see, e.g., Kocsis 2015). A large group of people advocates for stricter gun policies to prevent violence and crime related to guns, and many gun owners and nonowners have experienced or know someone who has experienced violence, injury, or death due to gun violence (Parker et al. 2017).

Emergency departments, especially in large cities, see much gun-related violence, injury, and death in youth, especially males, from ages 15 to 24, which is often thought to be because guns are so easy to access, although the complex relationship with many other variables is acknowledged (Downey et al. 2013). In addition, correlations between youth delinquency (including substance use), violence, and gun carrying behaviors have been found (see, e.g., Logan et al. 2016; Vidourek et al. 2016). The view on this side of the debate is characterized by the desire to look at the implications that the constitutional freedoms promote in modern times and to consider safety and logical restrictions without removing the freedoms (Kocsis 2015).

In the Caribbean culture, children are largely exposed to guns through acts of delinquency, crime, and violence, and gun use is often voiced as being for protection. Even when carried by law enforcement and used in response to crime and violence, guns are touted as being used for protection. When guns are visibly shown in everyday interactions with youth, it is associated with person or property protection. Protection is used loosely to often mean "demonstration of power" as in gang violence and drug trafficking. Conversely, protection is also viewed as to protect one's self against the unknown.

In the U.S., guns are also seen as a form of protection, and owning and carrying them is a constitutional right (Kocsis 2015; Parker et al. 2017). In addition, guns are prevalent in crime and violence, and not all gun owners are responsible gun owners (Kocsis 2015). However, the social, recursive, and freedom aspects of gun ownership and carrying are widely pervasive in U.S. gun culture (Parker et al. 2017). Thus, as the recursive cycle presupposes, in the U.S., a continuance of gun use and carrying is often perceived as being for social and preventative purposes and, in the Caribbean, gun use and carrying is often perceived as being for fear-driven protection. This distinction is not meant to pigeon-hole groups into specific categories, but to help us to understand that our perceptions must be shaped by what our culture of gun carrying, usage, and culture is. A culture impacts the society in the form of norms, values, beliefs, and traditions (Berger and Luckmann 1966). A culture can also dictate who is involved in gun use and carrying such as that of gender (identity, behaviors, roles, and interpersonal relationships). A society's cultural values may inhibit gender equality, suggesting that gender and age may aid in predicting victimization (Dixon et al. 2006).

GENDER DIFFERENCES IN GUN CULTURE

There are gender and age differences in gun carrying and usage. For instance, more males may go through the initiation process of learning how to shoot and kill for sport or food than females. This appears to be true in the U.S. where 58 percent of males who own guns are likely to participate in gun enthusiast activities as opposed to only 43 percent of females who own guns (Parker et al. 2017). In addition, males who own guns report that 54 percent of their peers also own guns, where only 40 percent of females who own guns report that their peers own guns (Parker et al. 2017). In the

U.S., 39 percent of male respondents in one study reported owning a gun, whereas only 22 percent of women reported owning a gun (Parker et al. 2017). There have even been campaigns devoted to recruiting more women into gun culture using both the argument for self-and-family-protection and that of feminism, because women are underrepresented in gun culture, but also because women tend to lead gun regulation efforts (Goss 2017). In a fear-driven, male-dominated culture, males may be armed more with guns for protection of themselves, their family, others, and property than compared to females and parents may take different stances with their girls than their boys.

Protective factors that have been noted in the U.S. include family and school connections and interventions (Logan et al. 2016). However, there are no current signs of slowdowns with gun-related incidents in either the U.S. or the Caribbean. In fact, both countries are reporting increase in the use of weapons in crime. Many of these incidences are the use of guns in crime linked with drug trafficking, with youth crime, violence, and gun usage overtaking all other challenges (Logan et al. 2016; Parra-Torrado 2014; UNODC and World Bank 2007). In the U.S., risk factors as reported by respondents include unstable family relationships; economics; influence of video game, movie, and television violence; and easy access (both legally and illegally) to guns (Parker et al. 2017). In the U.S., youth violence including homicides, violent crimes, rapes, and weapons charges continues to trend upward (Downey et al. 2013; Feder et al. 2007). Gender plays a role in youth violence in the U.S. as well. Boys tend to be socialized into stereotypically masculine roles including violence (Feder et al. 2007), and as Downey et al. (2013) found, young males are the largest group seen in gun-related violence in inner city hospitals. Risk factors for youth in the Caribbean include lack of employment for youth, a poor educational system, and early dropout (Imbusch et al. 2011; Parra-Torrado 2014; UNODC and World Bank 2007), poverty, mass migration to urban environments, unsafe neighborhoods, drug trafficking, unsuccessful policing, access to weapons, and gangs (Imbusch et al. 2011; UNODC and World Bank 2007). Parra-Torrado (2014) reports that the economic cost of youth crime in certain Caribbean countries is estimated to equate to between 3 percent and 4 percent of the GDP and is growing.

Individual risk factors of violence in Caribbean and Latin America include age, education, family, income, youth, male, gun ownership, and others (Imbusch et al. 2011). The community risk factors include many of the same challenges of high unemployment and residential mobility, closeness to drug trade, poverty, feeble policies in schools, gender inequality, customs supporting male dominance and general violence, weak criminal justice system, and access to weapons (Imbusch et al. 2011).

METHODS

The primary research for this study was conducted in the Caribbean school system with 512 students responding to a survey about youth-on-youth violence. The survey identified risk factors, protection factors, and community and school perceptions surrounding gang involvement and violence at school.

Sample

In November 2013, the CARICOM Secretariat (with funding from the Kingdom of Spain) embarked on a pilot project to reduce youth-on-youth violence in schools and communities in five CARICOM member states. The project was developed out of the concern for the escalation of gang violence and other related forms of violence in schools and the surrounding communities. Antigua and Barbuda, St. Kitts and Nevis, Saint Lucia, Jamaica, and Trinidad and Tobago were identified as the five member states in which to pilot the project. Using a set of criteria, each country was asked to identify one high school perceived to be at-risk. At each high school, principals were asked to identify 10 percent of their student population for participation in the study. From this group of students, 512 students completed the survey. Of the 512 students, 266 (51.8 percent) were females; 246 (48.2 percent) were males. Three hundred twenty-seven participants (65.7 percent) were in the 14–16 age group, 122 (24.5 percent) were in the 11–13 age group, and 49 (9.8 percent) were in the 17–19 age group. The largest ethnic group was Black (n = 336, 69.3 percent), followed by mixed ethnicity (n = 105, 21.6 percent), and a small number of various other ethnic groups (e.g., White, Chinese, and Indian). The majority of participants (n = 401, 80 percent) lived with their parents; the other students reported living with guardians (n = 37, 7.4 percent), grandparents (n = 28, 5.6 percent), or others (n = 35, 7 percent).

Data Collection and Procedures

Researchers in each country administered the survey at the identified schools. Survey responses were input into SPSS for factor analysis and descriptive statistics with some correlation analysis. We conducted a series of t-tests to assess whether gender groups have different perceptions of the various aspects of gun culture. Surveys were used to gather information from participating students during the summer of 2014. The principal investigator administered the survey in each school spending two days in each country. The survey was conducted using a fifty-one-item paper-based questionnaire, which included items assessing youth violence or gang problems developed by the Office of Juvenile

Justice and Delinquency (used with approval; OJJDP 2009). About 75 percent of the standardized questions were used to form the survey template. Two sets of questions were also included in the survey: the Adverse Childhood Experience study trauma scale (ACE; Felitti et al. 1998) and Perception of School Social Bonding (PSSB) Instrument (Gentle-Genitty 2009).

Gun Culture

Gun culture is a broad concept that encompasses people's behaviors, attitudes, and beliefs about gun ownership and gun usage (Utter and True 2000). We measured the three aspects of gun culture perceived by Caribbean youth. First, community norms against gun carrying were measured by a single item that asked youth how much they felt adults in their community would think it was wrong to carry a gun to school. Second, the access to guns was measured by a single item that asked them how much they felt it would be easy to get guns. Finally, peer involvement in gun carrying was measured by a single item that asked them how much they agreed that they had close friends who have carried a gun to school. All the variables were rated on a five-point Likert scale with higher scores representing positive or negative gun cultures.

Family Risk and Protective Factors

For a family risk factor, the family history of violence and crime was measured by three five-point Likert items that assessed the extent to which youth had lived with family members committed to violence and crimes. Family cohesion as a family protective factor was measured by six five-point Likert items about their perceptions of emotional bonding and positive relationships with their family members.

School Risk and Protective Factors

School risk factors include exposure to gang activity, being bullied, and unsafe school environments. The exposure to gang activity was measured by four five-point Likert items that assessed how often youth were exposed to or witnessed gang-related activities in their school. In addition, two five-point items were used to measure the extent to which youth were emotionally and physically bullied due to their low achievement in school. Unsafe school environments were measured by four five-point items that asked youth how much they felt their school was violent and unsafe. For a school protective factor, school social bonding was assessed using the short version of the PSSB instrument developed by Gentle-Genitty (2009). This instrument includes ten five-point items that measured the four subcomponents of school social bonding: attachment, commitment, involvement, and beliefs.

The overall instrument was first pilot-tested with a sample-set of students in Jamaica and then revised for the final use in the study of the five countries (Gentle-Genitty et al. 2017).

RESULTS

Results of this study show that, similar to U.S. culture, males in the Caribbean seem to have greater access to guns. Family history of violence and crime appeared to be a risk factor for both males and females, whereas family cohesion appeared to be a protective factor and, for males, this is especially true for reducing access to guns.

Gender Differences in Youth Gun Culture

There was no significant gender difference in community norms against weapon/gun carrying (see figure 4.2). However, figure 4.3 presents that male youth ($M = 2.11$, $SD = 1.59$)

reported a significantly higher score on the access to guns than did female youth ($M = 1.54$, $SD = 1.15$; $t = 4.18$, $p < .001$).

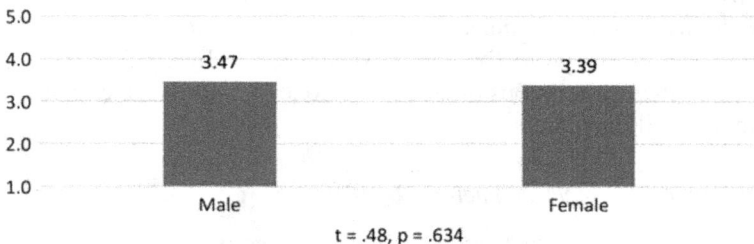

Figure 4.2　Gender difference in community norms against weapon/gun carrying.

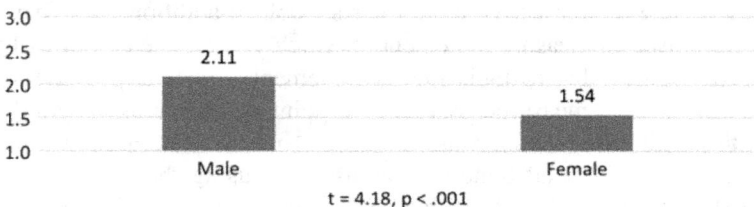

Figure 4.3　Gender difference in access to guns.

As can be seen in figure 4.4, perceptions of peer involvement in gun carrying did not significantly differ by gender. However, we found a significant interaction of gender and age in the perceived peer involvement by conducting two-way ANOVA ($F = 3.59$, $p < .05$). As youth become older, the peer involvement in gun carrying tended to be decreased among female youth, whereas it tended to be increased among male youth (see figure 4.5). The results imply that older and male youth may become the most at-risk population for having close friends who had carried a gun to their school.

Correlations between Youth Gun Culture and Risk/Protective Factors

A correlation analysis was employed to examine the overall relationships between youth gun culture and risk and protective factors at the family and school levels (see table 4.1). Overall, significant correlations with risk and protective factors varied across the different aspects of youth gun culture although family-level factors seemed more strongly correlated with the gun culture than school-level factors. More specifically, youth are more likely to report the access to guns in their school ($r = .28$, $p < .001$) and their peer involvement in gun carrying ($r = .30$, $p < .001$) when they had many family members committed to violence and crime. On the other hand, they tended to report a higher level of community norms against gun carrying ($r = .20$, $p < .001$)

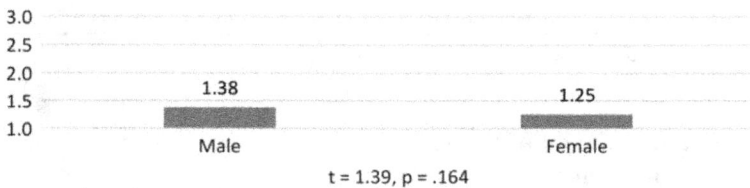

Figure 4.4   Gender difference in peer involvement in gun carrying.

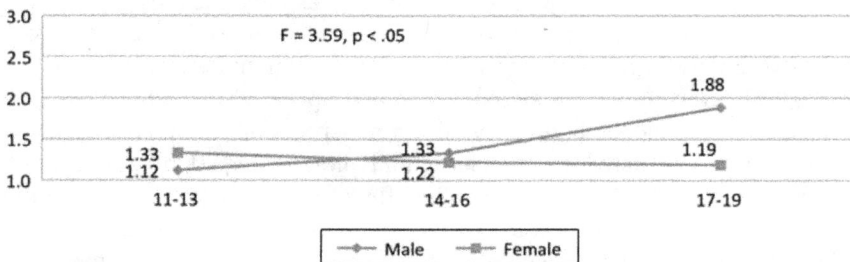

Figure 4.5   Interaction of gender and age in peer involvement in gun carrying.

Table 4.1 Correlations between Gun Culture Variables and Risk/Protective Factors

	Community Norms	Access to Guns	Peer Involvement
Family Factors			
Family history of violence/crime	−.04	.28***	.30***
Family cohesion	.20***	−.10*	−.08
School Factors			
Exposure to gang activity	−.07	.19***	.16**
Being bullied	.05	.08	.16**
Unsafe school environments	−.12*	−.00	.09
School social bonding	.20***	.11*	.07

Note: The numbers indicate Pearson correlation coefficients.
* < .05, ** p < .01, *** p < .001.

Table 4.2 Gender Difference in Correlations between Community Norms and Risk/Protective Factors

	Male Youth	Female Youth
Family Factors		
Family history of violence/crime	−.10	.02
Family cohesion	.23**	.15*
School Factors		
Exposure to gang activity	−.06	−.07
Being bullied	.04	.06
Unsafe school environments	−.15*	−.07
School social bonding	.20**	.18**

Note: The numbers indicate Pearson correlation coefficients.
* < .05, ** p < .01, *** p < .001.

and report a lower level of the access to guns (r = −.10, p < .05) when they had cohesive relationships with family members.

For school-level factors, the exposure to gang activity was positively correlated with the access to guns (r = .19, p < .001) and peer involvement in gun carrying (r = .16, p < .001). Being bullied was only positively correlated with the peer involvement (r = .16, p < .001), while unsafe school environments were only negatively correlated with the community norms (r = −.12, p < .05). Interestingly, school social bonding appeared to be both risk and protective factors depending on the different aspects of youth gun culture. It was positively correlated with the community norms (r = .20, p< .001), which was consistent with the previous studies' findings. However, it was found to be a risk factor that increased the access to guns (r = .11, p < .05).

We also conducted separate correlation analyses to better understand how the correlations differ by gender. Table 4.2 depicts the gender differences in the correlations between the community norms and risk and protective factors. Similar to the overall results, family cohesion and school social bonding were identified as significant protective factors of the community norms for both male and female youth; the strengths of the correlations were relatively greater for male youth than female youth. However, unsafe school environments were significantly correlated with the community norms only for male youth. Meaningful gender differences were also detected in the correlations between the access to guns and risk and protective factors.

Table 4.3 shows the gender differences in the correlations between the access to guns and risk and protective factors. Although, the family history of violence/crime was significantly correlated with the increased access to guns for both gender groups, the strength of the correlation was relatively greater for male youth than female youth (r = .39 vs. r = .22). Furthermore, family cohesion appeared to be a significant protective factor for reducing the access to guns for male youth, whereas the exposure to gang activity appeared to be a significant risk factor for increasing the access to guns for female youth.

Cross-Cultural Issues Related to Gun Culture

In the Caribbean, a family history of violence and crime showed an increase in peer involvement in gun carrying in females; however, this peer involvement declines as they get older. This could indicate that there are more similarities between U.S. female gun ownership and culture. More research would need to be done to assess this. In males, access to guns increases with age in the Caribbean. In both U.S. and Caribbean cultures, the family history of violence and crime is more strongly correlated with youth gun culture, however, unlike in the U.S. where social gun structure outside of crime is also strong, the Caribbean does not show this. Similar to the U.S. gun culture, however, the main factors in the Caribbean are also primarily the family history of

Table 4.3 Gender Difference in Correlations between Peer Involvement and Risk/ Protective Factors

	Male Youth	Female Youth
Family Factors		
Family history of violence/crime	.17*	.41***
Family cohesion	−.12	−.05
School Factors		
Exposure to gang activity	.16*	.16*
Being bullied	.08	.22**
Unsafe school environments	.04	.11
School social bonding	−.04	.16*

Note: The numbers indicate Pearson correlation coefficients.
* < .05, ** p < .01, *** p < .001.

violence and crime and peer behavior. We found that youth perceptions of access to guns were significantly higher and more favorable for males than females. Similar to the U.S. culture around gun carrying, this study also showed a significant interaction of gender in the perceived peer involvement in gun carrying. As youth become older, peer involvement in gun carrying tended to be decreased for females, whereas it tended to be increased for males. Overall, although family and school factors can be protective factors, family risk factors (e.g., family history of violence/crime and lack of family cohesion) were more strongly correlated with youth gun culture than school risk factors (e.g., exposure to gang activity, being bullied, and unsafe school environments). Interestingly, school social bonding appeared to be both risk and protective factors depending on the different variables of youth gun culture: it was a protective factor for improving community norms against gun carrying whereas it was a risk factor for increasing access to guns.

Finally, this study showed specific gender differences in the correlations with risk and practice factors. The family history of violence/crime was identified as a family risk factor for both gender groups; however, it was more strongly correlated with access to guns for males, whereas it was more strongly correlated with peer involvement in gun carrying for females. Family cohesion was found a protective factor for both gender groups, but it was an only significant factor for males to reduce access to guns. In contrast, exposure to gang activity led to significantly increased access to guns only for females although it increased peer involvement in gun carrying for both gender groups. Unsafe school environments were significantly correlated with decreased community norms for males, but not females.

This chapter concludes with a discussion of the implications for effectively addressing gender issues in addressing Caribbean youth's gun culture and violence. Additional research is needed to further compare U.S. gun culture and Caribbean gun culture, as the issues are multifaceted and deserve. The inner city U.S. gun culture seems to be more parallel to the Caribbean gun culture, since that research has shown the greatest amount of violence and crime in the U.S.. Although risk factors and protective factors may overlap, there are many complexities in the U.S. social gun culture that are not visibly present in this study of the Caribbean culture. Future studies could look at possible social gun culture in the Caribbean to see if any similarities with attitude can occur in any contexts. Additional research could include looking at individual issues including mental health and substance use in addition to family and social factors. Creating strategic prevention efforts and educational interventions including relationship-building and training has been shown to be effective in preventing violence (David-Ferdon and Simon 2014). Implementing these types of innovative prevention and education interventions in schools could promote fostering greater protective factors and bring a broader awareness to families, the community, and the school systems, especially in the Caribbean, about these issues.

Specific Implications for Practitioners in Caribbean Schools

There are definitely cross-cultural issues between U.S. gun culture and that of the Caribbean. Both cultures could benefit from work toward shifting the gun culture of youth and increasing the protective factors including family cohesion and school- and family-based interventions. However, understanding that males are more likely to carry guns and engage in youth violence given some of the risk factors associated with their environment in the Caribbean, and understanding that for females, this reduces as they age, we must establish greater support for males in school settings. There must be more protective factors instituted for males especially through adolescence. Families can be educated about these protective factors, and an awareness of these results may help with influencing a cultural shift. If we assume that males have fewer risks and let them be "boys" in the traditional sense, it is unlikely that the current gun culture will change. Males experience high rates of bullying and victimization perhaps hardening and acculturating them to plan retaliations and hold malice early manifesting in later gun carrying and usage. Mechanisms for males to report and get help early with victimization can aid, we believe, in reducing some of the gun violence. Solutions to a societal issue must involve gender analysis—founded on fact, not expectations (Schalkwyk 2000). Therefore, more research specifically on differentiation is a must.

We acknowledge CARICOM as the rightful owner of the aggregate data and ownership is distinct from the analysis of the data conducted by the authors. We would like to thank CARICOM and Spain for providing the funding to assess youth and youth violence in five Caribbean countries.

REFERENCES

Berger, Peter, and Thomas Luckmann. 1966. *The Social Construction of Reality.* Garden City, NY: Anchor Books.

Bindu, Kalesan, Marcos Villarreal, Katherine M. Keyes, and Sandro Galea. 2016. "Gun Ownership and Social Gun Culture." *Injury Prevention London*, 22, no. 3 (June), 216–226.

Caputi, T. L., S. Burd-Sharps, J. W. Ayers, M. Dredze, and N. Suplina. 2020. What Search Data Shows About Americans and Guns During the COVID-19 Crisis? Everytownresearch.org/covid-search.

Choi, N. G., D. M. DiNitto, and C. N. Marti. 2017. Youth Firearm Suicide: Precipitating/Risk Factors and Gun Access. *Children and Youth Services Review*, 83, 9–16. https://doi.org/10.1016/j.childyouth.2017.10.022.

Coker, Ann L., Heather M. Bush, Diane R. Follingstad, and Candace J. Brancato. 2017. "Frequency of Guns in the Households of High School Seniors." *Journal of School Health*, 87, 153–158.

David-Ferdon, Corinne, and Thomas R. Simon. 2014. *Preventing Youth Violence: Opportunities for Action*. Atlanta, GA: Centers for Disease Control and Prevention, Center for Injury Prevention and Control.

Dixon, Mike, Howard Reed, Ben Rogers, and Lucy Stone. 2006. *CrimeShare: The Unequal Impact of Crime*. Institute for Public Policy Research Website. http://www.ippr.org/files/images/media/files/publication/2011/05/crimeshare_1500.pdf?noredirect=1.

Downey, La Vonne A., Leslie S. Zun, Trena Burke, and Tangula Jefferson. 2013. "Does Gun Accessibility Lead to Violence-Related Injury?" *Southern Medical Journal*, 106, no. 2 (February), 161–172.

Feder, June, Ronald Levant, and James Dean. 2007. "Boys and Violence: A Gender-Informed Analysis." *Professional Psychology: Research and Practice*, 38, no. 4, 385–391.

Felitti, Vincent J., Robert F. Anda, Dale Nordenberg, David F. Williamson, Alison M. Spitz, Valerie Edwards, Mary P. Koss, and James S. Marks. 1998. "Relationship of Childhood Abuse and Household Dysfunction to Many of the Leading Causes of Death in Adults: The Adverse Childhood Experiences (ACE) Study." *American Journal of Preventative Medicine*, 14, no. 4, 245–258.

Gentle-Genitty, Carolyn. 2009. *Tracking More Than Absences: Impact of School's Social Bonding on Chronic Truancy*. Saarbrucken, Germany: Lambert Academic Publishing.

Gentle-Genitty, Carolyn, Jangmin Kim, Eun-Hye Yi, Douglas Slater, Beverly Reynolds, and Natasha Bragg. 2017. "Comprehensive Assessment of Youth Violence in Five Caribbean Countries: Gender and Age Differences." *Journal of Human Behavior in the Social Environment*, 27, no. 7, 745–759. https://doi.org/10.1080/10911359.2016.1273811.

Goss, Kristin A. (June 2017). "The Socialization of Conflict and its Limits: Gender and Gun Politics in America." *Social Science Quarterly*, 98, no. 2, 455–470.

Imbusch, Peter, Michel Misse, and Fernando Carrion. 2011. "Violence Research in Latin America and the Caribbean: A Literature Review." *International Journal of Conflict and Violence*, 5, no. 1, 87–154.

Kocsis, Michael. 2015. "Gun Ownership and Gun Culture in the United States of America." *Essays in Philosophy*, 16, 154–179.

Kondrat, Mary Ellen. 2002. "Actor-Centered Social Work: Re-Visioning 'Person-in-Environment' Through Critical Theory Lens." *Social Work*, 47, no. 4, 435–448. https://doi.org/10/1093/sw/47.4.435.

Logan, Joseph E., Kevin J. Vagi, and Deborah Gorman-Smith. 2016. "Combined Histories of Violent Behavior, Suicidal Ideation or Behavior, and Gun-Carrying." *Crisis*, 37, no. 6, 402–414. https://doi.org/10.1027/0227–5910/a000389.

Ministry of Justice. 2015. *Statistics on Race and the Criminal Justice System 2014*. https://www.gov.uk/government/uploads/system/uploads/ attachment_data/file/480250/bulletin.pdf.

National Rifle Association. 2017. https://home.nra.org/about-the-nra/.

New York Times. 2019, August 25. *How American Gun Laws Are Fueling Jamaica's Homicide Crisis*. https://www.nytimes.com/2019/08/25/world/americas/ one-h andgun-9-murders-how-american-firearms-cause-carnage-abroad.html.

Office of Juvenile Justice and Delinquency Prevention. 2009. *OJJDP Comprehensive Gang Model: Planning for Implementation*. Institute for Intergovernmental Research, U.S. Department of Justice Office of Justice Programs.

Pantin, Dennis. 1996. *The Challenge of Youth Unemployment in the Caribbean: The Role of Youth Employment Training Programmes*. International Labor Organization Website. http://www.ilo.org/wcmsp5/ groups/public/---americas/---r o-lima/---sro-port_of_spain/documents/ publication/wcms_224314.pdf.

Parker, Kim, Juliana Menasce Horowitz, Ruth Igielnik, Baxter Oliphant, and Anna Brown. 2017. "America's Complex Relationship with Guns: An In-Depth Look at the Attitudes and Experiences of U.S. Adults." *Pew Research Center Social and Demographic Trends*. http://www.pew socialtrends.org/2017/06/22/americas-com plex-relationship-with-guns/.

Parra-Torrado, Monica. 2014. "Youth Unemployment in the Caribbean." *World Bank Website*. http://documents.worldbank.org/curated/en/756431468012643544/pdf/ 883620WP0Box385224B00PUBLIC 00April02014.pdf.

Ruback, R. B., J. N. Shaffer, and V. A. Clark. 2011. "Easy Access to Firearms: Juveniles' Risks for Violent Offending and Violent Victimization." *Journal of Interpersonal Violence*, 26, no. 10, 2111–2138. https://doi.org/10.1177/0886 260510372948.

Schalkwyk, Johanna. 2000. *Culture*. Quebec, Canada: Culture, Gender Equality, and Development Cooperation. http://www.acdi-cida.gc.ca.

Schroeder, R. D., and T. J. Mowen. 2014. "Parenting Style Transitions and Delinquency." *Youth & Society*, 46, no. 2, 228–254. https://doi.org/10.117 7/0044118X12469041.

Stroope, S., and J. C. Tom. 2017. "In-Home Firearm Access Among US Adolescents and the Role of Religious Subculture: Results from a Nationally Representative Study." *Social Science Research*, 67, 147–159. https://doi.org/10.1016/ j.ssresearch.2017.06.001.

United Nations Office on Drugs and Crime [UNODC]. 2020. *Global Study on Firearms Trafficking*. https://www.unodc.org/unodc/en/firearms-protocol/ firearms -study.html.

United Nations Office on Drugs and Crime [UNODC] and World Bank. 2007. *Crime, Violence, and Development: Trends, Costs, and Policy Options in the Caribbean* (Report No. 37820). http://www.unodc.org/ pdf/research/Cr_and_Vio_Car_E.pdf.

Utter, Glenn, and James True. 2000. "The Evolving Gun Culture in America." *The Journal of American Culture*, 23, no. 2, 67–79.

Vidourek, Rebecca A., Keith A. King, and Ashley L. Merianos. 2016. "Impact of School Violence on Youth Alcohol Abuse: Differences Based on Gender and Grade Level." *Children & Schools*, 38, no. 2, 99–106. https://doi.org/10.1093/cs/ cdw006.

Chapter 5

A Woman's Place in Gun Advertisements

The American Rifleman, *1920–2019*

David Yamane, Riley Satterwhite, and Paul Yamane

A full-page advertisement placed by the Peters Cartridge Division of Remington Arms Co. features a large photo of Esther Sichler holding her target revolver and a large trophy. From the text of the ad, we learn the trophy is the Championship Cup from the Southern California Revolver League Matches. Sichler won the cup in record-setting fashion, shooting nineteen out of twenty bulls-eyes. The headline of the ad emphasizes that this "Lady Champion RELIES ON PETERS .38 SPECIAL 'TARGET' WAD-CUTTER" cartridges.

Although the advertisement is unremarkable in many ways, it nevertheless caught our attention. Why? Because everything we had learned from reading the scholarly literatures on gun culture and gender in advertising left us unprepared to find an ad depicting a female shooting champion in a nongendered fashion, especially not while perusing an issue of the National Rifle Association's (NRA) *American Rifleman* magazine from January 1937.

In the resurgence of scholarly interest in guns, of which this book is a part, gender has been a dominant analytical framework. Gun culture has largely been depicted as embodying "hegemonic masculinity," or, more specifically, "white hetero/cis-masculinity" (Light 2017, 15). Of course, gun culture is part of American culture, so to the extent it exists in gun culture, hegemonic masculinity is in part a reflection of American culture. This broader cultural influence is evident in the scholarly literature on gender in advertising which highlights the pervasiveness of negative stereotypical portrayals of women. Taken together, these led us to expect from gun magazines the worst possible gender advertisements. The Esther Sichler ad was far from that.

But is the 1937 Peters Cartridge advertisement merely the exception that proves the rule? To answer this question, we cannot turn to either the literature on guns or on advertising. Although there is a growing body of research on guns in U.S. society, it has yet to take the place of women very seriously. And the rich tradition of studying the portrayal of women in advertising does not extend to gun ads (but see Blair and Hyatt 1995). In this chapter, therefore, we create a bridge between the existing research on gun culture and on the portrayal of women in advertisements by looking at gender advertisements in *The American Rifleman* over a 100-year time period, from 1920 to 2019. In examining a woman's place in gun advertising, we offer some first steps toward understanding a woman's place in gun culture more broadly.[1]

HEGEMONIC MASCULINITY IN GUN CULTURE

The renaissance of scholarship on guns in the U.S. has arguably been led by scholars of gender. And by gender, we mean masculinity. Perhaps, the purest example of the focus on hegemonic masculinity in gun culture is Angela Stroud's (2016) book, *Good Guys with Guns.* Stroud argues that guns are symbolic tools for socially privileged men to enact hegemonic masculinity. Two key components of Stroud's analysis of "manhood" are significant here. The first is the ideal of men being the primary protectors of their families. This discourse is nearly universally invoked by the gun owners Stroud interviewed, like Adam: "I think my role is that I have to protect my family. That's my number one duty as a dad: to provide . . . food, shelter, and protection for my wife and my child. I mean that's what being a dad is" (p. 46). The second is overcoming the fear of being dominated by others which is tantamount to being "symbolically turned into a woman" (p. 51). Stroud is not the first to make this latter argument. Michael Kimmel (2017) also argues that guns allow men to perform masculinity by helping them overcome the emasculating effects of fear.

The argument that guns prevent men from being emasculated raises the specter of the common dismissal of guns as mere "phallic symbols" and male gun owners as using guns as "penis substitutes." This sort of psycho-sexual analysis of masculinity and guns actually predates the current renaissance in gun studies. A quarter century ago, James William Gibson (1994) analyzed defensive handgun ammunition in these terms. Gibson explains that "hollow point" bullets are designed to expand upon impact, and that an expanded bullet "has its shaft intact, but the head is folded back into a mushroom." This leads him to conclude, "A perfectly expanded bullet bears some resemblance to an erect penis." From here, Gibson moves on to a discussion of gun magazines' stories about hollow point bullet testing. "Bullets are fired into a simulation of human flesh called 'ballistic gelatin.' Sophisticated magazines show graphs contrasting bullet expansion and penetration, often accompanied by drawings of wound channels that look very much like vaginas" (Gibson 1994, 91–92).

Although the psycho-sexual approach never caught on in gun studies, analyses that place masculinity at the center abound. Scott Melzer's (2009) analysis of the NRA and its supporters provides an early example. He sees "the gun rights movement as a form of collective action in response to perceived challenges to conservative men's status and identities" (Melzer 2009, xii). Their response to this fear is to rally around the mythology of frontier masculinity. Jennifer Carlson's (2015) more recent analysis along these same lines highlights the roots of men's attraction to guns in their economic decline. In an "age of decline," carrying a gun allows men to engage in everyday political acts that reassert their masculinity and help them to "reclaim a sense of dignity" (Carlson 2015a, 24; see also Mencken and Froese 2019).

Most recently, Levi Gahman has written about *Settler Colonialism and Masculinity in the American Heartland*. When he discusses "the normalization of gun culture in the Heartland" (Gahman 2020, 34), the "normal" he is referring to is what he calls heteropatriarchal racist colonial-capitalism. He notes that the gun owners he spoke to highlighted the need for guns in rural areas where police are few and far between. Moreover, Gahman writes,

> guns were a farm/country tool. That is, interviewees noted the necessity of having a firearm on ready given that outside threats including wild animals, stray vermin, or rabid predators may attack or spread disease amongst their livestock, garden, or crops. "They [guns] are a way to hold down the fort" and "help rid the place [farm] of pests," as Everett, 54 years old, and Ricky, 48 years old shared; which are statements connoting that gun use makes men empowered and active agents. (Gahman 2020, 135–136)

He predictably slides straight from this statement to noting that "recent literature on gun use and manhood suggests the reasons men sometimes own guns are because of disillusionment, powerlessness, despair, and alienation they are experiencing as a result of their social standing, economic situation, and/ or just 'getting older'/less 'able'" (Gahman 2020, 136). So, guns are not normal tools that people in the Heartland use to have fun and/or to protect their lives and livelihoods. They are a normalized way that men compensate for their loss of masculinity. If Gahman were a psychoanalyst rather than a critical geographer, he might just come out and say that they are penis substitutes.

The idea that guns help privileged men compensate for lost heteropatriarchal dominance is accepted as conventional wisdom in gun studies today. On the one hand, this emphasis on masculinity makes sense considering the fact that men are much more likely to own guns than women (Wolfson et al. 2020) and therefore play a more central role in gun culture.

But what, then, is a woman's place in gun culture? As Wolfson et al. (2020, 49) observe, "Little is known about female gun owners in the USA." Nonetheless, a small social scientific literature attempting to understand contemporary women gun owners is beginning to emerge.[2] As with the existing scholarship on hegemonic masculinity in gun culture, this literature frequently seeks to understand how women negotiate gun culture as a masculine space (Carlson 2016) and how progun activism struggles to incorporate women, especially on equal terms (Carlson and Goss 2017; Goss 2017). Martha McCaughey (1997) sees female gun ownership as related to the rise of "physical feminism," France Winddance Twine (2013) argues that female gun ownership is antifeminist, and Jennifer Carlson (2015b) explores the "double-barreled" meaning of guns.

Examining the portrayal of gender in gun advertising provides a unique window onto the historical reality of women and guns and helps address the question of women's incorporation in gun culture. In simple terms: Is the 1937 Peters Cartridge advertisement featuring Esther Sichler the exception, the rule, or something else?

GENDER IN ADVERTISING

Scholarly interest in the portrayal of gender role stereotypes in advertising dates to Courtney and Lockeretz's (1971) pioneering study, "A Woman's Place." They examined 729 advertisements in seven general interest magazines (e.g., *Newsweek* and *Saturday Review*) published in April 1970. They found men were shown in working roles much more often than women: 45 percent vs. 9 percent. Women, by contrast, were more frequently depicted in domestic settings, unless they were accompanied by men. When women were portrayed outside the home, they were often "portrayed as decorations, as in one ad where an attractive and elaborately dressed woman was used to display an automobile" (Courtney and Lockeretz 1971, 93). These stereotypes of domesticity and passivity are consistently found in subsequent studies (e.g., Belkaoui and Belkaoui 1976; Conley and Ramsey 2011). In a meta-analysis of gender roles in advertising, Eisend (2010) found that women are much more likely than men to be occupationally stereotyped, set in a domestic environment, associated with domestic products, placed in a dependent role, and presented visually/not speaking.

Another major gendered stereotype found in advertising, often related to passivity, is the sexual objectification of women. In their pioneering study, Courtney and Lockeretz (1971, 95) found some indirect evidence that "men regard women primarily as sexual objects; they are not interested in women as people." Later work took up this stereotype more directly. In a study of

1,988 advertisements from fifty-eight popular magazines published in the U.S. in 2002, Stankiewicz and Rosselli (2008) found that slightly more than half of advertisements (51.8 percent) featured women as sexual objects. The feminist movement notwithstanding, the sexual objectification of women in advertising got worse through the 1970s and 1980s not better. For example, Kang looked specifically at "body-revealing clothes or nudity" and found it in 24.6 percent of the ads depicting women in 1979, increasing to 31.9 percent of the ads in 1991 (Kang 1997). Sullivan and O'Connor (1988) also find an increase in images of women in sexualized roles from 1958 to 1983.

Studies of the portrayal of women in advertising received a conceptual boost with the publication in 1979 of Erving Goffman's *Gender Advertisements*. Goffman (1979) introduced more subtle gendered characteristics found in advertising's visual imagery, such as relative size, feminine touch, function ranking, ritualization of subordination, and licensed withdrawal. Goffman's dramaturgical perspective suggested these "behavior displays" revealed ritualized forms through which gender is performed. For example, feminine touch directs attention to the ways in which women tend to be shown tracing or cradling objects in a delicate fashion, as opposed to the more masculine utilitarian touch in which objects are grasped and manipulated more forcefully.

Although conceptually rich, Goffman's methodology was criticized because he did not systematically operationalize his concepts so as to make them replicable (Kang 1997) and he sought out advertisements that exemplified his concepts rather than analyzing systematic samples of ads (Belknap and Leonard 1991). Still, many researchers use Goffman as a starting point for their studies. Belknap and Leonard (1991) analyzed over 1,000 advertisements from six magazines in 1985, comparing three each which they characterized as "traditional" (*Good Housekeeping, Sports Illustrated, Time*) versus "modern" (*Ms., GQ, Rolling Stone*). Unexpectedly, they found that more of the advertisements in the modern magazines had stereotypical portrayals of women than in the traditional magazines, especially feminine touch and ritualization of subordination, and to a lesser extent licensed withdrawal.

Kang (1997) also used Goffman's categories to analyze a sample of 504 advertisements in popular women's magazines, half from 1979 and half from 1991. She found that feminine touch was common, both cradling and caressing objects (41.8 percent of ads in 1979 and 41.4 percent in 1991) and self-touching (38.2 percent in 1979 and 40.2 percent in 1991). Function ranking—men being depicted in a superior role—was found in 35.3 percent of ads in 1979 and 38.1 percent in 1991. Ritualization of subordination was operationalized several ways, but "bashful knee bend" was among the most frequent gender displays in Kang's study, found among women in 31.7 percent of ads in 1979 and 37.5 percent in 1991. Head or body cant was also found in 31.7 percent of ads in 1979 and 37.5 percent in 1991. Last, Goffman's licensed withdrawal was seen in women covering their mouth or face with their hand in 6.3 percent of ads in 1979 and 8.7 percent of ads in 1991.

As Sullivan and O'Connor (1988) and Kang (1997) suggest, the stereotypical portrayal of women in advertising does not seem to be improving over time. Looking over an even longer time period, 1955 to 2002, Lindner (2004) examined gender displays in *Time* and *Vogue* magazines. Once again, she used the same coding scheme from Goffman, with the addition of body display, location, and objectification. She found that in *Vogue*, which is tailored more toward women, the stereotypical portrayal of women was more prevalent than *Time*, which is directed at the general public. Additionally, Lindner found that there was only a slight decrease in the stereotypical depiction of women across the studied period. Similarly, Mager and Helgeson (2011) examined nearly 8,000 portrayals of people from 1950 to 2000 and found women displaying feminine touch, suggestive poses, lower function ranking, ritualized subordination, and licensed withdrawal both more often than men and more frequently over time.

Still more recent studies have demonstrated similar results in the stereotypical portrayal of women in advertising. Tartaglia and Rollero (2015) studied gender differences in newspaper advertisements from two European countries. They found that women played more decorative roles than men, implying more passive behaviors, and were more sexualized. Taylor et al. (2019) analyzed the portrayal of women (and racial minorities) in Super Bowl advertisements. They found that ads with female main characters were more likely to feature home settings, sexual appeals, and emotional messages. Both of these studies lend further support to the idea that the stereotypical portrayal of women in advertisements has not changed considerably over time.

HYPOTHESES

Insofar as gun culture—like advertising—has been characterized as embodying the worst aspects of hegemonic masculinity, we expect to find all of these gender stereotypes in gun advertising over the entire 100-year period under study here. In this chapter, we analyze gender displays in gun advertising to test the following specific hypotheses:

1. Women will be *underrepresented* across the entire period under study and the gender gap will remain unchanged over time.
2. Women will be portrayed as *more passive* than men over the entire time period studied.

3. Women will be portrayed as *more submissive* than men over the entire time period studied.
4. Women will be shown in *lower function ranking* positions more often than men over the entire time period studied.
5. Women will be shown using *feminine touch* more than men, who will be shown using utilitarian touch more than women, over the entire time period studied.
6. Woman will be portrayed as *sexualized* more than men over the entire time period studied.
7. Women will be portrayed as *less determined* than men over the entire time period studied.

Overall, we expect there will be *no change in the stereotypical portrayal of women in gun advertisements across the entire time period studied.*

DATA AND METHODS

To test these hypotheses, this study analyzes advertising in the oldest and largest circulation general interest gun magazine in the U.S.: *The American Rifleman*. The magazine has been continuously published since 1885, as *The Rifle* until 1888, *Shooting and Fishing* to 1906, and *Arms and the Man* to 1923. In 1916, then-owner and former NRA president James A. Drain sold *Arms and the Man* to the NRA for $1. It has been published by the NRA since then, and given as a membership benefit since the 1920s, driving its circulation upward as the NRA's membership has grown (Hardy 2012; Rajala 2012; Trefethen 1967).[3]

Among those magazines submitting to audits by the Alliance for Audited Media in the six months ending June 30, 2020, *The American Rifleman's* circulation of 1,706,688 ranked first in the "Fishing & Hunting" category, tripling the circulation of the popular outdoor magazine *Field & Stream* (572,879) and dwarfing the next highest circulation general interest gun magazine, *Guns & Ammo* (369,682). Considering consumer magazines as a whole, *The American Rifleman* has a smaller circulation than *Sports Illustrated* (1,866,026) and *National Geographic* (2,129,477) but a larger circulation than *Golf Digest* (1,627,353) or *Car and Driver* (1,113,121).[4]

Just as America's sporting culture cannot be reduced to what appears in and who subscribes to *Sports Illustrated*, so too is American gun culture not reducible to *The American Rifleman* and its subscribers. Nevertheless, its broad audience and status as the official journal of the largest organization of gun owners in the U.S. (an estimated 4-million members) makes *The*

American Rifleman a good representation of American gun culture, if only one magazine is to be analyzed.

Sampling

The sample of advertisements analyzed in this study comes from a single randomly selected issue of *The American Rifleman* for each of the 100 years from 1920 through 2019. We used a random number generator set from 1 (January) to 12 (December) to determine which of the twelve monthly issues to examine for each year. We then acquired the specified issues either from the authors' collection (for more recent issues) or purchased them through eBay (for older issues).

To be included in the sample, an advertisement had to meet four main criteria. First, the ad had to use one or more human models, and show enough of the model(s) to determine their gender. Second, the ad had to be at least one-quarter of a page in size. Third, the ad had to be placed by the manufacturer, licensed dealer, or importer of the product (i.e., not a retailer like Midway USA or Brownell's). Fourth, the ad had to be for firearms (handguns, rifles, shotguns, or a variety of gun types), ammunition (but not separate parts of ammunition or reloading equipment), gun accessories (products designed to be attached to or affect the utility of a firearm in some way), or some combination of these products. These inclusion criteria yielded a total of 457 advertisements from 100 issues of *The American Rifleman*.

Coding

Following protocols established by previous studies of gender advertisements, basic characteristics of the models were recorded for each ad. These included the total number of models and total number of female models. Coders then identified the central model in the advertisement and recorded whether the central model was male or female. If there were multiple pictures but it was clear that it was the same model in each, this was coded as one model. If there were multiple models, the central model was determined using indicators such as: being located in the center of the ad or physically above other models, or playing the central or active role in the ad (e.g., holding or shooting a gun). If there was no clear central model, the ad was coded as "no central model." For example, when there were multiple pictures of different people, but they were all roughly the same size or doing roughly the same things. In these cases, we coded the first model from the left-hand side of the page (following Conley and Ramsey 2011).

If there were only male models in the advertisement, attributes of the central male model were coded. Because, we wanted to include as many female models in our analysis as possible, any time a female model appeared we coded the attributes of that model, even when she was not identified as the central model in the ad. This was the case for 33 of 61 ads we analyzed. (In the interest of time, we coded the attributes of only one model per advertisement.) If there were multiple female models in the ad, we determined which female model was most central using indicators noted above.

With the exception of a category we call "determination" (following Waller et al. 2014), qualitative attributes of the model being coded were derived from the existing literature on gender advertisements reviewed above. The coding scheme employed by coders in this study is summarized in table 5.1, which gives the specific codes, code definitions, examples, explanatory notes, and intercoder reliability statistics (about which more below).

These data were analyzed to test the hypotheses specified above. Because, there were so few women in advertisements, especially in the early years of this analysis, we combined our data into 10-year increments from 1920 to 1999, and 5-year increments from 2000 to 2019 (when women appeared in gun advertisements more commonly).

Intercoder Reliability Tests

As a test of the reliability of the coding scheme and instructions that were developed, three researchers coded thirteen advertisements meeting the selection criteria from the May 2019 issue and eleven advertisements from the June 2018 issue of *The American Rifleman*, for a total of twenty-four advertisements. Researchers coded each ad for the presence (=1) or absence (=0) of the attributes of interest. Krippendorf's α (alpha) was used to assess intercoder reliability. According to Krippendorf (2013), it is customary to require $\alpha \geq .800$ to conclude that the coding scheme and instructions are reliable.[5]

As reported in table 5.1, all of the attributes coded resulted in satisfactory levels of intercoder reliability. Krippendorf's α for all variables collectively was 0.962.

RESULTS

Hypothesis 1 stated: Women will be *underrepresented* in gun advertisements across the entire period under study and the gender gap will remain unchanged. We find support for the first half of this hypothesis (underrepresentation) but not the second (consistent gender gap). Over a 100-year period, just 61 of 457 advertisements in *The American Rifleman* that used human models featured *any* female model (13.3 percent). Only thirty-three of those advertisements (7.2 percent of coded ads) presented the female model as the central model.

Table 5.1   Gender Advertisements Coding Scheme

CODE	CODE DEFINITION	EXAMPLES/NOTES	α (3 CODERS)
Active vs. Passive	Model is presented in an active pose, as if actively engaging in an activity, or not.	*Model is shooting a gun (active) vs. model is sitting on a chair (passive).* Active: If model is at any stage of drawing or firing a gun (e.g., clearing cover garment, hand on gun in holster). Passive: If model is standing at the ready but not doing anything, walking but not doing anything with the gun.	0.815
Submissiveness (Ritualization of Subordination)	"Posture" of the model's body is subordinated or submissive, such as tilting (canting) of the head or body, being embraced so that movement or mobility is restricted, leaning on others for support, or occupying a lower physical position relative to another (kneeling, bending forward).	*Model is leaning or laying backward, or model's head is tilted and is looking off as if into space*	1.00
Function Ranking	The model is in an authoritative/superior/ executive role relative to other models depicted.	*Model is teaching another person how to shoot a gun.* Note: Code only if there is more than one model in the same picture in the ad.	0.885
Feminine vs. Utilitarian Touch	The model is touching self (e.g., hair, face, lips) or their clothing in a studied manner, or using fingers or hands to trace an object, cradle it, or caress its surface. This sort of touching is distinguished from a utilitarian kind that grasps, manipulates, and holds an object.	*Model is placing finger on gun instead of gripping it.* Note: Code only if model is touching self or object.	0.823

(Continued)

Table 5.1   Gender Advertisements Coding Scheme (*Continued*)

CODE	CODE DEFINITION	EXAMPLES/NOTES	α (3 CODERS)
Sexual Objectification	The model's sexuality is being used to sell the product, as evidenced by wearing revealing, hardly any, or no clothes at all; a sexualized posture or seductive facial expression; or being portrayed in such a way as to suggest that being looked at is their major purpose in the advertisement.	*Model is positioned with legs spread open*	1.00
Determination	Relates to being focused and actively involved in an activity (Waller et al. 2014). Facial expression shows determination, a high-approach-motivated positive emotion. Coded according to Facial Action Coding System (FACS) codes AU17: chin raiser and AU24: lip presser.	*Model is focused on aiming gun at target.* Note: Code only if enough of face is shown to assess.	0.895

(Recall our coding protocol which called for coding of the female model in any advertisement, even if the female model was not the central model.)

There is, however, fluctuation over the study period. In two decades (the 1920s and 1970s), women appeared in no coded advertisements, while in the 2010s, they appeared in nearly 30 percent of the coded ads (29 of 104). Indeed, almost half of the coded advertisements that included women (29 of 61, or 47.5 percent) were from 2010 to 2019. Figure 5.1 represents the overall pattern for the study period, with the best fitting trend lines shown for men (solid black line) and women (dashed black line). From the 1980s forward, the gender gap in gun advertising—though still substantial—shrinks, which we expect may continue as women become more involved in gun ownership and culture.

Our data support Hypothesis 2, that women will be portrayed as *more passive* than men over the entire time period studied. This conclusion needs to be cautiously interpreted, though. Figure 5.2 gives the trends lines for men and women, with both becoming more active/less passive over time. This likely reflects trends in advertising aesthetics, not limited to the firearms industry. Although, the best fitting trend lines show men (solid black) as more active than women (dashed black) over the entire 100 years covered, there are

Percentage of Advertisements With Any Female Model vs. Only Male Models,
The American Rifleman, 1920-2019

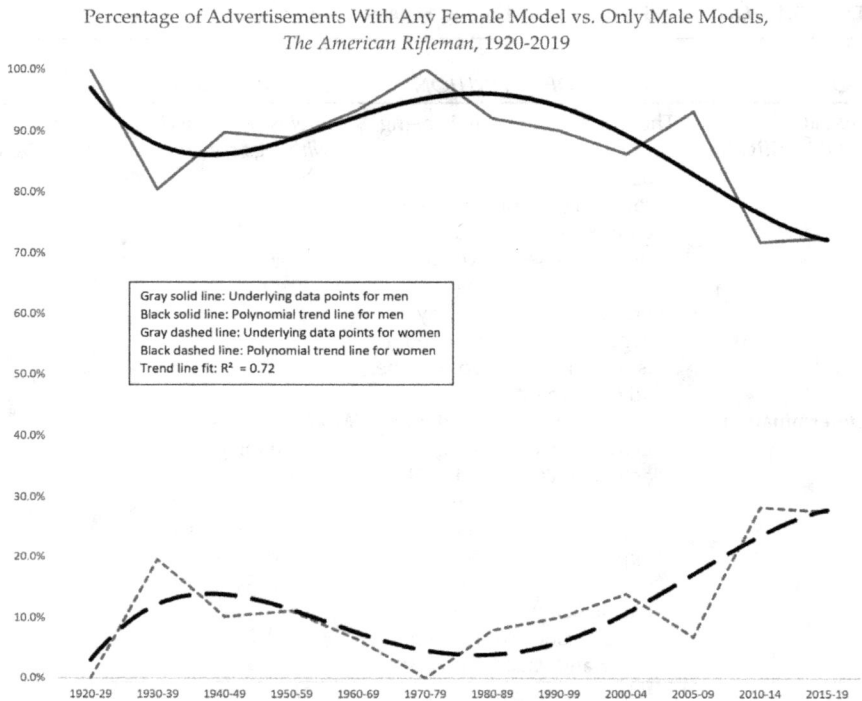

Figure 5.1   Percentage of Advertisements With Any Female Model vs. Only Male Models, *The American Rifleman*, **1920-2019.**

dramatic fluctuations in the activity/passivity of women from time period to time period. In four time periods (1920–1929, 1940–1949, 1970–1979, and 2005–2009), no advertisements in our sample depict women as active, and in three time periods (1980–1989, 1990–1999, and 2000–2004) women are portrayed as equally or more active than men. This explains why the trend line for women (black dashes) captures only 40 percent of the variance in the underlying data (R-square = 0.40), while the trend line for men (solid black) captures nearly three-quarters of the variance (R-square = 0.725).

Our data also offer qualified support for Hypothesis 3, that women will be portrayed as *more submissive* than men over the entire time period studied. Collectively, women were over four times more likely to be portrayed as submissive. Women are submissive in 9 of 61 advertisements (14.8 percent) and men in only 13 of 396 ads (3.3 percent). It is hard to see a clear trend in this portrayal, however, since there are many years in which no models, male (seven time periods) or female (eight time periods), are portrayed as submissive. The more submissive portrayal of women overall is driven by higher proportions of female submissive advertisements in the 1940s (3 of

Percentage of Advertisements that Depict Central Model as Active,
By Gender, *The American Rifleman*, 1920-2019

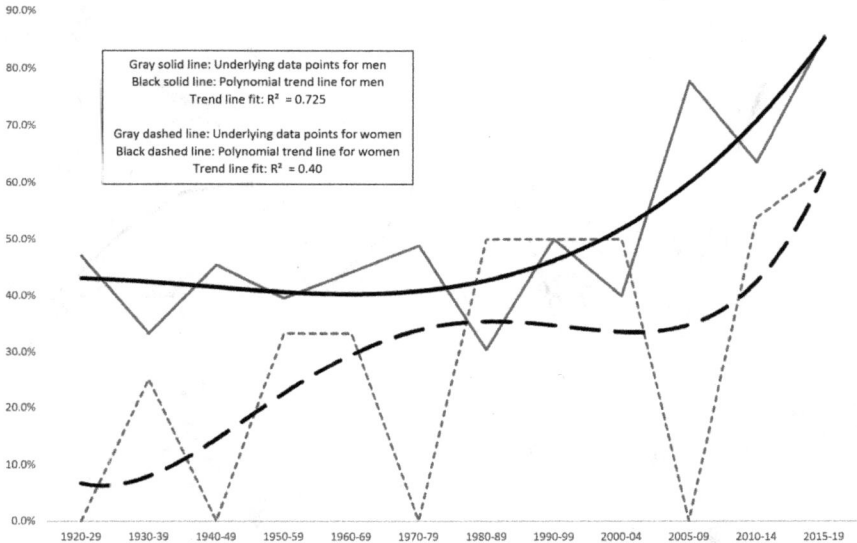

Figure 5.2 Percentage of Advertisements that Depict Central Model as Active, By Gender, *The American Rifleman*, 1920-2019.

5, or 60 percent), 1950s (2 of 6, or 33 percent), and 2010s (4 of 29, or 14 percent).

Our data generally support Hypothesis 4—women will be shown in positions of *lower function ranking* more than men over the entire time period studied—but again with some important caveats. Figure 5.3 shows the gender gap in portrayal of men vs. women as superior in function ranking. When the solid black line is above the horizontal dashed line (set at 0.0 percent gap), then the gender gap favors men, and when it is below the horizontal line, the gender gap favors women. For 12 of 16 data points, men are more commonly shown as superior than women; in 2 of 16 data points (interestingly, 1940–1949 and 1950–1959) women are more commonly shown as superior than men; and in 2 of 16 data points (1990–1999 and 2015–2019) the proportions are the same.

Our data do not support Hypothesis 5 that women will be shown using *feminine touch* more than men over the entire time period studied. This is in part because very few ads employ feminine touch as a gender display. In our sample, 375 ads show models touching products. Almost all of them employ utilitarian touch (364, or 97 percent). Of the eleven ads showing feminine

David Yamane et al.

Percentage Gender Gap in Portrayal of Men vs. Women as Superior in Function
Ranking, *The American Rifleman*, 1920-2019

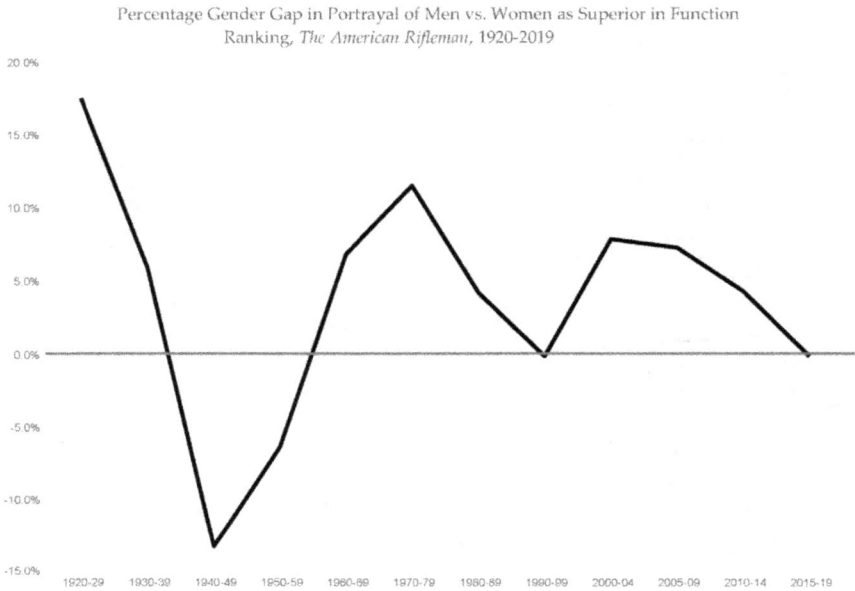

Figure 5.3 Percentage Gender Gap in Portrayal of Men vs. Women as Superior in Function Ranking, *The American Rifleman*, 1920-2019.

touch, only five (45.5 percent) involved female models, and almost all of these appeared in the 20 years from 1946 to 1967.

Hypothesis 6 stated that women will be portrayed as *more sexualized* than men over the entire time period studied. Sexual objectification of models as a form of gender display is so uncommon in gun advertising, at least in *The American Rifleman,* that we cannot claim support for this hypothesis. Of 457 advertisements coded over the 100-year period, only four advertisements in total were coded as sexually objectifying the model. To be sure, in three of those four advertisements women rather than men were sexualized. But, just 5 percent of all ads involving female models (3 of 61) is a smaller proportion of sexual objectification than scholars have found in other magazines, as discussed above.

Our data also do not support Hypothesis 7, that women will be portrayed as *less determined* than men over the entire time period studied. To the contrary, in our sample of advertisements women are portrayed as determined 37.7 percent of the time (23 of 61 advertisements) and men 33.8 percent of the time (134 of 396 advertisements). As in figure 5.3, when the solid black line in figure 5.4 is above the horizontal dashed line (set at 0.0 percent gap), then the gender gap favors men, and when it is below the horizontal line the gender gap favors women. Figure 5.4 does not show a clear trend over the years,

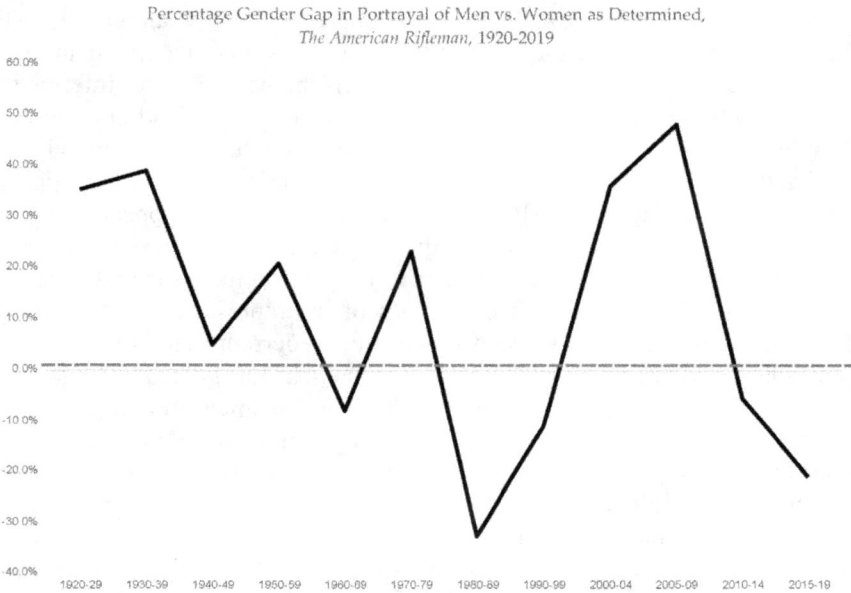

Figure 5.4   **Percentage Gender Gap in Portrayal of Men vs. Women as Determined,** *The American Rifleman,* **1920-2019.**

as the gender gap fluctuates from the 1950s forward, with men portrayed as determined more commonly than women in four time periods (1950–1959, 1970–1979, 2000–2004, and 2005–2009) and women as determined more commonly than men in five time periods (1960–1969, 1980–1989, 1990–1999, 2010–2014, and 2015–2019).

DISCUSSION AND CONCLUSION

Although, no one had systematically studied the portrayal of gender in gun advertising when we began this work, based on the existing literatures on American gun culture and gender in advertising, we expected to see a consistently stereotypical portrayal of women in gun advertising in *The American Rifleman* magazine over the entire 100-year time period we examined. What we found was substantially more complex.

Reflecting gun culture itself, gun advertising as a whole is largely the domain of men, though the gap in gender representation is shrinking, especially from the 1980s forward (half support for Hypothesis 1). Moreover, when women do appear in gun advertising, at least in *The American Rifleman,* some of the most stereotypical gender displays we find in the world of print advertising more broadly are more muted or absent altogether. We find qualified support for the portrayal of women as more passive than men (Hypothesis 2), more submissive than men (Hypothesis 3), and inferior to men in function ranking (Hypothesis 4). Our data do not support our hypotheses that women would use feminine touch more often than men (Hypothesis 5), that they would be sexualized (Hypothesis 6), and that they would appear less determined than men (Hypothesis 7). In fact, women appear as more determined than men overall, especially in recent decades.

We conclude here with some further reflections on the issue and caveats. We began our analysis with the question of the representation of women in gun advertising. To say that women are "underrepresented" raises the question, "Relative to what?" Relative to men in the general population, women are definitely underrepresented. But are women underrepresented relative to their proportion of the gun owning population? Here, the lack of historical gun ownership statistics by gender makes it impossible to answer this question definitively. But, Parker et al. (2017) find about 22 percent of women report personally owning a gun. As Yamane (2019) has argued that surveys underestimate gun ownership rates in the U.S., the rate of representation of women in gun advertising in the most recent period (27.6 percent in 2015–19) may actually be very close to the rate of female gun ownership during this time. Moreover, the inclusion of women in 28 percent of advertisements in the 2010s overrepresents women relative to the readership of *The American Rifleman*. According to the 2021 media kit prepared by the NRA (2021) for potential advertisers, 85.3 percent of the magazine's readers are men.

The greater inclusion of women in advertising (in the later time periods especially) in ways that are not grossly stereotypical reflects the gun community's and industry's conscious effort to better incorporate women into gun culture. One study of this is Noah Schwartz's "Called to Arms: The NRA, the Gun Culture and Women." Schwartz (2019) examines three online television series that the NRA has produced under the label of NRA Women: *Armed & Fabulous, Love at First Shot*, and *New Energy*. Despite the overall failure of NRATV, these particular shows consciously sought to overcome social barriers to women's involvement in gun culture created by masculinist norms. They did so by framing participation in gun culture as enjoyable and empowering for women, highlighting role models, and providing practical advice specifically for women.

Other examples of the effort to build a more inclusive gun culture abound. Among the women who play prominent roles in gun culture are Julie Golob, who serves as Captain of Team Smith & Wesson (the gun company's professional shooting team), and Jessie Harrison, who does the same for Brazilian gun manufacturer Taurus. Tamara Keel is the handgun editor for *Shooting Illustrated* magazine and Lara Cullinan Smith is the national spokesperson for the Liberal Gun Club. Prominent women in the civilian gun training industry include Kathy Jackson (The Cornered Cat, retired), Annette Evans (On Her Own Life), Tiffany Johnson (Citizens Safety Academy), and Melody Lauer (Citizens Defense Research). These few examples highlight the fact that female representation in gun culture is increasing.

Although some, like Goss (2017), question whether these efforts at inclusion have been successful at expanding female gun ownership, we do see an increasing proportion of women getting concealed carry permits (Lott and Wang 2020), and a recent national survey found no difference in the proportion of male and female respondents who say they have them (Wolfson et al. 2020). Organizations such as *A Girl and a Gun Women's Shooting League* (144 chapters in thirty-six states) and *The Well Armed Woman* (345 chapters in forty-seven states) also continue to expand, suggesting that women's involvement in gun culture is growing. Whether these examples will or should lead to the development of alternatives to the dominant scholarly narrative of hegemonic masculinity in gun culture remains to be seen.

Some important caveats apply to this study as well. Although it is the only study of gender advertisements in gun magazines to date, this work is certainly not definitive. For one, it looks only at arguably the most mainstream of all gun magazines, of which there are many (Jacobs and Villaronga 2004; Saylor et al. 2004). The gender displays in advertisements placed in newer magazines like *Recoil*—which characterizes itself as a "firearms lifestyle publication for the modern shooting enthusiast"—may differ. Also, our study looks only at "dead tree" media. It may, therefore, overlook some more stereotypical depictions of gender in social media advertising, which can tend toward the lowest common denominator. This would include "gun bunny" social media influencers on Instagram like American Gun Chic, Lea "Speed6," and Tactical Yoga Girl, as well as companies that lean heavily on the sexual objectification of women like Taran Tactical Innovations, We the People Holsters, and Weapon Outfitters.

Also, this study did not make any comparisons between ads based on product type. It would be interesting to compare gender displays in advertisements targeted toward different subcultures within the larger gun culture. For instance, advertisements for products associated with Gun Culture 1.0 (especially hunting) could be different than those associated with Gun Culture 2.0 (self-defense), which according to Yamane (2017) has the potential to be more demographically inclusive.

This content analysis of *The American Rifleman* from 1920 to 2019 highlights some seemingly unique aspects of gun advertising in comparison to previous studies of gender in nongun media advertising. In highlighting a woman's place in gun advertising, it also takes some first steps toward a broader understanding of the place of women in gun culture. We hope it inspires other scholars to develop this work further.

NOTES

1. One challenge in trying to understand the place of women in American gun culture is having systematic data over a long period of time. Two of the authors of this chapter have elsewhere shown the utility of using gun advertising as a consistent source of data representing different priorities in gun culture over time (Yamane et al. 2019, 2020).

We recognize this project embodies cisnormativity, the assumption that people conform to a gender binary: "The social and biological classification of sex and gender into two distinct oppositional forms of masculine and feminine selfhood" (Sumerau et al. 2016, 294). However, with trans* people representing just 0.6 percent of the U.S. population today (Flores et al. 2016), we did not judge it to be the best use of our time to include gender nonconformity in our study, especially in gun advertising and especially when looking over a 100 year time period.

2. Much of what has been written about women and guns actually comes from outside the social sciences proper, including book-length works by Religious Studies professor Mary Zeiss Stange and Carol K. Oyster (2000), writer and English professor Deborah Homsher (2001), freelance journalist Caitlin Kelly (2004), English professor Laura Browder (2006), and photography professor Nancy Floyd (2008).

3. Today, NRA members can opt to receive *American Hunter* (published since 1973, current circulation 873,444), *America's First Freedom* (published since the 1990s, current circulation 595,522), or *Shooting Illustrated* (official NRA publication since, 2016, current circulation 582,260), instead of *The American Rifleman*.

4. Circulation data is the Alliance for Audited Media average for the six months ended 30 June 2020, retrieved from https://abcas3.auditedmedia.com/ecirc/magtitl esearch.asp on on 20 January 2021.

5. We used the free reliability calculator, ReCal3: Reliability for 3+ Coders, on Deen Freelon's web page: http://dfreelon.org/utils/recalfront/recal3/.

REFERENCES

Belkaoui, Ahmed, and Janice M. Belkaoui. 1976. "A Comparative Analysis of the Roles Portrayed by Women in Print Advertisements: 1958, 1970, 1972." *Journal of Marketing Research* 13(2): 168–172.

Belknap, Penny, and Wilbert M. Leonard. 1991. "A Conceptual Replication and Extension of Erving Goffman's Study of Gender Advertisements." *Sex Roles* 25(3): 103–118.

Blair, M. Elizabeth, and Eva M. Hyatt. 1995. "The Marketing of Guns to Women: Factors Influencing Gun-Related Attitudes and Gun Ownership by Women." *Journal of Public Policy & Marketing* 14(1): 117–127.

Browder, Laura. 2006. *Her Best Shot: Women and Guns in America*. Chapel Hill: University of North Carolina Press.

Carlson, Jennifer. 2015a. *Citizen-Protectors: The Everyday Politics of Guns in an Age of Decline*. New York: Oxford University Press.

Carlson, Jennifer Dawn. 2015b. "Carrying Guns, Contesting Gender." *Contexts* 14(1): 20–25.

Carlson, Jennifer. 2016. "Troubling the Subject of Violence: The Pacifist Presumption, Martial Maternalism, and Armed Women in Contemporary Gun Culture." In *Perverse Politics? Feminism, Anti-Imperialism, Multiplicity. Political Power and Social Theory*, Vol. 30, pp. 81–107. Bingley, UK: Emerald Group Publishing.

Carlson, Jennifer, and Kristin Goss. 2017. "Gendering the Second Amendment." *Law and Contemporary Problems* 80(2): 103–128.

Conley, Terri, and Laura Ramsey. 2011. "Killing Us Softly? Investigating Portrayals of Women and Men in Contemporary Magazine Advertisements." *Psychology of Women* 35(3): 469–478.

Courtney, Alice E., and Sarah Wernick Lockeretz. 1971. "A Woman's Place: An Analysis of the Roles Portrayed by Women in Magazine Advertisements." *Journal of Marketing Research* 8(1): 92–95.

Eisend, Martin. 2010. "A Meta-Analysis of Gender Roles in Advertising." *Journal of the Academy of Marketing Science* 38: 418–440.

Flores, Andrew R., Jody L. Herman, Gary J. Gates, and Taylor N. T. Brown. 2016. *How Many Adults Identify as Transgender in the United States?* Los Angeles: The Williams Institute.

Floyd, Nancy. 2008. *She's Got a Gun*, illustrated edition. Philadelphia, PA: Temple University Press.

Gahman, Levi. 2020. *Land, God, and Guns: Settler Colonialism and Masculinity in the American Heartland*. London: Zed Books.

Gibson, James William. 1994. *Warrior Dreams: Violence and Manhood in Post-Vietnam America*. New York: Hill & Wang.

Goffman, Erving. 1979. *Gender Advertisements*. Cambridge: Harper & Row.

Goss, Kristin A. 2017. "The Socialization of Conflict and Its Limits: Gender and Gun Politics in America." *Social Science Quarterly* 98(2): 455–470.

Hardy, David T. 2012. "American Rifleman." In *Guns in American Society: An Encyclopedia of History, Politics, Culture, and the Law*, edited by Greg Lee Carter, 2nd edition, pp. 29–30. Santa Barbara, CA: ABC-CLIO.

Homsher, Deborah. 2001. *Women and Guns: Politics and the Culture of Firearms in America: Politics and the Culture of Firearms in America*. Armonk, N.Y: M.E. Sharpe.

Jacobs, James B., and Domingo Villaronga. 2004. "Mapping the U.S. Gun Culture: A Content Analysis of Gun Magazines." *Journal on Firearms and Public Policy* 16: 135.

Kang, Mee-Eun. 1997. "The Portrayal of Women's Images in Magazine Advertisements: Goffman's Gender Analysis Revisited." *Sex Roles* 37(11): 979.

Kelly, Caitlin. 2004. *Blown Away: American Women and Guns*. New York: Gallery Books.

Kimmel, Michael. 2017. *Angry White Men: American Masculinity at the End of an Era*, 2nd edition. New York: Bold Type Books.

Light, Caroline. 2017. *Stand Your Ground: A History of America's Love Affair with Lethal Self-Defense*. Boston: Beacon Press.

Lindner, Katharina. 2004. "Images of Women in General Interest and Fashion Magazine Advertisements from 1955 to 2002." *Sex Roles* 51(7): 409–421.

Lott, John R., and Rujun Wang. 2020. *Concealed Carry Permit Holders Across the United States: 2020. SSRN Scholarly Paper ID 3703977*. Rochester, NY: Social Science Research Network.

Mager, John, and James G. Helgeson. 2010. "Fifty Years of Advertising Images: Some Changing Perspectives on Role Portrayals Along with Enduring Consistencies." *Sex Roles* 64(3–4): 238–252.

McCaughey, Martha. 1997. *Real Knockouts: The Physical Feminism of Women's Self-Defense*. New York: New York University Press.

Melzer, Scott. 2009. *Gun Crusaders: The NRA's Culture War*. New York: New York University Press.

Mencken, F. Carson, and Paul Froese. 2019. "Gun Culture in Action." *Social Problems* 66(1): 3–27.

National Rifle Association. 2021. "Media Kit." http://www.nrapublications.org/adve rtising. Accessed January 21, 2021.

Parker, Kim, Juliana Horowitz, Ruth Ingelnik, Baxter Oliphant, and Anna Brown. 2017. "Guns in America: Attitudes and Experiences of Americans." *Pew Research Center's Social & Demographic Trends Project*. https://www.pewsocialtrends.org /2017/06/22/americas-complex-relationship-with-guns. Accessed February 8, 2020.

Rajala, Tiia. 2012. "Gun Magazines." In *Guns in American Society: An Encyclopedia of History, Politics, Culture, and the Law*, edited by Greg Lee Carter, 2nd edition, pp. 351–353. Santa Barbara, CA: ABC-CLIO.

Saylor, Elizabeth A., Katherine A. Vittes, and Susan B. Sorenson. 2004. "Firearm Advertising: Product Depiction in Consumer Gun Magazines." *Evaluation Review* 28(5): 420–433.

Schwartz, Noah S. 2019. "Called to Arms: The NRA, the Gun Culture & Women." *Critical Policy Studies*. DOI: 10.1080/19460171.2019.1697892.

Stange, Mary Zeiss, and Carol K. Oyster. 2000. *Gun Women: Firearms and Feminism in Contemporary America*. New York: New York University Press.

Stankiewicz, Julie M., and Francine Rosselli. 2008. "Women as Sex Objects and Victims in Print Advertisements." *Sex Roles* 58(7–8): 579–589.

Stroud, Angela. 2016. *Good Guys with Guns: The Appeal and Consequences of Concealed Carry*. Chapel Hill: University of North Carolina Press.

Sullivan, Gary L., and P. J. O'Connor. 1988. "Women's Role Portrayals in Magazine Advertising: 1958–1983." *Sex Roles* 18(3): 181–188.

Sumerau, J. E., Ryan T. Cragun, and Lain A. B. Mathers. 2016. "Contemporary Religion and the Cisgendering of Reality." *Social Currents* 3(3): 293–311.

Tartaglia, Stefano, and Chiara Rollero. 2015. "Gender Stereotyping in Newspaper Advertisements: A Cross-Cultural Study." *Journal of Cross-Cultural Psychology* 46(8): 1103–1109.

Taylor, Charles R., Alexander Mafael, Sascha Raithel, Carissa M. Anthony, and David W. Stewart. 2019. "Portrayals of Minorities and Women in Super Bowl Advertising." *Journal of Consumer Affairs* 53(4): 1535–1572.

Trefethen, James B. 1967. *Americans and Their Guns: The National Rifle Association Story Through Nearly a Century of Service to the Nation.* Harrisburg, PA: Stackpole Books.

Twine, France Winddance. 2013. *Girls with Guns: Firearms, Feminism, and Militarism.* New York: Routledge.

Waller, Bridget M., Antonia Misch, Jamie Whitehouse, and Esther Herrmann. 2014. "Children, But Not Chimpanzees, Have Facial Correlates of Determination." *Biology Letters* 10(3): 20130974.

Wolfson, Julia A., Deborah Azrael, and Matthew Miller. 2020. "Gun Ownership Among US Women." *Injury Prevention* 26(1): 49–54.

Yamane, David. 2017. "The Sociology of U.S. Gun Culture." *Sociology Compass* 11(7): e12497.

Yamane, David. 2019. "Why Surveys Underestimate Gun Ownership Rates in the U.S." https://guncurious.wordpress.com/2019/02/11/why-surveys-underestimate-gun-ownership-rates-in-the-u-s/. Accessed January 21, 2021.

Yamane, David, Paul Yamane, and Sebastian L. Ivory. 2020. "Targeted Advertising: Documenting the Emergence of Gun Culture 2.0 in Guns Magazine, 1955–2019." *Palgrave Communications* 6(1): 1–9.

Yamane, David, Sebastian L. Ivory, and Paul Yamane. 2019. "The Rise of Self-Defense in Gun Advertising: The American Rifleman, 1918–2017." In *Gun Studies: Interdisciplinary Approaches to Politics, Policy, and Practice*, edited by Jennifer Carlson, Kristin Goss, and Harel Shapira, pp. 9–27. New York: Routledge.

Chapter 6

Confronting Christian Nationalism with the True Meaning of the Second Amendment and Example Set by Jesus Christ

Matt Stolick

A Christian nationalist believes that guns are a God-given right to Americans in a Christian country. They think of the U.S. Constitution as they do the Ten Commandments, equally inspired by God. In their recent study of the relationship between Christian nationalism and support for stricter gun control, Andrew Whitehead, Landon Schnabel, and Samuel Perry recently found that Christian nationalism is a "key determinant of American opposition to stricter gun control" (Whitehead et al. 2018). In this paper, I confront the Christian nationalist and specifically two core beliefs inherent in the position: that the Second Amendment to the Constitution is about an individual right to a gun and that a "Christian," one who aspires to live as Christ did, would so vociferously identify Christian faith with killing machines.

I first present some basic information about guns in the U.S. from the time of the colonists at the end of the eighteenth century to the present day. I focus on the Second Amendment, the birth and development of the gun business in the U.S., the National Rifle Association (NRA), the landmark Supreme Court Heller decision of 2008, and Stand Your Ground Laws including a contextualization of these laws as going well beyond the castle doctrine and duty to retreat of traditional self-defense laws. Second, I present a Christian defense of gun rights using one key text, the Sixth Commandment, and Just War Theory. Third, I present a response to the Christian gun rights position. Arguing for a gun control position, I introduce and apply four Biblical passages most relevant to guns: turning the other cheek, the sanctity of human life, the commissioning of the twelve apostles and sending them out into the world with no weapons, and the "two swords" passage. I conclude arguing

that Christians have got themselves entangled in a cultural movement espous-
ing a false reading of the Second Amendment and one inconsistent with their
defining beliefs, values, and way of understanding their lives and this world
as Christians.

A BRIEF HISTORY OF THE GUN INDUSTRY
AND GUN LAW IN THE U.S.

In the two hundred years before America began, there was in the new world
from the 1600s to the Revolutionary War a tradition of gun *control* in the
country. Controls included concealed and open carry restrictions, prohibition
on dueling, firing firearms near towns, after dark, on Sundays, and near roads,
and there were restrictions on gun access to minors. Robert Spitzer recently
clarified that America is a country that has a history of gun control laws and
works to dispel the myth that the right of individuals to own guns without any
controls or limits on this right is a return to the past of American tradition:

> The prevailing gun law movement in America in the last three decades toward
> the relaxing of gun restrictions (e.g., the reduction of gun sale inspections, the
> shielding of manufacturers and dealers from criminal and civil liability, the rise
> of unregulated Internet gun and ammunition sales), as well as the spread of
> concealed carry laws, the open carry movement, and most recently stand your
> ground laws are not a return to the past. They are refutation of America's past,
> a determined march away from America's gun regulation traditions. And these
> changes have nothing to do with improving safety or security in society, but
> they have everything to do with politics. (Spitzer 2015, 16)

After researching guns in America, I have come to believe that the Second
Amendment, and an accurate understanding of the meaning and purpose of
this Amendment, is the central point in the current raging gun rights/gun
control debate in the U.S.. Advocates of gun rights managed to recently
reinterpret the Second Amendment through law review articles to eventually
the Supreme Court as including an individual right to bear arms, overcoming
over two hundred years of clear legal precedent against such a reading, and
for a militia interpretation. That the militia view of the Second Amendment is
the clear precedent interpretation from before the founding fathers on to 1960
can be understood by focusing on the centrality of the militia to the lives of
those in mid-to-late eighteenth century America.

Michael Waldman, in his very illuminating book, *The Second Amendment:
A Biography*, points out militias as military units were commonplace and
very important to colonists in the mid-late 1700s.

Militias were military forces drawn from the citizenry . . . In England, and then even more so in the colonies, militia service was a universal expectation. Men from sixteen to sixty were required to join a company, and train intermittently. They were expected to own and bring their own gun. (Waldman 2014, 6)

Owning a gun was not considered an "individual right" but rather was a duty and responsibility, something that people had to be encouraged to do in order to strengthen the whole and to be prepared to help defend the other colonists in the militia. "People of 1775 did not see the army the way we might today . . . they saw the army as tyranny in the making, authoritarianism on the march" (Waldman 2014, 8). The colonists' experience of an "army" (what we think of as "the military") was as the tool of an authoritarian king. A *militia* was what protected the people against such an army, in their minds a real immediate threat, given the great revolution about to take place in the 1700s among the colonists.

Tom Lansford, in *The Early History of Guns: From Colonial Times to the Civil War*, further explains how central the militia was for those living at the beginning of America and the immediate years before. The militia was active and the leading force in protecting the frontier, and locally responding to emergencies or disturbances.

After the end of the French and Indian War, the British reduced their troop strength throughout the North American colonies. One result was new pressure on colonial militias to take a more active role in protecting the frontier and responding to emergencies or disturbances. Militias had acquired new weapons in the years preceding the Revolutionary War, including cannons and other artillery pieces, and built new facilities to store weapons and ammunition. (Lansford 2016, 16–17)

These facilities were targeted by the British, as they recognized how crucial guns and ammo were to the colonists protecting themselves from British forces enforcing oppressive measures from the King.

At the end of August 1774, British general Thomas Gage ordered troops to raid militia storehouses and confiscate firearms, artillery, powder, and shot. . . . The importance of the militia within colonial society cannot be overestimated. . . . Efforts to suppress militias and remove their weapons and ammunition became a casus belli. (Lansford 2016, 16–17)

Trying to read a twenty-first century "individual right to guns" into this context seems contrived. There are also practical problems with such a reading. Consider that the colonists used flintlock muskets that had to be loaded in a manual process, shoving gun powder and pellets or balls into a tube, then aiming and igniting a shot, maybe getting off two shots a minute. This would not seem to be a prudent process with an intruder in the house. Although mandatory to own a musket, many did not (for the hefty expense of purchasing a gun, among other reasons). It was also recognized that gunpowder was something that was more safely kept outside of the home, also making it difficult to have a musket at hand for self-defense. Individual colonists, instead of fearing being accosted by other colonists (as it would be in an individual right to bear arms interpretation of the Second Amendment), were united as a group against British, French, Native Americans, and others.

The exact twenty six words of the Second Amendment are as follows: "A well-regulated Militia, being necessary to the security of a free State, the right of the people to keep and bear Arms, shall not be infringed." This is about a militia and the security of a whole state, and uses the plural "people" having a right to form a militia. It seems simply unacceptable, for anyone seeking the true meaning of this Amendment, to paraphrase it with only the last part: ". . . the right of the people to keep and bear Arms, shall not be infringed." Supporting this sturdy pre-1960 interpretation of the Second Amendment as pertaining to a militia, a military, and not individual gun users, consider that the phrase "bear arms" is solely used at this time in reference to military uses.

> Searching a Library of Congress database containing all official records of debates in the Continental and U.S. Congresses between 1774 and 1821 reveals thirty uses of the phrase "bear arms" and "bearing arms" and in every single one of these uses, the phrase has an unambiguously military meaning . . . Another scholar looked at databases containing all surviving books, pamphlets, and newspaper articles from the period. He found 202 uses of phrase "bear arms" in a military context, eight otherwise. In 2013, the National Archives launched a searchable database of all the writings and papers of six key founders (Washington, Adams, Jefferson, Hamilton, Franklin, and Madison). A search for the phrase "bear arms" produces 153 mentions—again, all in the military context. (Waldman 2014, 62)

At the end of the 1700s, a continuing problem for militias was a shortage of guns. Haag explains, "In the 1790s, during the first, craft phase of the American gun business, the United States had a gun problem, but of another sort—it did not have enough of them" (Haag 2016, 8). There was a scarcity of gunsmiths at the start of the Revolutionary War. "George Washington had noted the 'scarcity of gunsmiths' as well as guns at the start of the war" (Haag 2016, 9). This issue was addressed by the new country. Eli Whitney got involved in 1798, applying his ideas on machine production to gun production, in early 1801 to creating gun molds and machines to mass produce guns.

The August 1814 Burning of Washington, with militias unable to protect the federal government by the British during the War of 1812, was a major impetus for the creation of the U.S. military. The war demonstrated the need to replace the unreliable state militias with a professional U.S. military. This is what the Second Amendment recognizes, the need of a free state to have a military, to have groups of people willing to dedicate their lives to defense of the country as the nation's defenders (Butler 2012). At this point, after the War of 1812, the militias and the Second Amendment became irrelevant in so far as after 1812 militias were replaced by the most powerful military in the world, one fulfilling the purpose of the Second Amendment.

Moving into the nineteenth century, where the U.S. gun business is born, I find most enlightening Pamela Haag's *The Gunning of America: Business and the Making of American Gun Culture.* She repeatedly emphasizes that the gun business from its beginnings in the nineteenth century has always been *amoral*, acting with a "commercial agnosticism." That is, there are no qualms about who buys guns or the purpose of using them. We are invited to see this as an accurate interpretation even for the present time. "For the United States, the gun culture was forged in the image of commerce. It was stamped, perhaps indelibly, by what historian John Blum called the 'amorality of business'" (Haag 2016, xiii). "Indelibly" implies that the gun business is *still* (and will always be) amoral. "Amoral" implies a complete lack of social consciousness and sense of responsibility for the consequences of using products one had created, marketed, and sold for a profit. This point strongly supports the need to protect society from the gun industry, given that their product is by design a killing machine, and therefore a tool of potential havoc and tragedy in society unlike most any other consumer product.

At the turn of the nineteenth century, the pressing concern in addressing the need for guns was mass production of arms with interchangeable parts. For wartime, this would be invaluable for having working weapons, repairing them if needed, and staying effectively armed. This idea, mass production of guns, would bring with it the whole world of guns we know today. Skipping ahead a bit to the early 1860s, consider another innovation, the repeating rifle. We each in our current twenty-first century consciousness harbor in our memories images of horrific mass shootings that have taken place at schools, workplaces, and other areas. With the move from the single-shot muskets and pistols to the repeating rifle, there was suddenly the possibility of killing many people in a matter of seconds and minutes. This was a major change in killing and what was required of a killer to take another person's life. Now killing was much more impersonal, easier, quicker, cleaner, efficient, and distant. The idea of mass killing all at once brought with it consideration of what was at the time called the "moral effect" of the gun. This "moral effect" of killing many people at once is one we currently in the U.S. experience on a regular basis, with several dozen mass shootings in the news every year. The new social danger, of the "army of one," emerges with the invention and mass production of repeating rifles: "Semiautomatic repeaters made every individual, in a twenty-first-century phrase, an 'army of one' . . . the repeater invited and emboldened the individual, lone gunman, whether guerrilla, soldier, or civilian—and Winchester sensed this early in his gun enterprise" (Haag 2016, 89).

The repeater rifles were becoming available for the first time at the end of the U.S. Civil War. There were two notable battles signaling the beginning of the time of the repeater rifle. First, there was "Tennessee's Waterloo":

> At the "army of Tennessee's Waterloo," the last great Confederate charge at the end 1864, 20,000 rebel infantry advanced . . . they charged into Henry-armed soldiers of 65th Indiana Infantry, Company A, and 12th Kentucky unit armed with Colt revolving rifles. (Haag 2016, 88)

In a matter of minutes thousands of soldiers were killed, when only months before killing required a single shot from a weapon that shot a couple of manually loaded shots a minute. Imagine the complete discombobulation of units that had only known muskets to be facing off against the new repeating rifle technology, and what a complete slaughter and gruesome scene it would have been for these people at this time.

The second battle (really series of battles between Russians and Turks) known as the "Plevna Delay," where the "delay" was this much smaller army of 10,000 being able to hold off an army of 40,000 Russian for five months.

> In a first assault by Russians, Turks lost 12 men, 30 wounded; Russians lost 74 and 2,771 wounded in a 20 minute firefight . . . subsequent attacks were just as horrific . . . They unleashed an unheard of 20,000 shots per minute in one battle. Russia's coalition lost 14,000 men and 356 officers. Reporters wrote of the scene of Battle of Plevna that it would be difficult to recall "another instance of a corps being so rapidly destroyed" as this "frightful slaughter." (Haag 2016, 140)

Word of the "Plevna Delay" spread quickly throughout other countries and "Winchester's foreign sales thrived" (Haag 2016, 141).

> As part of the ongoing gun evolution to faster shooting, practically every European nation replaced outdated and single-shot rifles with rapid-fire ones. Gun innovation moved almost invariably in the direction of greater speed, lethality, and power in the commercial arms race. The Plevna Winchesters had inaugurated irreversibly the age of the semiautomatic rifle. (Haag 2016, 141)

After the Civil War, with the ability to sell repeating rifles, the next step was finding buyers. The major gun capitalists relied on international markets for their very survival from the mid-1800s to the 1860s and 1870s. "Winchester survived initially by selling internationally—as did Colt's, E. Remington & Sons, and Smith & Wesson" (Haag 2016, xvi). Colt sold to Turkey, Austria, Russia, and Italy (Haag 2016, xvi).

Winchester won a huge Turkish government contract on November 9, 1870. As Haag describes it, Winchester and the sultan's minister of war agreed:

> Winchester would sell 15,000 muskets and 5,000 repeating carbines for $28 and $20 each, respectively, with a discount of 5 percent . . . the Turkish contracts brought Winchester gross income of over 1,360, 000 for 1870 contract and 1871 contracts. (Haag 2016, 136)

Haag explains that the number of companies producing guns was quickly narrowed down in massive takeovers. "Of the 239 firms in 1860 that produced small arms, only 26 survived to 1900. Of those 26, 2 would become American icons of the West: Colt and Winchester" (Haag 2016, 164), and "Winchester zealously took over, bought out, and eliminated rivals" (Haag 2016, 165).

From 1879 to World War I was the time when the gun business became domestic and advertising efforts began.

> During this phase of the American gun industry the domestic markets, from sporting to frontier warfare to home defense, were cultivated and nourished. Likewise, Winchester's reliance on foreign markets declined, falling to no more than 10 or 15 percent of total sales by 1890. (Haag 2016, 166)

Winchester envisioned a "scattered" civilian market and one that needed to be developed. Haag goes to great pains to point out that there was not a huge demand for guns, so that the markets for guns had to be created and were not merely located or found.

Very popular dime novels at the turn of the twentieth century brought a romanticized version of the lone gunman hero that grew substantially into the twentieth century. I believe that many current supporters of gun rights in the name of American tradition are harkening back to these fictional stories. Dime novels and gun legends "roughly 100 pages, were sensational stories, but they were generally presented as real, thrilling, authentic, and true tales of the West. They flourished in the 1860s and through to the early 1890s" (Haag 2016, 189). Also, before the turn of the twentieth century were a couple of events worth mentioning in light of what is to follow. First, The ("NRA")

was founded in 1871 "after alarm arose over the poor marksman- ship of
National Guard members" (Haag 2016, 249). Although, the NRA claims to
be the oldest civil rights organization, it began to teach people how to shoot.
Also, the NRA "died in obscurity in 1892, but it did not stay dead." It came
back in 1904, "with an agenda to bolster Americans' atrophied rifle skills"
(Haag 2016, 249). Second, the Supreme Court's first Second Amendment
case, *United States v. Cruikshank*, was in1876. This case concerned the state
restricting the right of blacks to bear arms. The court upheld the state's right
to pass civilian firearms controls and legislation. As Haag explains, "In this
ruling, the Court upheld the right of states to pass civilian firearms controls
and legislation" (Haag 2016, 197). This decision, along with two others,
would affirm the militia-reading of the Second Amendment. "*Cruikshank*
. . . . held that the right to keep and bear arms was *not* endowed in individuals but rather in state militias. "'The right of bearing arms . . . is not a right
granted by the Constitution,' explained Chief Justice Morrison R. Waite in
his majority opinion" (Light 2017, 51).

Early 1900s advertising was very effective in increasing gun sales. From
the vantage point of business, gun cultures are gun markets. Remington,
Colt, and Winchester understood market segmentation, and they understood
the gun's distinct potential uses and customers. During the years after the
Civil War, when the industry established itself, advertisements were a powerful influence in creating a gun culture (Haag 2016, 167). Gun sellers also
knew early on that "self-defense sells" and used this rationale in one form or
another to persuade customers to purchase guns. Color lithography in advertisement coincided with the growth in Winchester gun net sales, from $1.8
million in 1885 to $11 million in 1912 (Haag 2016, 251). Promotional calen-
dars were very effective and part of the milieu of the time. Gun manufacturers
also hired "missionaries" or "business getters" to market and sell guns at the
turn of the century, such as skilled marksmen, trick shots, and "expert enter-
tainers" (Haag 2016, 255).

In the twentieth century, federal gun laws passed in three waves, each
driven by an uptick in firearms violence and very visible examples of horrific and shocking gun violence. The first wave followed the St. Valentine's
Day Massacre in 1927. It included a ban on shipments of handguns using the
United States Postal Service, the 1934 National Firearms Act that made it a
requirement to register machine guns and sawed off shotguns, and the 1938
Federal Firearms Act which created national licensing for gun dealers and
manufacturers and banned sales to known felons. The second wave followed
the assassinations of JF Kennedy, Martin Luther King Jr., and others, leading
to the Gun Control Act of 1968 "the foundation of today's most prominent
national gun laws," expanded "prohibited purchases," banning the sales of
firearms to those "adjudicated as a mental defective" or "committed to mental

institution," and the 1986 Firearm Owners' Protection Act. And the third wave was sparked by President Reagan's aide James Brady being shot while defending President Reagan, which eventually in the early 1990s became the Brady Bill which most notably introduced background checks, and the 1994 law banning future production of assault weapons, feeding devices with more than ten bullets, including nineteen specific guns (Cook and Goss 2014, 80, 99).

The Supreme Court's last direct ruling on the Second Amendment, *the* precedent-setting Supreme Court case for the monumental *Heller* decision in 2008, was *United States v. Miller* (1939). In *Miller*, the government argued, unopposed, that the Second Amendment "gave sanction only to the arming of the people as a body to defend their rights against tyrannical and unprincipled rulers" and "did not permit the keeping of arms for purposes of private defense" (Brief of the United States at 12, U.S. v. Miller 307 U.S. 174, 1939).

Diaz explains that the individual right to bear arms view of Second Amendment first appeared in a law review article in 1960. He also explains that prior to 1960 the militia view was *the sole basis* for understanding and analyzing the Second Amendment in the thirteen law journal articles published from 1874 to 1959 that examined the Second Amendment (Diaz 2013, 73). Waldman discovers the same thing. He cites one political scientist who examined law review articles on the Second Amendment from the time the reviews were first indexed in 1888 to 1960. He found every single article concluded the Second Amendment did not guarantee an individual right [to bear arms] (Waldman 2014, 97).

At this point, the obvious question to ask is, What happened in 1960? (And perhaps a second question is, Where did the individual rights interpretation of the Second Amendment come from?) The NRA was not much of a political force up until the late 1960s into the 1970s. Before then the NRA supported many gun control initiatives, staying quite silent in the first two federal waves of legislation. It is as if the gun industry saw an opening in the late 1960s and early 1970s, a possibility to reinterpret the Second Amendment, to make it about an individual right to own guns. This would be very powerful in marketing and selling guns, convincing people to take advantage of a "Second Amendment right to personally bear arms." Again, this amendment had become irrelevant after the War of 1812, and today's militia would face the strongest federal military the world has ever known. A rather shocking point from a 2020 perspective, where this issue is certainly deeply divided between Democrat–gun control and Republican–gun rights, is that this is a relatively new division. Not until 1968 did the two major parties first include positions on gun control in their platforms (Cook and Goss 2014, 184).

Several individuals and groups got in ahead of the NRA on this reinterpretation effort. The first was the Second Amendment Foundation (SAF), created by Alan Gottlieb in 1974. This was the first "foundation," an entity devoted to research and education to qualify for tax deductions, something the NRA would not do until 1990. Also, the SAF began sponsoring annual conferences where scholars could come together and strategize about strengthening gun rights (Hardy 2016, 149). Simply put, the SAF "specializes in producing and publishing research that favors gun rights" (Hardy 2016, 149).

However, "The NRA did not begin pushing an individual right to bear arms theory of the Second Amendment until the 1970s" (Hardy 2016, 149). The NRA changed into the political force it currently is in 1977, at the annual meeting in the event that has come to be known as "The Cincinnati Revolt." Leadership was replaced and new leaders and members agreed to seventeen new bylaws as well as a new emphasis on legislative activism. Its member ship skyrocketed in response, going from about one million in 1977 to three million in 1985 (Hardy 2016, 152). It is hard to emphasize enough how important this meeting was. The leadership and new direction and approach of the NRA that still exists today started at this 1977 meeting. And this is the core force behind the reinterpretation of the Second Amendment.

Light gives a complementary explanation of this major shift in purpose of the NRA, from a shooting and hunting group to activism. She points out that although this organization was originally founded to support marksman-ship, hunting, and gun safety, it underwent a radical transformation in the late 1970s. It was at that time when the leaders of the organization changed focus to being political activists for gun rights. She explains that in addition to insisting that the Second Amendment pertained to an individual right to bear arms, advocacy of "gun rights" was also developed through the construction of a perceived urgent need for individual citizens to own guns for self-defense (Light 2017, 127). She explains that in the 1970s NRA advertisements there is clear evidence of the political transformation of this organization. Included was the suspicion that the government would eliminate the individual right to own guns. In continuous images and words, they emphasize the threat of urban crime and home invasion, (Light 2017, 150) and

> By mid-to-late 1980s, the organization's scare tactics had intensified. It was then that NRA ads, appearing in *Guns and Ammo, American Rifleman*, and *Guns* magazine, began to reflect the reactionary, antigovernment tone that would char-acterize the organization of the twenty-first century. (Light 2017, 151)

However, to actually change the Second Amendment, there needed to be built *some* rational, legal foundation for doing so, given the utter lack of precedent for this individual rights interpretation, as I have pointed out above. The main vehicle discovered for this purpose was the law review article. Gun rights organizations like the NRA paid for law review articles that defended the individual rights view. These law review articles apparently give credibility to interpretations of the Second Amendment in turn made by federal judges. Whether this should be the case for judges seems debatable, given that these articles can apparently be used to create and fabricate self-serving interpretations of the law, which in turn seem to carry some weight in judicial decisions. This is a way to bypass lack of previous precedent interpretations of the Second Amendment (or any amendment). Through the law review article, one can provide a new, unfounded interpretation of the Second Amendment.

> From 1970 to 1989, twenty-five articles adhering to the collective right view were published . . . but so were twenty-seven articles endorsing the individual rights model . . . at least sixteen of these articles—about 60 percent—were written by lawyers who had been directly employed by or represented the NRA or other gun rights organizations, although they did not always so identify themselves in the author's footnote. (Waldman 2014, 97–98)

The Second Amendment was being targeted for transformation, reinterpretation, change in meaning, from being about militia to being about an individual right to bear arms. And NRA membership was strong, between 1993 and 2013 there were roughly 3 million members, fluctuating lower and higher during this time (Kessler 2013; Harkinson 2013).

Jack Rakove ("A Faulty Rethinking of the 2nd Amendment") explains the significant role played by Attorney General John D. Ashcroft in 2002 (Rakove 2002). Rakove observes that Ashcroft's interpretation of the Second Amendment included an individual right to bear arms: "This posture represents an astonishing challenge to the long-settled doctrine that the right to bear arms protected by the Second Amendment is closely tied to membership in the militia" (Rakove 2002). Rakove explains that the individual rights interpretation was "once seen as marginal" but "has become an article of faith on the right, and Republican politicians have in turn had to acknowledge its force" (Rakove 2002). He explains the Supreme Court "last examined this issue in 1939 in *United States v. Miller*. There it held that the Second Amendment was designed to ensure the effectiveness of the militia, not to guarantee a private right to possess firearms. The *Miller* case, though it did not fully explore the entire constitutional history, has guided the government's position on firearm issues for the past six decades" (Rakove 2002). He also emphasizes two major points for the militia reading of the Second Amendment, first that "The amendment refers to the right of the people, rather than the individual person of the Fifth Amendment. And the phrase "keep and bear arms" is, as most commentators note, a military reference" (Rakove 2002).

Also relevant to the originalist interpretation of the Second Amendment are legislative concerns at the time. Relevant proposals offered in 1787 and 1788 by state ratification conventions were all focused on the necessity of a militia as an alternative to a standing army. And the only recorded discussion of the Second Amendment in the House of Representatives was about requiring religious dissenters to serve in the militia. (Rakove 2002). And the Senate in 1789 deleted a clause defining the militia as "composed of a body of people," showing that the Senate gave militia a narrower meaning than it otherwise had, more evidence against the individual right to bear arms interpretation of the Second Amendment (Rakove 2002).

Briefly, also note that in 2005 Congress passed the so-called Tiahart Amendments, disallowing lawsuits against the gun industry! "[T]he NRA succeeded in pushing through Congress the Protection of Lawful Commerce in Arms Act, which President George W. Bush signed into law in 2005. This extraordinary federal law shields the gun industry against all but the most carefully and artfully crafted private lawsuits." They also forbid ATS from releasing to the public information about gun trafficking and gun crimes. Not only a shield from lawsuits that any other consumer product is subject to, but also this law stores crucial information about the guns used in crimes (Cook and Goss 2014, 117). There is no apparent social good being promoted through these laws, and they seem quite clearly and primarily laws to empower the profit interests of those in the gun industry. Cook and Goss come to no good rationale for these laws protecting guns, of all consumer products to be protected: "Why aren't guns treated like other consumer products—cars, toys, even cigarettes?" Answer: "Politics mostly" (Cook and Goss 2014, 118).

With the right Supreme Court make-up, 2008 would become the year when the reinvention of the Second Amendment would be complete. Justice Scalia was "hailed by an adoring gun lobby as 'the best friend gun-rights has up there' and was well known to be a long time gun enthusiast and supporter" (Diaz 2013, 46). To appreciate the extreme bias of long-time gun rights advocate Justice Scalia, consider this one example, where he is given a prestigious award, gives a speech, and even meets those who will argue for gun rights in the Supreme Court the very next year!:

In 2007, the World Forum on the Future of Sport Shooting Activities (WFSA) gave Scalia its "Sport Shooting Ambassador Award," along with a solid silver reproduction of a sixteenth-century pistol with its powder flask. He accepted the award and gave the keynote address in Nuremberg, Germany, at the forum's annual meeting . . . an international gun industry trade organization, uses its annual ambassador award to improve the gun industry's image by "making public recognition of the social contribution made by some of the many public figures who have a longstanding interest in the shooting sports" . . . Scalia was photographed at the meeting with Alan Gottlieb, who is head of the pro-gun Second Amendment Foundation. At the very moment of the cozy Scalia-Gottlieb "grip and grin" photo, Gottlieb's foundation would be using Alan Gura as the lawyer to argue the *Heller* case before Scalia. (Diaz 2013, 47)

On June 26, 2008, the Supreme Court affirmed the Court of Appeals for the DC Circuit in *Heller v. District of Columbia*. The 2008 *Heller* decision was the culmination of roughly fifty years from that first 1960 law review article suggesting an individual rights reading of the Second Amendment. Briefly put, in *District of Columbia v. Heller*, 554 U.S. 570 (2008), the Supreme Court held in a 5–4 decision that the Second Amendment protects an individual's right to possess a firearm, unconnected with service in a militia, for traditionally lawful purposes, such as self-defense within the home. It found that Washington, DC's handgun ban and requirement that lawfully owned rifles and shotguns be kept "unloaded and disassembled or bound by a trigger lock" violated this guarantee. The Supreme Court struck down provisions of the Firearms Control Regulations Act of 1975 as unconstitutional, determined that handguns are "arms" for the purposes of the Second Amendment, and found that the Regulations Act was an unconstitutional ban.

To justify his overcoming the clear precedent view of the Second Amendment as pertaining only to the militia, to ignore the clear precedent Supreme Court case of *Miller*, Scalia in the majority decision in *Heller* centrally employed the theory of "originalism." This term was apparently first used in the mid-1980s, making a rather modest appearance as a sort of meme. Originalism has three serious problems as a way of interpreting the Constitution: originalism is not itself prescribed by the Constitution, it does not reflect a convincing picture of the founders' intent, and it does not prevent judicial activism (Levy 2017). Also, Scalia himself did not write other opinions using this theory of "originalism," but instead seems to reserve use of this theory for interpreting the Second Amendment (Waldman 2014, 115).

In his majority opinion on *Heller*, Scalia spends 2 out of 64 pages on the militia. Although this does not mean that his ruling is therefore wrong, it is significant that precedent cases and the militia interpretation are only briefly considered. Another problem with the *Heller* ruling is that in dealing with the Second Amendment, it does not engage with the very words of the amendment itself, specifically the first part dealing with the militia. This is beyond a question of interpretation, and is now one of ignoring text. As Waldman explain, this negligence of Scalia as a justice is mirrored by the NRA as well:

But he has a surprising way to deal with that prefatory clause, the homage to the "well-regulated militia being necessary to the security of a free state," so important to the framers. He skips right over it. Scalia simply lops off the first half of the amendment, just as in the bowdlerized quote in the NRA headquarters lobby. (Waldman 2014, 108)

To summarize Scalia's imaginative read of the Second Amendment, *The New Yorker*'s Jeffrey Toobin writes that, "Scalia translated a right to military weapons in the eighteenth century to a right to handguns in the 21st" (Waldman 2014, 127).

Along with *Heller* and the reinvention of the Second Amendment, there has been from then until the present time a continued push to eliminate gun control measures and expand the availability of firearms to citizens. After the *Heller* decision, the NRA is more emboldened. Two major changes are worth mention. First, there has been a major loosening of concealed carry laws.

The NRA's most decisive political victory in the states has been reflected in a sea change in states "concealed carry" laws. In 1981, only two states allowed; 19 states barred entirely, 28 had "may issue" laws; . . . by 1988, shall issue in 9 states; by 2014, 36 states had "shall issue" laws; 4 states no permit requirement and the rest "may issue." (Spitzer 2015, 113–114)

Second, broadening the right to bear arms even further, something else never before seen has emerged, namely "Stand Your Ground" laws, the first being in Florida in 2005.

Florida Statutes, Section 776.013(3): "A person who is not engaged in an unlawful activity and who is attacked in any place where he or she has a right to be has no duty to retreat and has the right to stand his or her ground and meet force with force, including deadly force if he or she reasonably believes it is necessary to do so to present death or great bodily harm to himself or herself or another or to prevent the commission of a forcible felony." (Spitzer 2015, 117)

These laws are replacing self-defense laws and restrictions on the use of violence that seemed to be working well enough. Most importantly, self-defense laws and restrictions on use of deadly force are defended consistently with one major rationale, to *respect the sanctity of human life*. Diaz explains of the common law tradition that the general rule has been,

First, try to dis-engage or retreat, if attacked, which was often a prerequisite for a claim of self-defense. This rule, a duty to retreat, places a priority on human life. This rule is followed by those who would rather retreat than kill and have to live with the consequences, which may include killing an innocent third party. (Diaz 2013, 124)

Caroline Light deftly explains how in the last four hundred years we have gone from a self-defense law with a duty to retreat to a Stand Your Ground law that protects persons who kill in defense of property. She charts this change through several precedent legal cases that continued to expand the original law. How this happened is not a clear and distinct story, but, as Light puts it, "the story of how we evolved from a society restrained by the duty to retreat from danger to one where some possess the right to kill is a complex, nonlinear tale" (Light 2017, 16). She reiterates that the starting point of lethal self-defense is English common law. The framers of the U.S. legal system used this. Common law held that one was obliged to retreat if threatened, rather than respond with lethal violence (Light 2017, 19). Light explains.

> The chief exception to the English duty to retreat was the castle doctrine, which originated in a 1604 case involving an officer of the Crown who had forcibly entered the house of a man. . . . This decision popularized the expression "A man's home is his castle" . . . . Under the castle doctrine, a man did not have to retreat before fighting back against an intrusion on his home. (Light 2017, 20)

The major precedent-setting case that broadened the castle doctrine was that of Thomas Selfridge, who in 1806 published a statement in the newspaper calling a man named Austin a "coward." Austin sent an 18-year-old tough to beat up Selfridge. Selfridge heard about this ahead of time, being weak physically, and wanting to protect his honor against such a public beating, armed himself. When the tough approached him, Selfridge shot and killed him. The jury in the case found Selfridge not guilty. Light points out how important this case was:

> The trial would serve as a precedent for nineteenth-century efforts to adjudicate cases of lethal self-defense . . . this famous case provided legal foundation for the gradual decay of the duty to retreat" (Light 2017, 30).

> Through this case the "right of an individual to protect himself from attack. . . . has the castle doctrine's defense of retaliation extended to a right to defend one's own person. (Light 2017, 28)

One particular justification for the use of lethal force at the time of the early nineteenth century was an offense to one's honor, and specifically defending one's honor through dueling. We should pay careful attention today in the twenty-first century to this same defense of honor as a reason for individuals standing their ground in defense of themselves and their property. This is because the same arguments made against dueling could be made against use of lethal force while standing one's ground. Light explains that dueling was widespread and was something people wanted to eliminate. They did so by mainly coming to hold that "dueling constituted murder and that allowing a man to kill another over an assault on his honor would effectively legalize dueling" (Light 2017, 29). Among arguments against allowing duels was that killing in defense of one's honor is "incompatible with a liberal democracy" and "violent chaos would reign supreme" (Light 2017, 29). However, supporters of dueling argued

> Turning the other cheek when faced with an insult to one's honor was not compatible with the "manly independence" expected of white male citizens. While such "exercise of great Christian forbearance" was laudable, it was "utterly repugnant to those feelings which nature and education implanted in the human character." (Light 2017, 35)

The main point here is how long-standing, traditional views of self-defense, ones including a duty to retreat, were rejected for other values. Light explains that in the nineteenth century "retreat from confrontation was increasingly considered a value incompatible with rugged independence, white masculine honor, and the nation's early investment in armed self-defense" (Light 2017, 38). She also points out that "Over the course of the nineteenth century, the law shifted selectively to allow some men to use defensive violence when they felt threatened outside of the protective confines of their 'castle'" (Light 2017, 57).

Light explains that the *Erwin* and *Runyan* decisions "legitimated a 'true man's' right to use lethal violence in self-defense, even in spaces beyond his 'castle'" (Light 2017, 62). These cases would further broaden the castle doctrine beyond the castle. That is, the cases establish a justification for killing a person even though the killing takes place outside of the castle-home. In the first case, Ohioan James W. Erwin, in January 1872, at 55-years old, killed his 23-years-old son-in-law in an argument over a storage shed on Erwin's property. Erwin was convicted of second-degree murder, appealed to the Ohio Supreme Court, where it was overturned and ordered for retrial in 1876. Ultimately, Erwin was acquitted. "This landmark case established the right of the 'true man' to stand his ground against an attacker, even if the attack took place outside of the man's home" (Light 2017, 58). In the second case, John Runyan in Indiana was found guilty of manslaughter, sentenced to eight years, and appealed to Indiana Supreme Court, which ordered a retrial (Light 2017, 58–59). Judge Neblack explained in his justification for the retrial that the lower court was improperly instructed on the duty to retreat. "Judge Neblack reasoned that retreat was incompatible with American values of rugged independence and self-suffering" (Light 2017, 59). And also Neblack cites natural law as the foundation for self-defense and that using lethal force was consistent with the "true man" who does not back away from danger. On retrial, John Runyan was acquitted.

Into the twentieth century, there was further broadening of the castle doctrine and right to use of lethal force beyond the castle. In 1921, the Supreme
Court would effectively eliminate the duty to retreat in *Brown* v. *United
States*. Delivering the majority opinion, Justice Oliver Wendell Holmes actually uses the words "stand your ground" (which Florida used to create the first
"Stand Your Ground" law in 2005) when he explains "if a man reasonably
believes that he is in immediate danger of death or grievous bodily injury
from his assailant, he may stand his ground and that if he kills him he has not
exceeded the bounds of lawful self-defense" (Light 2017, 84–85).

Moving back to our current Stand Your Ground laws, we can see how far
we have come from English common law in the 1600s, where self-defense
was inside the castle and there was a duty to retreat elsewhere. Lethal force
was a last resort, and this all was in the name of the sanctity of human life.
In her section called, "The Birth of A Stand-Your-Ground Nation" Light
explains that "Misrepresentations, which minimize the harm done by the
person claiming self-defense and exaggerate the threat posed by the person
who has been killed have long been common among advocates of lethal self-
defense" (Light 2017, 158). Instead of representing the early traditions of the
U.S., Stand Your Ground laws are innovations; The legal scholar Mary Anne
Franks summarizes the Florida law's three main ones:

1. Merely need the "commission of a forcible felony" to use lethal force,
   which means mere robbery can justify use of lethal force;
2. Expands the castle beyond a person's home;
3. Law offers criminal and civil immunity from prosecution (Light 2017,
   161–162).

As the results of these new laws begin to show themselves, consider
that "evidence suggests that the law has increased the incidence of lethal
violence . . . a 7 to 9 percent increase in homicides since the law's passing"
(Light 2017, 162). The American Bar Association in 2015 recommended the
repeal of the Stand Your Ground laws as they provide a "low cost license to
kill." In the end, the ideology of lethal self-defense "encourages all people
. . . to use lethal violence in defense of their expanded castles" (Light 2017,
173).

Stand Your Ground laws and the lethal force used is based on the individual killer's own belief, even if unfounded and extreme, albeit sincere.
It gives much too much power to shooters. It is exponentially easier to kill
now and pay no penalty than it was under the guise of self-defense. Another
major departure from traditional self-defense law: autonomic presumption of
"reasonable fear" to justify the use of lethal force (Light 2017, 162). It dangerously relaxes a restraint on the use of violence in retaliation. Before the

new law, 16,000 Floridians had a concealed carry license. After the law, as of 2012, 1,151,537 licenses (Diaz 2013, 122).

The results of these laws and increase in the number of people carrying guns have been more deaths. Spitzer explains

> A primary consequence of castle doctrine laws [when applied to public places] is to increase homicide by a statistically and economically significant rate. . . Stand your ground laws reduced the costs associated with the use of lethal force, thereby encouraging more of it. (Spitzer 2015, 130)

Also, justifiable homicides doubled from 2000 to 2010 and tripled in Florida (from 12 per year to 33 per year) (Spitzer 2015, 129).

Stand your ground laws in essence lead us all in a society with such laws to have *less* regard for human life. The main beneficiaries of this law are violent criminals. This is because they can now kill and simply claim they had the requisite fear under the Stand Your Ground law to take a life. A review of over 100 stand your ground cases in Florida "found that nearly half of those invoking self-defense had been arrested at least three times— many for violent offenses—before they killed someone" (Hardy 2016, 157). Hardy attempts to sum up concisely many negative consequences of these laws:

> In short, the effects of Florida's stand-your-ground law have been an increase in homicides, protection for repeat criminals, aggravated racial and general disparities, and heightened confusion created by the immunity provision for the use of justifiable force. Perhaps unsurprisingly given these effects, 60 percent of Floridians want the law to be amended (ABA Report, 18). (Hardy 2016, 160)

A DEFENSE OF THE CHRISTIAN
GUN RIGHTS POSITION

In the first, more informational section, I argued that the Second Amendment is only about the militia, the NRA transformed itself into a political machine for gun industry in 1977, the Heller decision in 2008 created a new right in the Constitution, and stand your ground laws go well beyond traditional self-defense law and in effect primarily protect violent killers. The gun industry, amoral from the start to now, is mostly if not only interested in profit and is the business of selling killing machines. With no clear actions motivated by love, service, helping others in society, and apparent dishonesty and politicking at the expense of the integrity of the Second Amendment, the burden is great for Christians supporting gun rights. Here, I attempt to present a defense of the Christian gun rights position. Currently, Christian nationalism provides strong political support for the view that the Second Amendment is about an individual right to own guns and furthermore that this Amendment, along with the U.S. as a country, was a product of a Christian God's creation.

The attempt to provide some scriptural and other support for gun rights from a Christian worldview seems most strongly based on the two swords text, Just War Theory (and defending the position of Christian realism over pacifism), and on a proper understanding of the Sixth Commandment.

Christians who advocate to the right to bear arms as individuals argue that this gives justification for owning a gun and using it. Luke 22:7–38, where this text is located, is in the context of The Last Supper, where Jesus will reveal to his disciples his future death, certainly not a plan for the use of weapons. Let us pick up at verse 24:

A dispute also arose among them as to which one of them was to be regarded as the greatest. But he said to them, "The kings of the Gentiles lord it over them; and those in authority over them are called benefactors. But not so with you; rather the greatest among you must become like the youngest, and the leader like one who serves. For who is greater, the one who is at the table or the one who serves? Is it not the one at the table? But I am among you as one who serves. You are those who have stood by me in my trials; and I confer on you, just as my Father has conferred on me, a kingdom, so that you may eat and drink at my table in my kingdom, and you will sit on thrones judging the twelve tribes of Israel. Simon, Simon, listen! Satan has demanded to sift all of you like wheat, but I have prayed for you that your own faith may not fail; and you, when once you have turned back, strengthen your brothers." And he said to him, "Lord, I am ready to go with you to prison and to death!" Jesus said, "I tell you, Peter, the cock will not crow this day, until you have denied three times that you know me." He said to them, "When I sent you out without a purse, bag, or sandals, did you lack anything?" They said, "No, not a thing." He said to them, "But now, the one who has a purse must take it, and likewise a bag. And the one who has no sword must sell his cloak and buy one. For I tell you, this scripture must be fulfilled in me, 'And he was counted among the lawless'; and indeed what is written about me is being fulfilled." They said, "Lord, look, here are two swords." He replied, "It is enough." (Luke 22:24–38, NRSV)

Here, Jesus says that although they did not need swords when he sent them out before, now they will need swords. And this is urgent, as they are even to sell their cloak to get a sword. Jesus seems to be recommending that they arm themselves, and by extension we should arm ourselves. Furthermore, here Jesus approves of the disciple who shows him two swords. In general, this text has Jesus promoting our arming ourselves, consistent with the gun rights position. Just War Theory is not merely about war, but its moral principles extend to the realm of postwar and nonwar activity. As such, Just War Theory can be used to formulate and defend a position on the individual right to own and use guns. There are times when war is justified, and times when individual killing is justified, but there are certain conditions that must be met. Before presenting those conditions of Just War Theory, I will consider the "Christian realist" position.

A Christian realist believes "there *are* occasions in which, reluctantly, we may need to apply coercive force, even if this means going to war, for the protection and preservation of a third party" (Brown 2008, 20). Two extreme positions, militarism and pacifism, exist alongside of Christian realism. There exist major problems for each of these two, making Christian realism seem the most justified for Christians on the use of lethal force in war (Brown 2008, 19).

The militarist considers war and coercive force to be justified in any circumstance. For this position, there are no moral limits to what can be done for political purposes. On the other hand, the pacifist believes that war and coercive force are never justified and that war is never an option (Brown 2008, 19). The problems with militarism are many: the

> Failure to distinguish between religion and statecraft (i.e., between duties of the individual and the state), its inadequate and distorted understanding of God (whether through theology proper or though some skewed form of civil religion), its disregard for natural moral law, its merely simplistic approach to morality by which it reduces all things to a clear conflict of good over evil, its failure to realize that justness is only approximate and not pure in the present life, and its indiscriminate attitude toward human life. (Charles 2005, 125–126)

The problems for pacifism seem just as strong, as for pacifism, "in its refusal to resist evil directly through actions, in practice it bestows on evil and tyranny an advantage in the present life" (Charles 2005, 127). Also, "Pacifism overestimates the effectiveness of nonviolence and nonresistance at the same time that it underestimates—it does not fully deny—the fact that an ethics of protection issues out of Christian charity" (Charles 2005, 127). Pacifism suffers from a "lack of realism," not acknowledging violent, criminal people who "have no interest in being reasonable" and will not be persuaded (Charles 2005, 128). Also, the flip side of this weakness of the pacifist is that he or she fails to appreciate charity is an "ethics of protection" (Charles 2005, 128). The pacifist can justifiably forgo self-defense. But to forgo defending innocent others, as an obligation, seems strained, especially from a Christian perspective. This gets into the distinction between attitudes for individuals in day-to-day life in the text (e.g., Romans 12, Sermon on the Mount) and other passages that deal with authorities and countries and public policy. In short,

"While pacifism may be the dictate of private conscience . . . it cannot be public policy" (Charles 2005, 130). Also, "religious pacifists give too little attention to the church's rich and broad history, which affirms, rather than negates, the worth of the soldier and the magistrate alongside all vocations" (Charles 2005, 128). Further, the pacifist is weak theologically, not accounting for God as Warrior, with the Bible "filled with allusions to this divine Warrior and his activity" (Charles 2005, 129). Finally, the pacifist seems to fail to recognize that "not all killing is outlawed by Scripture and the Christian tradition. The Sixth Commandment applies to the killing of innocent, not moral retribution against those who do evil" (Charles 2005, 129).

Just War Theory represents Christian realism, a position defended by Christians who see as most justified the use of violence that mediates between the absolutes of pacifism and militarism. I do not aim to summarize the massive literature of Just War Theory here. Instead, in light of the gun control position, I want to establish here that there are cases of justified killing by Christians, given certain criteria are met,

> Just war principles as they have developed in the Christian tradition proceed from charity. The right response to injustice is a response "in kind." A law of reprisal exists for retribution and restoration. Just reprisal is a moral good. It is rooted in natural moral laws. (Charles 2005, 138)

Martin Luther argues that it is "work of Christian love to protect and defend a whole community with the sword and not let people be abused" (Charles 2005, 50). And consider,

> Consistent with Ambrose, Augustine and Aquinas before him, Luther believed that bearing the sword was not inconsistent with Christian discipleship. It is not for the purpose of "avenging yourself or returning evil for evil, but for the good of your neighbor and for the maintenance of the safety and peace of others." (Charles 2005, 52)

Charles points out that the government is accountable to God to restrain evil (Charles 2005, 15). Augustine sees Just War as a duty of citizenship, working for justice motived by charity. Both Ambrose and Augustine believed that there was an obligation of Christian love to defend and protect innocent third parties (Charles 2005, 41). Augustine's famous phrase here is "benevolent harshness." Augustine had "little patience for the notion that Christianity will possibly tolerate evil based on a particularly distorted understanding of Jesus' 'teaching'" (Charles 2005, 146) and keep in mind that "Christian moral traditions concur in acknowledging justifiable forms of homicide, such as self-defense, protecting civilians and resisting insurrection" (Charles 2005, 146).

In Just War Theory, there are seven criteria to justify the use of violence in war. The first three "core conditions represent the heart of just war theory" (Charles 2005, 135) and St. Thomas Aquinas identified these three (Charles 2005, 132). These first three conditions for a war to be just are just cause, proper authority, and right intention. The last four are last resort, reasonable chance of success, proportionate means, and peace as ultimate aim. As support for the gun rights position, the point is that with these conditions met, gun use is justified from a Christian perspective. Very briefly put, consider the meaning of all seven conditions:

1. An injury or injustice inflicted. Rights to sovereignty are violated. Key here is whether one believes in inalienable rights worth defending. Charles states pacifists do not consider rights inalienable and worth defending (Charles 2005, 133).
2. "Proper authority" means only "sovereign authorizers" can wage war. If the magistrate is the authority, not mere individuals, then what results is anarchy and tyranny. The magistrate uses the sword against criminals and unjust states. Coercive force may be necessary to preserve justly ordered peace. Charles explains that both militarism and pacifism "miss the essence of moral responsibility, militarism by running roughshod over moral considerations, while pacifism negates political power that exists to preserve the peace" (Charles 2005, 134).
3. "Right intention" "which is justly ordered peace and a greater good. Intentions failing to qualify include those for pride, aggrandizement, or reputation" (Charles 2005, 134).
4. Reasonable efforts to use nonmilitary (e.g., diplomatic, economic, and political) alternatives should be exhausted before resorting to war.
5. "Reasonable chance of success," so that there should be calculation involved and a greater good in mind to be promoted. Futile efforts would fail to meet this condition, as well as wars that caused more harm than good.
6. "Proportional means" weighs costs included in war and benefits to be attained, and benefits should outweigh costs.
7. Peace as the ultimate goal, so that the establishment of social order and political stability are goals (Charles 2005, 133–135).

Getting to the gun debate, among the gun control defenders "there are not a few Christians who stubbornly maintain that retribution—whether in the criminal justice system or among the nations—is unjust and immoral. It is not morally responsible to relegate matters of justice to non-believers" (Charles 2005, 140). Gun rights Christians are defending retribution, not revenge. That is, the use of guns for self-defense is doing justice, not done out of a vicious attitude.

In using guns for self-defense, one is acting out of charity, "if it has moral backbone and is not sloppy sentimentalism—with what is best for the criminal and for the public at large" (Charles 2005, 144). "It is virtuous, not vicious, to feel anger at moral evil" (Charles 2005, 145). The difference between retribution and revenge is that revenge is based on real or perceived injury, is wild and not subject to limitations, and delights in and derives pleasure from injury of the offender. Retribution is based on objective wrong, has upper and lower limits, takes no pleasure in punishment, and is impersonal and impartial (Charles 2005, 145). Gun rights advocates are for retribution, not revenge.

A DEFENSE OF THE CHRISTIAN
GUN CONTROL POSITION

Here, I will provide a brief response to the gun rights Christian defense of the gun rights position, based on a proper understanding of the Sixth Commandment, Christian realism, and Just War Theory. Then, I will provide a brief scriptural argument for the Christian gun control position.

A key assumption in the gun rights/gun control debate is that gun control Christians are pacifists. The arguments against Christian pacifism as public policy are many and strong. However, a gun control Christian can be a Christian realist. The arguments rejecting gun control Christians as pacifists is therefore a strawman caricature of the stronger Christian realist position.

Gun control Christians can consistently recognize that the Sixth Commandment tacitly allows killing, just not "murder," a certain type or subset of all killings. However, that still leaves unaddressed the question of whether Christians should be standing their ground with guns. The attitude and intention of Christians standing their ground is too extreme and represents the other extreme to the pacifist, the militaristic Christian.

This takes us to an application of the Just War Theory to the gun rights position, including advocating Stand Your Ground laws:

1. An injury or injustice inflicted. Inalienable rights worth defending have been violated.
   This seems to lend support to individuals using a gun in self-defense.
2. "Proper authority" means only "sovereign authorizers" can wage war (Charles 2005, 133). The magistrate is authority, not mere individuals.
   This seems to be violated when individuals are using lethal force on their own, with no official social capacity.
3. "Right intention" "which is justly ordered peace and a greater good. Intentions failing to quality include those for pride, aggrandizement, or reputation."

There are many cases of people standing their ground for pride and reputation, not clearly thinking about the consequences and greater good.

4. Reasonable efforts to use nonmilitary (e.g., diplomatic, economic, and political) alternatives should be exhausted before resorting to war.

This condition is also not clearly met, especially with Stand Your Ground laws, where there is at least implicit encouragement to go to the gun, a killing machine, before all other alternatives, including retreat, have been exhausted. The very existence of Stand Your Ground laws implies an inability to civilly resolve social conflicts.

5. "Reasonable chance of success"

Let us assume that success is saving one's life and fending off an attacker. In that case one has success. However, if a person is killed, and killed when they did not have to be killed (under condition 4), then although successful in a sense, it also seems tragic and a failure when a life is lost. This gets into the value of a human life; if the gun rights position also respects the sanctity of human life, then any killing of any person would be viewed as a terrible loss.

6. "Proportional means" weighs costs included in war and benefits to be attained, and benefits should outweigh costs.

This condition is also not clearly met by the gun rights position, as using guns and therefore lethal force will result in ending another person's life, so that as with the previous condition, the sanctity of human life makes going to a gun something to do only as a last resort in self-defense. The costs can be innocent bystanders killed, and someone being killed when retreat may have been possible.

7. Peace as the ultimate goal.

In Stand Your Ground cases, many who have been killed seem to be involved in situations where there is no desire for such peace. This condition would seem to be quite limiting to individuals using lethal force in self-defense, and it also shows how strained an application of Just War Theory to individuals is when applied to self-defense situations.

Stand your Ground laws push way beyond self-defense; they empower, and embolden armed citizens. Now, it is merely a "perceived threat" that is enough to justify killing. As policy, this is contrary to the respect and value for the sanctity of human life, one that would show in the rejection of guns for use in a variety of ways and in a variety of contexts, including schools. Killings under Stand Your Ground have inclinations including rage and anger, offensiveness on the part of the killer, and attitudes contrary to that proscribed by Christ in the Sermon on the Mount.

Consider now four central Christian texts and basic tenets. Let us not go to the Old Testament, but beyond it into the life and teachings of Christ. First, the most relevant text to be considered from a Christian perspective given the use of guns in self-defense, is of "turning the other cheek" in response to an offense. This is the method and message of Jesus, so very contrary to their laws and their human nature. Here, I present the New Revised Standard Version from Matthew and then from Luke:

> You have heard that it was said, "An eye for an eye and a tooth for a tooth." But I say to you, Do not resist an evil-doer. But if anyone strikes you on the right cheek, turn the other also; and if anyone wants to sue you and take your coat, give your cloak as well; and if anyone forces you to go one mile, go also the second mile. Give to everyone who begs from you, and do not refuse anyone who wants to borrow from you. (Matthew 5:38–42, NRSV)

> But I say to you that listen, Love your enemies, do good to those who hate you, bless those who curse you, pray for those who abuse you. If anyone strikes you on the cheek, offer the other also; and from anyone who takes away your coat do not withhold even your shirt. Give to everyone who begs from you; and if anyone takes away your goods, do not ask for them again. Do to others as you would have them do to you. (Luke 6:27–31, NRSV)

Jesus Christ radically teaches persons to respond to offenses, dare I say violence, with blessings and love, so utterly counter to the idea of self-defense, let alone arming oneself with killing machines to respond to offenses. Jesus demands love and forbids spite or retaliation. "Turning the other cheek" is *contrary* in attitude and action to standing one's ground with a killing machine. According to Jesus, not only should ground be given, but also so should property, to anyone who asks for it, begs for it, or even takes it away. Perhaps, we have become much too protective of our property and our ground. So, for a Christian to stand his or her ground with a gun out in public, assuming a mindset and incredible responsibility and self-control that should exist for possessing such lethal force that takes so much away in so very little time, in seconds lives are ended and families and communities traumatized.

Secondly, the sanctity of human life is quite relevant to the gun rights debate. The self-defense laws replaced by stand your ground laws were founded on sanctity of human life. The long-recognized right to self-defense clearly demands using violence only in a last resort, retreating if possible. Stand Your Ground laws make violence something much more likely to happen; they invite violence as way to deal with a situation. Instead of protecting the sanctity of human life, they protect those who kill others, needing only to be based on their belief, not fact that they were in danger. So, many Christians identify as prolife in the abortion debate, quite a striking contradiction is apparent. The bottom line justification is the sanctity of human life, precious and protected even from the moment of conception, before sentience or ability to experience pleasure or pain. However, some of these same Christians are also strong gun rights advocates (Protestantism is a major predictor of gun ownership). Guns are killing machines, designed to take life, and more guns means more lives are lost, less guns, less lives lost. To respect the sanctity of human life means preventing the killing of humans. In the gun rights de- bate, this means fighting against the proliferation of guns and ammo. As Rob Schenck concludes in his notable 2015 documentary, *The Armor of Light*, on the very question motivating my paper: "You can't be pro-life and pro-gun."

As a third text relevant to guns, consider how Jesus commissioned the twelve according to Matthew 10:9–10 (NRSV): "Take no gold, or silver, or copper in your belts, no bag for your journey, or two tunics, or sandals, or a staff . . ."—and no swords. A major point of this arrangement is they had to depend upon God, not upon weapons and other worldly things. Christians should reflect deeply upon how Jesus sent these disciples out unarmed in light of the gun debate. And as for the swords used at the arrest at Gethsemane, in Matthew, focus on Jesus's rebuke: "Suddenly, one of those with Jesus put his hand on his sword, drew it, and stuck the slave of the high priest, cutting off his ear. Then Jesus said to him, 'Put your sword back into its place; for all who take the sword will perish by the sword'" (Matthew 26:51–52; NRSV). Here, a disciple acts on his own in using the sword, and Jesus rebukes him. He seems to advise also never to use a sword unless one wants to die the same way (relevant to those today who buy guns and then have a fatal accident). The disciples did not understand that Jesus would be victorious through suffering, willingly accepting his death, then coming back to life. He clearly teaches in word and deed not to match violence with violence. The true "sword" of a Christian is "the sword of the Spirit, which is the word of God" (Ephesians 6:17; NRSV).

A fourth and final text is one especially employed by gun-advocating Christians. In this text, Jesus seems to allow for the taking of "two swords." Christians who advocate for the right to bear arms as individuals argue that this gives justification for owning a gun and using it. Reconsider Luke 22:35–38 (NRSV):

[Jesus] said to them, "When I sent you out without a purse, bag, or sandals, did you lack anything?" They said, "No, not a thing." He said to them, "But now, the one who has a purse must take it, and likewise a bag. And the one who has no sword must sell his cloak and buy one. For I tell you, this scripture must be fulfilled in me, 'And he was counted among the lawless'; and indeed what is written about me is being fulfilled." They said, "Lord, look, here are two swords." He replied, "It is enough."

Immediately striking to me in this is that Jesus says, "That's enough!" as if screaming it, or exasperated with them. It may be that he was being metaphorical in his use of "sword" here, and that his reply is ironic on his part. And the disciples just don't get what is about to happen. They just acknowledged that when he sent them out without a bag or purse or sandals (or other things, including swords) that they did not lack anything. The implication here seems to be that if you don't lack anything, then you should not want something else (namely a sword, or a gun). I believe the gun rights reading of this is that when Jesus says, "That's enough!" he means that with two swords they will be able to defend themselves adequately and perhaps kill others. I find this an extremely strained reading, and this seems totally contrary to what Jesus is saying in this context, especially as he just said that they lacked nothing when he sent them out before. The context of this is The Last Supper and Jesus foretelling what was about to happen to him. He says to sell the cloak to buy a sword, perhaps because in the age to come, post-Jesus's crucifixion and resurrection Christians will be brutalized and killed. Christians would have quite a price to pay to live as believers in the world in the next three hundred years, and certainly for these disciples. Ultimately, even if this "two swords" text grounds the right to self-defense (which above was shown in common law tradition to only allow violence as a last resort, consistent with the sanctity of human life, unlike stand your ground laws) this text alone is hardly enough to ground a Christian gun rights position.

Finally, note that in three of four gospels, Jesus explains: "He who finds his life will lose it, and he who loses his life for my sake will find it" (Matthew 10:39; Luke 17:33; John 12:25). Also, in all four gospels Jesus teaches that true greatness is in humility not in "standing one's ground" (Matthew 18:1–5; Mark 9:33–37; Luke 9:46–48; John 3.3, 5; 13:20), "for he who is the least among you all is the one who is great" (Luke 9:48). These texts are consistent with Pope Francis's recent and repeated condemnation of the gun industry, seeing them essentially trusting in guns rather than in God. "Losing their lives" will entail forfeiting the idol of the gun. Pope Francis said,

> "If you trust only men you have lost . . . It makes me think of . . . people, managers, businessmen who call themselves Christian and they manufacture weapons. That leads to a bit of distrust, doesn't it?" The crowd applauded and he went on to criticize those who invest in weapons industries, saying, "Duplicity is the currency of today . . . they say one thing and do another. (Hartmann 2015)

Pope Francis called those of the gun industry "merchants of death," and said they perpetuate war to make money, declaring that the devil "enters through our wallets" (Hartmann 2015). In addition, these comments have

certainly upset the NRA, which "listed the United States Conference of
Catholic Bishops on its enemies list" (Hale 2016).

Pope Francis is focused on the motivation of those in the gun industry,
that of profit for money. There are certainly major passages that warn against
greed, the love of money, and this motivation. Reflect on 1 Timothy 6:6–10,
2 Timothy 3:2, and Hebrews 13:5, about not only the profit motivated makers
of the gun industry but also those who support and follow them:

1 Timothy 6:6–10 (NRSV):

Of course, there is great gain in godliness combined with contentment; for we
brought nothing into the world, so that we can take nothing out of it; but if
we have food and clothing, we will be content with these. But those who
want to be rich fall into temptation and are trapped by many senseless and
harmful desires that plunge people into ruin and destruction. For the love of
money is a root of all kinds of evil, and in their eagerness to be rich some
have wandered away from the faith and pierced themselves with many pains.

2 Timothy 3:2–5 (NRSV):

For people will be lovers of themselves, lovers of money, boasters, arrogant,
abusive, disobedient to their parents, ungrateful, unholy, inhuman, impla-
cable, slanderers, profligates, brutes, haters of good, treacherous, reckless,
swollen with conceit, lovers of pleasure rather than lovers of God, holding to
the outward form of godliness but denying its power. Avoid them!

Hebrews 13:5 (NRSV):

Keep your lives free from the love of money, and be content with what you
have; for he has said, "I will never leave you or forsake you."

CONCLUSION

A colleague of mine recently attended his fiftieth high school reunion. While
there, he went to a church service and at the altar were approximately twenty
American flags and one cross. This was deeply disturbing to him. I believe
that the same reason he was disturbed by the flags applies to Christians who
are gun rights advocates. This gets to the core problem with the current
Christian nationalism movement in the U.S., the major resistance to gun control laws. They confuse the Second Amendment with the teaching of Christ.
And they misinterpret and misuse the Second Amendment as referring to an
individual's right to own guns. We saw that the first guns of the colonists
were controlled in various ways. The militia was the main protection of the
colonists from authoritarian kings. The Second Amendment represents the
importance of the militia for the U.S. in its first decades. It is clear on many
different counts that the Second Amendment is about militias and not about
an individual right to bear arms. This new individual rights interpretation was

the product of a gun business, amoral and profit-driven from the outset to the present day, as Pope Francis has repeatedly pointed out. Through a concerted, intentional effort culminating in the *Heller* decision, gun rights activists successfully reinterpreted the Second Amendment. As the federal law of the land, this decision justifies many other measures to loosen gun control measures in society. This loosening has certainly happened to self-defense laws, which originally were limited to the castle doctrine and a duty to retreat. It is especially relevant to Christians, who value the sanctity of human life, that our current stand your ground laws have *moved away from* the duty to retreat, and from Christian realism to Christian militarism. The reason for conducting duels in the early nineteenth century was in order to defend one's honor, and this reason was ruled insufficient to take another human life. However, defense of one's honor and being a "true man" are major reasons for the expansion of the castle doctrine to places outside of the home, and moves away from the duty to retreat. But, the duty to retreat shows respect for the sanctity of human life, and so moving away from this duty seems a move away from Christian faith.

REFERENCES

American Bar Association, National Taskforce on Stand Your Ground Laws. 2014. "Preliminary Report and Recommendations" (August 8).

Brown, Davis. 2008. *The Sword, the Cross, and the Eagle: The American Christian Just War Tradition.* New York: Rowman & Littlefield.

Butler, Stuart. "War of 1812 Transformed American Military." *Richmond Times: Dispatch*, January 22, 2012.

Charles, J. Daryl. 2005. *Between Pacifism and Jihad: Just War and Christian Tradition.* Downers Grove, IL: InterVarsity.

Cook, Philip J., and Kristin A. Goss. 2014. *The Gun Debate: What Everyone Needs to Know.* Oxford: Oxford University Press.

Diaz, Tom. 2013. *The Last Gun.* New York: The New Press.

Editorial Board. "Despair Over Gun Deaths is Not an Option." *NY Times*, December 12, 2015.

Editorial Board. "The Death of Michael Brown." *NY Times*, August 12, 2014.

Editorial Board. "The Hidden Gun Epidemic: Suicides." *NY Times*, January 9, 2017.

Editorial Board. "The President Acts on Gun Violence." *NY Times*, January 4, 2016.

Editorial Board. "The Right to Sue the Gun Industry." *NY Times*, March 4, 2016.

Falwell, Jerry Jr. "Trump is the Churchillian Leader We Need." *Washington Post*, August 19, 2016.

Franks, Mary Anne. 2016. "How Stand-Your-Ground Laws Hijacked Self-Defense." In *Guns in Contemporary Society: The Past, Present, and Future of Firearms and Firearm Policy, Volume 2: Cultural Issues Related to Firearms in the United States*, edited by Glenn H. Utter. Denver: Praeger.

Gabriel, Trip. "Donald Trump and Hillary Clinton Set for Clash on Gun Control." *Washington Post*, May 19, 2016.

Guns in Contemporary Society: The Past, Present, and Future of Firearms and Firearm Policy. Volume 1: Background to the Current Debate over Firearms. 2016. Edited by Glenn H. Utter. Denver: Praeger.

Guns in Contemporary Society: The Past, Present, and Future of Firearms and Firearm Policy. Volume 2: Cultural Issues Related to Firearms in the United States. 2016. Edited by Glenn H. Utter. Denver: Praeger.

Haag, Pamela. 2016. *The Gunning of America: Business and the Making of American Gun Culture*. New York: Basic Books.

Hale, Christopher J. "Gun Control Is a Pro-Life Value." *Time.com*, January 6, 2016. http://time.com/4170126/gun-control-is-a-pro-life-value/.

Hardy, David T. 2016. "Evolution of the National Rifle Association and Other Gun Rights Organizations." In *Guns in Contemporary Society: The Past, Present, and Future of Firearms and Firearm Policy. Volume 1: Background to the Current Debate over Firearms*, edited by Glenn H. Utter. Denver: Praeger.

Harkinson, Josh. "Does the NRA Really Have 4 Million Members?" *Mother Jones*, January 14, 2013. http://www.motherjones.com/crime-justice/2013/01/nra-me mbership-numbers/.

Hartmann, Margaret. "Pope Francis Says Weapons Manufacturers Shouldn't Call Themselves Christians." *New York Magazine*, June 21, 2015.

Johnson, Nicholas J. 2016. "*Heller* as *Miller*: Court Decisions Dealing with Firearms" In *Guns in Contemporary Society: The Past, Present, and Future of Firearms and Firearm Policy. Volume 1: Background to the Current Debate over Firearms*, edited by Glenn H. Utter. Denver: Praeger.

Kessler, Glenn. "Does the NRA Really Have More Than 4.5 Million Members?" *Washington Post*, February 8, 2013.

Lankford, Adam. "What Drives Suicidal Mass Killers?" *NY Times*, December 17, 2012.

Lansford, Tom. 2016. "The Early History of Guns: From Colonial Times to the Civil War." In *Guns in Contemporary Society: The Past, Present, and Future of Firearms and Firearm Policy. Volume 1: Background to the Current Debate over Firearms*, edited by Glenn H. Utter, 1–32. Denver: Praeger.

Levy, Ken. "The Problems with Originalism." *New York Times*, March 22, 2017.

Light, Caroline E. 2017. *Stand Your Ground: A History of America's Love Affair with Lethal Self Defense*. Boston: Beacon Press.

Martin, James. "SJ Gun Control is a Pro-Life Issue." *NY Times*, December 17, 2012.

Miller, Hayley. "There Have Been Over 200 School Shooting Incidents Since The Sandy Hook Massacre." *Huffington Post*, December 14, 2016.

Nocera, Joe. "Guns and Mental Illness." *Washington Post*.

———. "Guns and Their Makers." *NY Times*, December 21, 2012.

———. "What Did the Framers Really Mean?" *New York Times*, May 26, 2014.

Rakove, Jack. "A Faulty Rethinking of the 2nd Amendment." *New York Times*, May 12, 2002.

Rob, Schenck. "I'm an Evangelical Preacher. You Can't Be Pro-Life and Pro-Gun." *Washington Post*, December 28, 2015.

Robinson, Eugene. "The Tragic Choice We Make About Guns." *Washington Post*, December 3, 2015.

Spitzer, Robert. "The NRA Wants to Suppress One Of Guns' Most Important Safety Features." *Washington Post*, January 22, 2017.

Spitzer, Robert J. 2015. *Guns Across America: Reconciling Gun Rules and Rights*. New York: Oxford University Press.

Stack, Liam. "President of Liberty University Urges Students to Get Gun Permits." *New York Times*, December 5, 2015.

Waldman, Michael. 2014. *The Second Amendment: A Biography*. New York: Simon & Schuster.

Whitehead, Andrew L., Landon Schnabel, and Samuel L. Perry. 2018. "Gun Control in the Crosshairs: Christian Nationalism and Opposition to Stricter Gun Laws." *Socius: Sociological Research for a Dynamic World* 4: 1–13.

Wood, Robert H. 2016. "A History of Firearms Legislation at the State and Local Levels." In *Guns in Contemporary Society: The Past, Present, and Future of Firearms and Firearm Policy. Volume 1: Background to the Current Debate over Firearms*, edited by Glenn H. Utter. Denver: Praeger.

Chapter 7

The American Gun Culture

Potential Impact on K–12 School Violence

Gordon Arthur Crews and Garrison Allen Crews

INTRODUCTION

While most modern school violence and disturbance incidents result from daily acts of bullying and mistreatment of children. Sadly, it appears that events in which high-powered semiautomatic weapons are used and extensive physical harm is caused seem to receive the most attention. Many argue that if weapons in general were less available then there would be less violence. This has led to great debate about "gun control" in the U.S. Each new school-related shooting brings about renewed controversy about the vast number of weapons readily available to juveniles across the nation.

The increasing number of K–12 school violence incidents seems to have only been mitigated starting in March 2020 due to various "shelter in place" orders enacted requiring schools to switch to an "online format" in their teaching of students in response to the COVID-19 pandemic (Crews and Crews, 2021). Eventually, all students will fully return to the traditional classroom setting thus reviving the fears and concerns over violent attacks at and upon American schools.

This chapter is the result of a comprehensive and on-going research projects investigating myriad causes of violence and disturbance in American K–12 schools. It involves an extensive examination of 78 incarcerated U.S. K–12 school violence offenders and their acts between 1979 and 2011 in thirty-three states. Each of the incidents examined in this study involved the use of some type of weapon (e.g., small knife, .22 caliber pistol, high-powered semiautomatic rifle, or even propane tanks).

We present select findings that focus on: weapons used and injuries incurred, the availability of guns, where the gun or weapon was obtained, the number of weapons used, the rounds of ammunition available, the number of potential victims, and the number killed or injured. In addition, these findings are presented as they relate to an author-developed typology of K–12 school violence perpetrators: traditional, gang-related, associated and nonassociated.

We intend for this study to contribute to the international debate about the American Gun Culture and the impact of interest in and availability of guns and other weapons on K–12 school violence in the U.S.

REVIEW OF THE LITERATURE

Since 16 years old Brenda Spencer used "I don't like Mondays" as her justification for killing two and injuring nine people with rifle fire at Cleveland Elementary School across from her home in San Diego, California, in 1979, researchers have attempted to determine correlates for this extreme type of juvenile delinquency and school violence.

While school shootings remain, especially on a large scale, relatively rare (Crews, 2016, 2020; Crews et al., 2013) in the percentage and type of school violence in general, they cause the most concern for parents, teachers, law enforcement, and educational administrators. In addition to the fear these types of events cause, they also bring about a great deal of debate on proper responses. Some feel that stringent zero-tolerance policies are the answer while others argue for more gun control in society (Lawrence and Birkland, 2004). Some argue that increased counseling and service to young people is the answer while others argue for the increased use of school expulsion and the building of more juvenile correctional facilities (Haider-Markel and Joslyn, 2001).

Research on agenda setting is useful for examining the media's role in elevating these issues to the national spotlight. Research in agenda setting (Haider-Markel and Joslyn, 2001) (*i.e.,* a process through which the mass media communicate the relative importance of various issues and events to the public) has demonstrated that dramatic news events (such as a high school shooting) can drive particular issues (such as gun control) to the top of media and governmental agendas. Debates and discussions about school shooting often see varying views converging on the gun-control aspect of the problem, but they often substantially diverge on other understandings of what kind of problem such events represent and how to address it.

Many argue that the differing institutional structure and incentives of the news media and politicians can create or inhibit interinstitutional positive feedback in the problem-defining process often based on personal political agendas (*i.e.,* framing issues to move issues forward in desired direction) (Haider-Markel and Joslyn, 2001). Agenda divergences are amplified when prominent politicians cue the media to follow particular story lines that depart from actual effective and meaningful legislative activity. Obviously, political events and policy discussion set parameters for debate and help to determine how an issue comes to be defined. Although existing research has examined the effects of alternative representations of political issues on public opinion, less attention has been given to highly salient issues, such as gun policy, and the potential effect of framing on causal attributions of blame for tragic events (Lawrence and Birkland, 2004).

The debate about solutions to school violence incidents where firearms are used is interesting and ironic at the same time. Many argue for more firearms on school grounds such as armed security or police to combat the issue, while others argue for less (Crews et al., 2013). Studies suggest that mass shootings often share two common characteristics. The shooters are very often mentally ill and many use guns with large-capacity magazines, allowing them to fire multiple rounds of ammunition without reloading (Kimmel and Mahler, 2003). As policymakers consider options to reduce such gun violence, many argue (Crews and Crews, 2020; Crews et al., 2013) they should understand public attitudes about various violence-prevention proposals, including policies affecting persons with mental illness; past research findings on Americans' attitudes about policies for curbing gun violence need to be updated.

Conducting any type of research regarding school violence and disturbance occurring in K–12 American schools is extremely difficult (Crews, 2019). It is difficult to locate information due to inconsistencies in definitions of school violence versus school disruption and lack of proper record-keeping. No system for recording and enumerating individual acts of crime existed until 1933, when the Federal Bureau of Investigation's Uniform Crime Report was developed. Most early information on school disturbance and problems is primarily anecdotal or simply not available, with even the very definition of "school" changing over time.

Further, many forms of individual aggression, such as juvenile misbehavior, were not a matter of great public concern and attention until the 1960s. It was not until the 1970s that many school districts started keeping comprehensive data on student criminality on their campuses. This is primarily due to the increased demand after the civil rights movement and anti-Vietnam war efforts from the general public for institutions and governmental agencies to be more accountable and transparent.

Throughout history, even definitions of what constituted school disturbance have varied. Reporting procedures have varied, and continue to vary, among school districts across the U.S. Local school administrators have historically played down their problems to give the impression that they controlled their school situations completely.

We have found that as of late 2017, no other study has surveyed or interviewed as many perpetrators or examined as many events as have been studied in this research. The Federal Bureau of Investigations' Threat Assessment Team (O'Toole, 1999) did not interview any actual perpetrators directly and only examined case studies of fourteen schools where shootings had occurred following the Columbine High School shooting as the foundation for their extensively utilized report entitled,. *The School Shooter: A Threat Assessment Perspective.*

Trying to determine the number of potential victims for any type of violence is difficult. This is definitely the case when studying school-related violence. The number of potential victims may be reported as only the students in a particular classroom or hallway (*e.g.*, 2 to 10) or, in some random shootings, the entire study body (*e.g.*, 150 or more) might be at risk. Attempting to examine the number of potential victims is difficult given the myriad types of school violence incidents. It can be argued that when a violent act occurs on or near a school's property, all children are at risk.

It is obvious that more research is needed into the true underlying causes of juvenile violence in general in schools, but especially these horrific types of events. There is also the need for more research related to Americans' fears about school violence and the inherent policy debates. The majority of the studies dealing with this topic demonstrate a strong tendency to group all school violence together because it is something that scares people so much, rather than think about it in a more nuanced fashion and consider how policy may also need to be nuanced. This study attempts to address the need to examine incidents of school violence in greater detail to foster more nuanced understanding of events and perpetrators to inform the policy debate.

THEORETICAL PERSPECTIVE

For the overall research project, the theoretical perspective used is the concept of Functionalism, also known as Structural-Functional Theory. The structural-functional approach is a perspective in sociology that sees society as a complex system whose parts work together to promote solidarity and stability (Spencer, 1898). It asserts that human lives are guided by social structures, which are relatively stable patterns of social behavior. One of the key ideas in Structural Functionalism is that society is made up of groups or institutions, which are cohesive, share common norms, and have a definitive culture.

Functionalist theorists examine social practices and their impact on society and its constituent subgroups and define these social practices as any social occurrences that have a pattern and are repetitive in their nature (Khromina, 2007). These social practices include social roles, social structures, social norms, and social institutions. The application of Structural Functionalism to issues of school violence require that we remember that the individuals who commit these crimes are neither aberrant one-offs nor their demonized depictions in media coverage of such events, but individuals within a greater demographic of young people and students that as a whole have similar motivations, strains, and aptitudes concerning stress management. In this way, Functionalism allows us to view these instances as extreme manifestations of stressors and value norms prevalent throughout society, but more overtly and simply expressed by a subset of that society that is more impressionable and less experienced in the nonviolent resolution of conflict and stress.

It is difficult to pinpoint the exact influences on any one act or actor; it is less difficult to show the relationship between a culture's value system regarding firearms and the use of those firearms by one demographic within that society, in this case students. It can also be argued that this relationship goes both ways. Various studies argue that politicians use the perception of high crime rates as a platform for their elections (Takacs, 2009). These false uses of important issues are visible in poll data through participants' higher interpretation of crime rates during election years. Taking attention away from the real issues at hand and concentrating instead on crime and violence which is usually "battled" with the increase of incarceration rates (Hollander, 1991).

Juveniles use violence and therefore crime to serve many functions: in order to belong to a group, to defend themselves against their environment, in order to get monetary benefits that they are unable to attain through other means, and as a way to express and filter out their internal rage (Tetlack, 1984). Simplifying this issue for political motives creates a potential feedback loop between the fear of gun violence and the need for guns to protect ourselves from violence.

This chapter is a piece of a larger body of research focusing on individuals who commit extreme forms of violence in K–12 institutions. This research aims to shed light on the specific motivations of these individuals, as well as the context within which they acted. This is often set in contrast to public perception, our understanding of both these acts of violence and the actors heavily skewed by social outrage, the media's framing, and our own general ignorance due to lack of such nuanced research. The use of Structural Functionalism in light of this more nuanced understanding of school shooters allows us to analyze the beginnings of violence, or at least the means by which this violence is perpetrated, as a function of social norms and values, rather than an outlier that exists in spite of it.

METHODOLOGY

In order to consider possible relationships between gun culture and school violence, this study set out to examine instances of school violence in greater depth, starting with a survey of convicted perpetrators and then conducting a content analysis of media sources about the events in which they were involved. The following is a brief overview of the research population and methods used to gather information on the myriad potential causes of K–12 school violence and disturbance in America.

The desired population for this study was convicted school violence perpetrators who had committed violent acts in American K–12 schools and on school property and who were alive and incarcerated at the time of the study. Between 2008 and 2011, all publicly available lists and news reports (*i.e.*, news reports, governmental sites, and school violence research sites) were scoured to obtain a population of names of perpetrators who committed violence on Kindergarten to 12th grade school property or at a school function since the 1700s, resulting in approximately 500 incidents initially identified.

Then, the deceased, released, unadjudicated, and otherwise unlocatable individuals were eliminated from the sample, decreasing cases to approximately 120 incidents. Finally, once the list of offenders of these 120 incidents was identified, the appropriate state correctional system database was extensively searched to determine which of these offenders were still alive, incarcerated, and able to be contacted. This resulted in a list of seventy eight school violence incidents and offenders who committed their acts of violence in thirty three states across the U.S. between 1979 and 2011.

Next, descriptive data from publicly available secondary sources (*e.g.*, court transcripts, news reports, journal articles, school violence research sites, etc.) related to the resulting seventy eight identified incarcerated perpetrators of school violence (mostly school shooters) were gathered. This was conducted to analyze their acts of school violence and the aftermaths of their acts to develop a more comprehensive portrait of K–12 school violence in the U.S. in comparison to the way that school violence is typically reported in the U.S.. It also allowed the separating of offenders by "type" of school violence perpetrator for more in-depth analysis. From extensive review of the cases, surveys, and interviews, four types of offenders were identified.

Traditional school violence perpetrators were defined as those who were current students and essentially "striking back" at the students and school which they attended at the time of the violent act. *Gang-related* school violence perpetrators were defined as those who were identified (either through self or law enforcement identification) involved in the gang lifestyle and committed their acts as part of such lifestyle on school grounds or at school functions.

In contrast, associated or nonassociated school violence perpetrators were identified as offenders who were generally much older and targeted a school with which they may (associated) or may not (nonassociated) have had involvement. These are either past students who returned to their former school to commit a violent act or targeted a school with which they had no association but targeted it for other reasons (e.g., as a symbol of innocence or revenge against society as a whole).

For this study, the following was the population sample:

- *Traditional School Violence Perpetrators* (42 of the 78 offenders in this sample)
- *Gang-related School Violence Perpetrators* (24 of the 78 offenders in this sample)
- *Associated School Violence Perpetrators* (7 of the 78 offenders in this sample)
- *Nonassociated School Violence Perpetrators* (5 of the 78 offenders in this sample)

STUDY LIMITATIONS

Regarding the entire research study (much of which is not discussed in this chapter), the potential limitation for this particular study is that various conclusions are drawn from a small sample of respondents. There could also be concerns over the timespan of 1979 to 2011 (*i.e.*, no "recent" cases examined).

We feel that limitations are minimized in parts of the overall research project given the extensiveness of a survey instrument (involving 365 variables), number of personal interviews and other on-going efforts to maintain contact with research population (e.g., phone calls and letters). As for the dates of events examined, incarcerated offenders are not generally a population which desires to discuss their past actions except to plead their innocence. This is very much the case for those who are involved in current types of appeals and postconviction relief hearings. Considering these considerations, a decision was made to limit the sample for the overall research project to incarcerated individuals whose offenses were committed in or before 2011.

For this chapter, the data analysis did not exceed simple percentage calculation based on results from original research. While this data was eventually entered into a database, the findings presented here do not offer the results of more extensive statistical analysis or tests.

RESULTS

The following is an overview of the results of this research as it relates to the potential impact of the American Gun Culture and the resulting interest in, knowledge of, and availability of guns and weapons in the U.S. upon K–12 American school violence. Results are presented as they relate to each of four categories of offenders (*traditional, gang-related, associated*, and *nonassociated*), and a summary of characteristics relating to each category of offender is also offered.

Availability and Source of Weapons

The following is an overview of the availability, source, and type of weapon used in the school violence incidents studied. Overall, the findings call into question many commonly held beliefs about school violence.

Availability of Weapons

The following examines the findings as they relate to where the weapons used were obtained. A comparison of the overall findings and each of the four types of offenders is presented.

Not surprisingly, overall, 96 percent of those in this study reported that weapons were readily available to them (see Figure 7.1). Almost all (98 percent) of the *traditional* school violence perpetrators reported that they could obtain the weapon (whether handgun, long gun, knife, etc.) very easily. Most often the weapons they used were found in their own home, either using a weapon which was a gift to them or stealing one or more from their parents. An interesting phenomenon about parental behavior was found in examining these incidents. There was a small but significant percentage of offenders who had been given a handgun or rifle as a present by their parents in order to give them a "hobby" (such as target shooting or hunting). Some parents had been advised to choose a hobby that they could do together with their troubled child—some chose sharing firearms.

The *gang-related* school violence perpetrators followed this trend but most often reported that they had obtained their weapons from prior thefts (21 percent) or from friends (41 percent). Being generally older many *associated* school violence perpetrators reported that they simply used weapons that they legally owned (6 percent), while *nonassociated* school violence perpetrators also owned the weapons used, but these weapons were mostly items such as vehicles, propane tanks, and machetes.

Source of Weapons

It is obvious and not surprising that weapons of all types are readily available in the U.S.. It is argued by many that only "criminals" have weapons and that they illegally enter the homes of "law abiding" individuals and steal them. The following is an overview of where the school violence perpetrators obtained the weapon which was used in their violent act.

No
4%

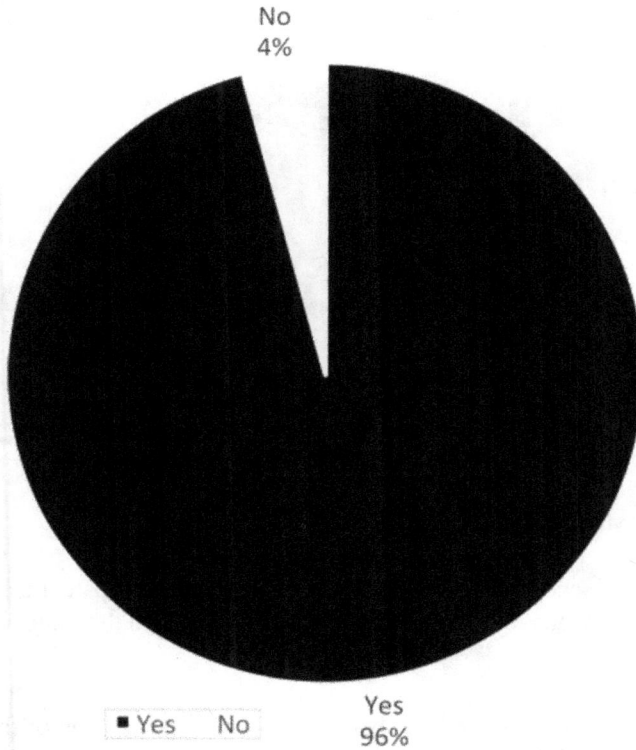

Yes   No

Yes
96%

Figure 7.1   Were weapons readily available?

As is evident, weapons are not difficult to obtain for those who wish to use them to cause violence (see Figure 7.2). Overall, most weapons (27 percent) were stolen from parents, but many (17 percent) were reported to be provided by friends. Almost half (47 percent) of the *traditional* school violence perpetrators obtained their weapons by stealing them from their parents. While almost half (41 percent) of the *gang-related* school violence perpetrators received theirs from friends. The generally older *associated* school violence perpetrators reported that most of them (21 percent) were obtained as gifts from their parents. Interestingly, the *nonassociated* school violence perpetrators almost equally (14 percent) reported that their weapons were obtained as gifts from parents, stolen from parents, gifts or loans from friends, and purchased legally.

Number and Types of Weapons

Incidents where large caliber or large numbers of weapons are used seem to receive the most attention and resulting headlines. While the number of weapons

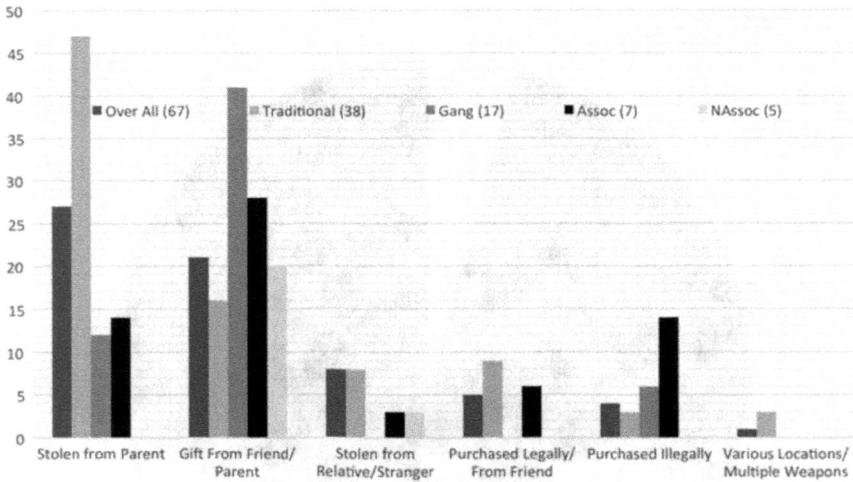

Figure 7.2   **Where weapons were obtained.**

used in acts of school violence varies greatly, it becomes apparent that the variance is probably due to the various types of offenders and their intentions.

Number of Weapons

The following examines the number of weapons in possession of the various types of school violence perpetrators at the time of their violence (see Figure 7.3). The vast majority (85 percent) used only one weapon during their act of violence. The great majority (88 percent) of the *traditional* school violence perpetrators was found to have used one weapon, but 5 percent did have at least five weapons at their disposal during the commission of their act. *Gang-related* school violence perpetrators were also mostly (87 percent) found to have used a single weapon.

In contrast to these groups, *associated* school violence perpetrators had one weapon a little over half the time (57 percent) and two weapons 29 percent of the time, but 14 percent did have at least six weapons with them at the time of their offense. The *nonassociated* school violence perpetrator was less likely than the associated perpetrator to possess two weapons, doing so only 20 percent of the time.

Types of Weapons

The following is a brief examination of the types of weapons used in the school violence incidents explored in this study. Given the use of varying types of weapons, this topic is broken down into use of pistols/handguns,

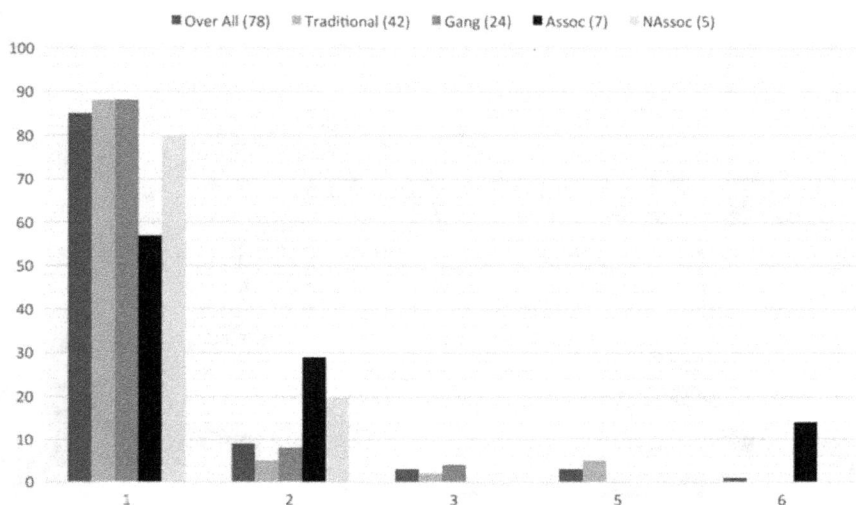

Figure 7.3   Number of weapons.

shotguns/rifles, weapons other than firearms, and the use of multiple weapons.

Types of Weapons Used: Pistols/Handguns

As for handguns, overall, 11 percent of offenders used a .22 caliber pistol (see Figure 7.4). Although, a 9-mm semiautomatic handgun was a very close second choice (10 percent) for offenders. The choice of handgun used by *traditional* school violence perpetrators ranged from a .22 caliber pistol (15 percent) to the somewhat uncommon M-11 pistol (2 percent). This may be due to the fact that most of these weapons are obtained from their parents who may have a variety of interests in weapons.

Gang-related school violence perpetrators mostly (19 percent) preferred the 9-mm semiautomatic pistol. But they also used guns ranging from .22 caliber pistols to .45 caliber pistols. This may be due to the fact that many of the weapons are stolen from various homes, business, or vehicles. The *associated* school violence perpetrators were almost evenly distributed between use of .22 caliber pistols (14 percent) and .45 caliber handguns (14 percent). *Nonassociated* school violence

perpetrators were divided evenly between .22 caliber pistols and 10-mm pistols (20 percent) and were more likely to use other types of weapons.

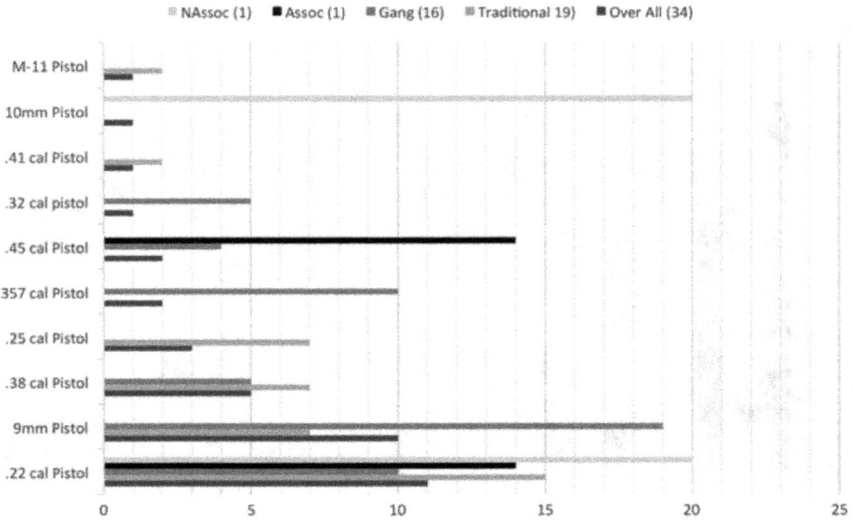

Figure 7.4   Use of pistols and handguns.

Types of Weapons Used: Shotguns/Rifles

While not used as often overall, shotguns and rifles made up a significant percentage of the types of weapons used. In these incidents, 12 percent involved weapons ranging from a common 12-gauge shotgun to the less common AK-47 (see Figure 7.5). The *traditional* school violence perpetrators used the .22 caliber rifle (7 percent) and 30–30 rifle use was a close second (5 percent).

The only weapon of this type reported to be used by *gang-related* school violence perpetrators was the AK-47 (14 percent). Interestingly, the *associated* school violence perpetrators used the 12-gauge shotgun, .44 caliber rifle, and AK-47 equally at 14 percent. For the *nonassociated* school violence perpetrators, only 20 percent used a long gun, a .22 caliber rifle.

Types of Weapons Used: Multiple Weapons

The vast majority of the incidents (85 percent) only involved one weapon (see Figure 7.6). Overall, only 5 percent of the incidents found the offender to have more than one weapon (the remaining 5 percent utilizing something that would not conventionally be considered a weapon, such as their hands). *Traditional* school violence perpetrators averaged having more than one weapon approximately 2 percent of the time. From this study, *gang-related* school violence perpetrators were found to only have one weapon used during their violence. Unfortunately, *associated* school violence perpetrators were found to have at

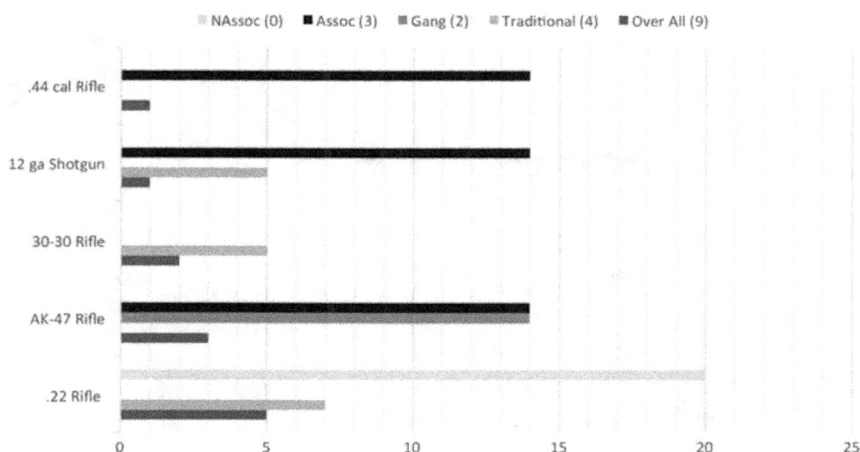

Figure 7.5   Use of rifles and long arms.

least two weapons 20 percent of the time, and *nonassociated* school violence perpetrators were found to be the same, at 14 percent of the time.

Types of Weapons Used: Other than Firearms

This study found that 15 percent of these incidents involved common household items being used as weapons (see Figure 7.7). Overall, 10 percent of the incidents involved the use of a knife of some type. *Traditional* school violence perpetrators followed this trend with 21 percent using a knife of some type (sometimes being obtained from the school cafeteria). Interestingly, *gang-related* school violence perpetrators were not found to have used any other type of weapon except a firearm in this study.

For *associated* school violence perpetrators, 14 percent used work tools (most often a machete) or common household items such as baseball bats to harm students at the schools they attacked, while *nonassociated* school violence perpetrators used a knife (20 percent) or their own car (20 percent) most of the time.

Rounds of Ammunition Available

An examination of these incidents found that, overall, 39 percent of the offenders had 1 to 10 rounds available to them, generally based on the capacity and number of bullets the particular weapon would hold (see Figure 7.8). This was true for 54 percent of the *traditional* school violence perpetrators, but 38 percent had over 200 rounds with them at the time of their act.

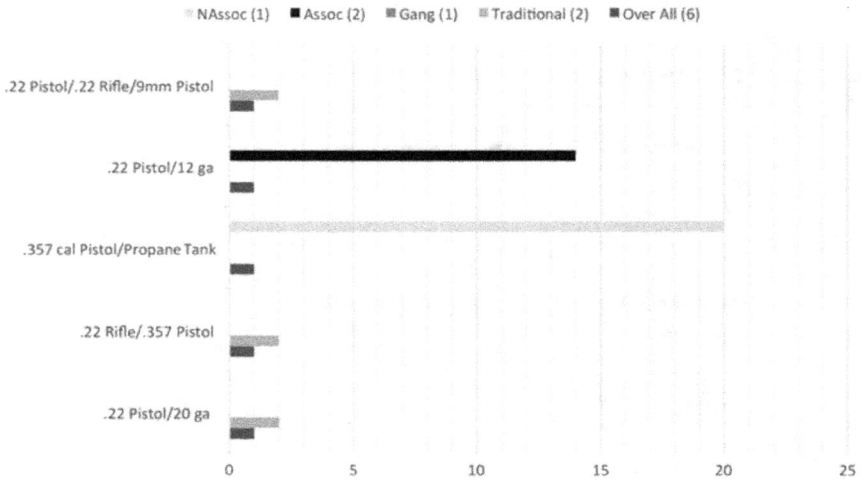

Figure 7.6   Use of multiple weapons.

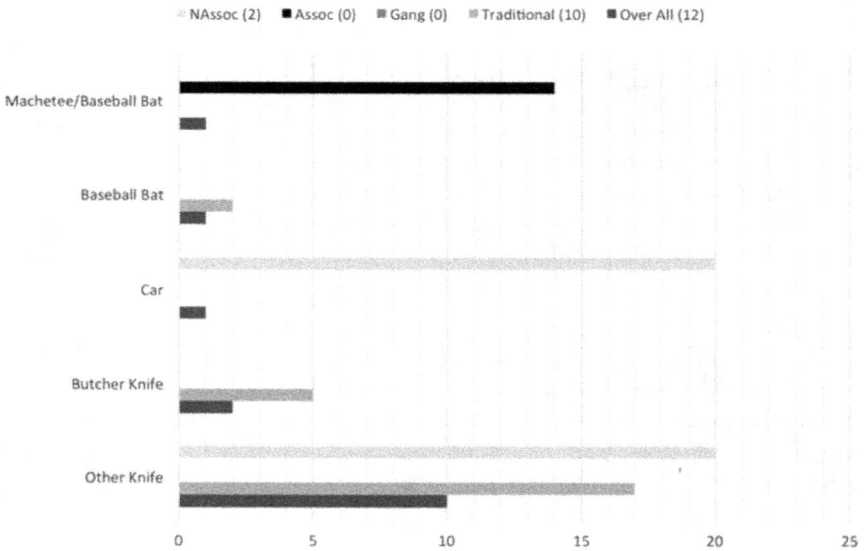

Figure 7.7   Use of other types of weapons.

Most *gang-related* school violence perpetrators used one weapon during the commission of their act, so 83 percent of these incidents involved 1 to 10 rounds of ammunition. The *associated* school violence perpetrators findings are interesting in that 33 percent of these offenders had 1 to 10 rounds, but the same percentage had 11 to 20 and over 200 rounds. *Nonassociated* school violence perpetrators were similar for those that used actual handguns or long arms; 50 percent had 1 to 10 rounds, but 33 percent had over 200 rounds available.

Potential Victims, Injuries, and Deaths

Much of the horror of a school violence or disturbance event becomes evident when examining the number and types of injuries and deaths.

Potential Victims

Overall, 14 percent of the incidents had 2 to 10 potential victims and 4 percent had over 1,500 potential victims (see Figure 7.9). *Traditional* school violence perpetrators committed acts almost evenly where 2 to 300 students were potential targets, but 21 percent committed acts which put an entire student body at risk (such as random shooting in schools).

Gang-related school violence perpetrators occurred with only 2 to 30 potential victims approximately half the time (53 percent). This is probably due to the fact that most of these types of acts involved one or two targets with only a few bystanders present during an attack. *Associated* school violence perpetrators ranged equally (14 percent) between potential victims from 21 to 300. This is probably due to the fact that most of these types of offenders have a target in mind (e.g., past teacher, coach, or principal) and seek that individual out upon whom to commit their violence. *Nonassociated*

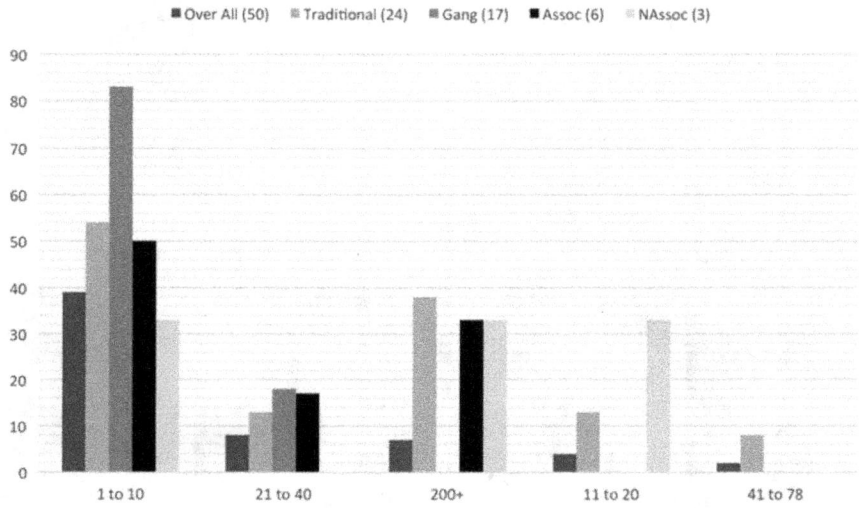

Figure 7.8   **Rounds of ammunition available.**

school violence perpetrators follow this same pattern (20 percent), although they are simply targeting the entire school, often smaller rural or suburban schools.

In almost all the school violence incidents reviewed in this study, some form of physical harm was incurred by one or more victims. All, of course, resulted in some type of mental or psychological harm to those involved.

Some incidents even involved others killed or injured prior to or after the school violence incident but not on school grounds. In a few cases, offenders had harmed others before coming to school and others while fleeing the scene of their crime.

Killed or Injured Anyone Outside School
Before or After School Incident

Overall, the vast majority (91 percent) of offenders did not harm anyone else before or after their school-related episode, but some did (8 percent) (see Figure 7.10). This is true for *traditional* school violence perpetrators (93 percent), but a small percentage (7 percent) did kill or injure a family member prior to arriving at the school to commit their violence there.

Gang-related school violence perpetrators only did this 4 percent of the time. This trend changed when examining the actions of other types of offenders. For *associated* school violence perpetrators, almost half (42 percent) did hurt others prior to seeking their target at a school, but *nonassociated* school violence perpetrators did not do so at all (100 percent).

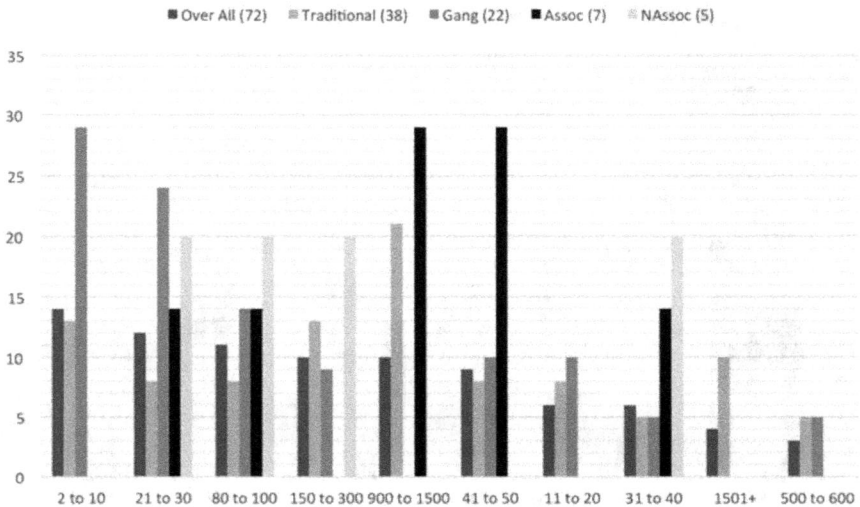

Figure 7.9   Number of potential victims.

Number Killed

Overall, in at least 22 percent of the incidents researched, no one lost their lives, but 78 percent of the events ended with at least one life lost (see Figure 7.11). *Traditional* school violence perpetrators did not cause death in 17 percent of the incidents examined but did in over half (59 percent) of the incidents.

Gang-related school violence perpetrators followed this trend in that they did not kill anyone in 21 percent of their acts but did in the vast majority (75 percent) of their acts. This is probably due to the fact that they often have one or two targets and seek just those targets out and no others. *Associated* school violence perpetrators did not take a life in 29 percent of their incidents but were responsible for at least four deaths in 14 percent of their acts. A similar trend is found in *nonassociated* school violence perpetrators. This group did not take a life in 60 percent of their attacks but took two in 40 percent of the attacks.

Number Injured

The above chart examines the findings related to the number physically injured during the events researched (see Figure 7.12). This does not include the number of individuals who lost their lives, which was examined in the prior discussion. Overall, 47 percent of the incidents resulted in no injuries, but 42 percent did have at least one individual injured.

Over half (57 percent) of the *traditional* school violence perpetrators incidents found no injuries, but 35 percent did have at least one person injured.

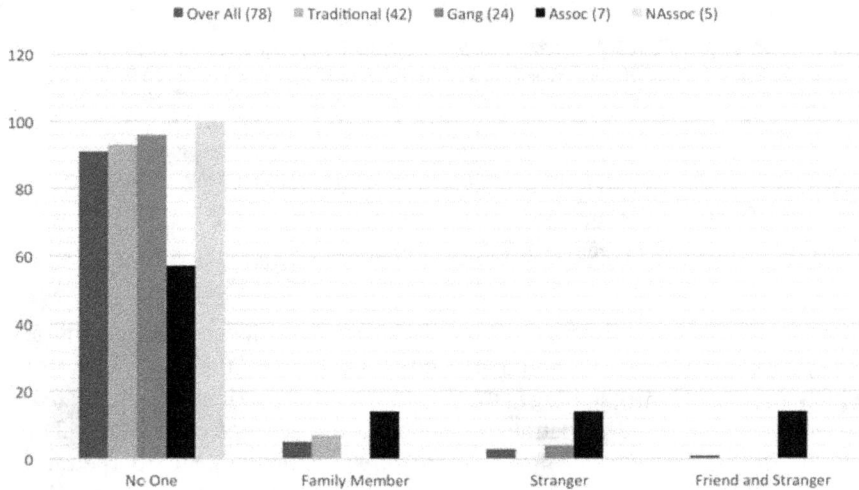

Figure 7.10 Violence committed before act.

NAssoc (5)   Assoc (7)   Gang (24)   Traditional (42)   Over All (78)

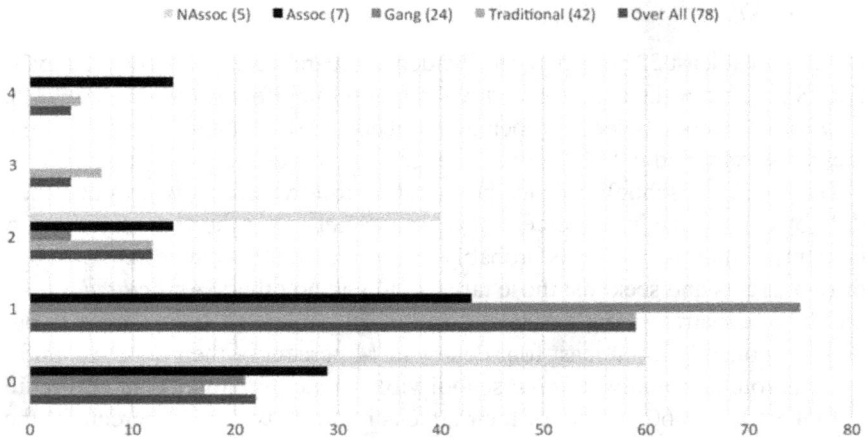

Figure 7.11   Number killed.

NAssoc (5)   Assoc (7)   Gang (24)   Traditional (42)   Over All (78)

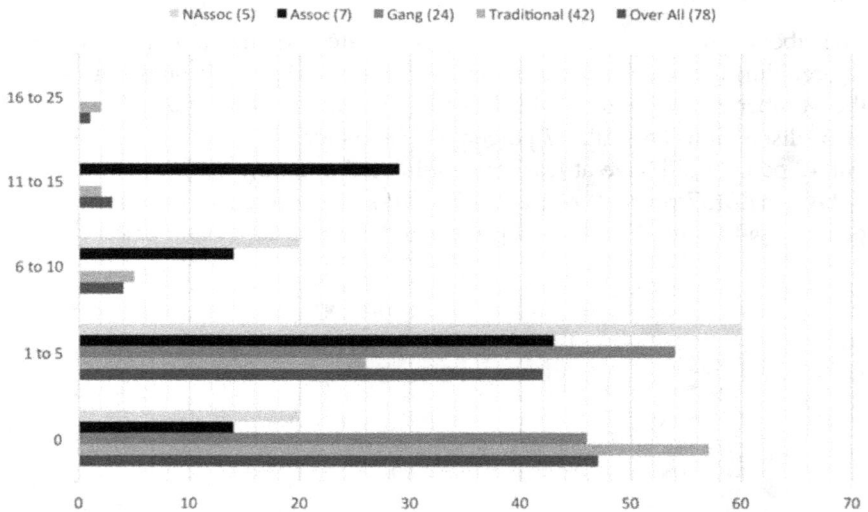

Figure 7.12   Number injured.

Gang-related school violence perpetrators saw 46 percent with no injuries, but one to five individuals were harmed in 54 percent of their events. A trend which is extremely frightening is the fact that 86 percent of all attacks by *associated* school violence perpetrators resulted in the harm of others at a school. This finding was the same for *nonassociated* school violence perpetrators, with 80 percent of their attacks resulting in one to ten individuals harmed.

Summary of Characteristics Displayed by Each Type of Perpetrator

Traditional School Violence Perpetrators

Based on this study, it appears that the *traditional* school violence perpetrator most often uses one weapon, and if a firearm, it was most often a .22 caliber pistol with 1 to 10 rounds of ammunition in their possession (see Table 7.1). Again, these events most often seem to happen at larger schools which inherently offer larger numbers of potential victims. They will generally not kill or injure anyone before their violent act on the K–12 campus but will most often take at least one life during their attack.

It also appears that this type of offender is the most likely to keep their plans secret until violence occurs. Most find that they cannot be readily identified nor do they act out too much until their violent act in many cases. This type of offender might not even be on anyone's radar—they are probably not in legal trouble, not in counseling, and not in therapy. It appears from this research that in the vast majority of incidents, one day they reached their final straw and committed their violent act. If they decided to use a weapon it was most often from their own home or the home of a friend.

Gang-Related School Violence Perpetrators

It is extremely interesting that this type of offender seemed not to suffer from many of the issues that other types of school violence perpetrators did regarding views of self and others (see Table 7.2). They appeared often to be the type of offender who was most worried about the consequences of their actions upon loved ones.

As with all types of offenders they appeared to have ease in locating a weapon to use, most often obtaining one from a friend or associate. Based on this study, it appears that the *gang-related* school violence perpetrator most often will generally have one weapon, very often a 9-mm pistol with 2 to 10 rounds available. The vast majority will not have killed or injured anyone immediately prior to their act and will most often not kill an individual at the school but will injure at least one bystander.

Associated School Violence Perpetrators

This type of offender was the first group of offenders in this study to use varying types of weapons from handguns to baseball bats (see Table 7.3).

Based on this study, it appears that the *associated* school violence perpetrator's weapons were easily found and were very often legally owned and usually given as gifts by others. Interestingly, they seemed to be much more prevalent in smaller student bodies with lower amounts of potential victims.

Table 7.1   Characteristics of Weapons Used and Injuries Incurred by *Traditional* **School Violence Perpetrators**

Were Weapons Readily Available to Offender?	Yes
Where Was Gun/Weapon Obtained	Stolen from parents
Number of Weapons	1
Rounds of Ammunition Available	1 to 10
Types of Weapons Used	.22 caliber pistol
Number of Potential Victims	900+
Killed or Injured Anyone outside School before or after School Incident	No
Number Killed	1
Number Injured	0

Table 7.2   Characteristics of Weapons Used and Injuries Incurred by *Gang-related* **School Violence Perpetrators**

Were Weapons Readily Available to Offender?	Yes
Where Was Gun/Weapon Obtained?	From friend
Number of Weapons	1
Rounds of Ammunition Available	1 to 10
Types of Weapons Used	9mm pistol
Number of Potential Victims	2 to 10
Killed or Injured Anyone outside School before or after School Incident	No
Number Killed	0
Number Injured	1

Table 7.3   Characteristics of Weapons Used and Injuries Incurred by *Associated* **School Violence Perpetrators**

Were Weapons Readily Available to Offender?	Yes
Where Was Gun/Weapon Obtained?	Stolen, gifts, legally owned
Number of Weapons	1
Rounds of Ammunition Available	1 to 10
Types of Weapons Used	.22 caliber pistol, .45 caliber pistol, AK-47, 12-gauge shotgun, .44 caliber rifle, machete, and baseball bat
Number of Potential Victims	41 to 50
Killed or Injured Anyone outside School before or after School Incident	No
Number Killed	0
Number Injured	1

It also appeared that they had not injured anyone prior to their act of school violence but did injure at least one during the event.

Nonassociated School Violence Perpetrators

The *nonassociated* school violence perpetrator, on an intellectual level, may be the most interesting of all types of offenders (see Table 7.4). They are also the type of offender who is most reluctant to offer any true insight into why they chose the K–12 school as a target for their violence. A great deal of this is obviously due to the high percentage of these offenders who were and remain mentally ill.

Regarding the weapons used and harm caused, this type of offender had easy access to weapons in that they generally used items which they legally own.

Based on this study, it appears that the *nonassociated* school violence perpetrators often use a .22 caliber pistol or rifle, but more often the weapon of choice was a vehicle. When a vehicle is used, they appeared to most often crash into school property locations and then attack students with other items such as propane tanks and machetes. When they did use firearms, the study suggests they are the one group to bring the most ammunition. Again, they most often appear to attack smaller schools with smaller numbers of potential victims. They also appear to be the type of offender who will do the most harm and injuries to others at 1 to 5.

DISCUSSION

As discussed in this chapter, not all school violence perpetrators are the same, not all violent acts are the same, and not all causes are the same. The resulting

Table 7.4 Characteristics of Weapons Used and Injuries Incurred by *Nonassociated* **School Violence Perpetrators**

Were Weapons Readily Available to Offender?	Yes
Where Was Gun/Weapon Obtained?	Gift from family or legally owned
Number of Weapons	1
Rounds of Ammunition Available	1 to 200
Types of Weapons Used	.22 caliber pistol, .22 caliber rifle, knife, vehicle, and propane tank
Number of Potential Victims	21 to 300
Killed or Injured Anyone outside School before or after School Incident	no
Number Killed	0
Number Injured	1 to 5

harm or death can be the same, but the road leading to it can come from many different directions. As with all types of offenders, weapons will be readily available, most often found in their own homes and stolen from parents. The following is a seldom examined topic in school violence research: the actual number of rounds with and available to the offender.

The number of weapons during an incident is, of course, important, but the amount of ultimate damage that weapon can do will vary with the amount of ammunition available. It is a common perception that in most school violence incidents a long gun, like the AK-47, is the weapon of choice. Based on the findings of this study, this does not appear to be the case for all types of school violence perpetrators.

There is a common perception that most school violence incidents involve semiautomatic high-powered weapons. It appears that, in the vast majority of incidents, weapons were readily available to the perpetrator. This was true for all four types of school violence offenders. These weapons were more than likely obtained from the offender's home or given to them by a family member or friend. In the case of *traditional* and *gang-related* perpetrators, they were most often stolen. Fortunately, most offenders of all types used only one weapon, but those who were older and targeted the school for other reasons (as a symbol or place of innocence) often attacked the schools with multiple weapons including vehicles and propane tanks.

Data from this study suggest that the typical offender will commit their act of violence with only one weapon but may have up to 200 rounds of ammunition with which to do so. They will most often use a small caliber handgun, but some do use up to and above the power of a high-powered automatic weapon. It must be noted that some offenders who target schools for other than rational reasons such as the *nonassociated* type offenders will attack schools with vehicles and other incendiary devices.

The number of potential victims will be determined by the location of the event. There is a vast difference between an event on a school bus holding 20 students and a cafeteria holding 100 students. There are also the incidents in which a drive-by type of shooting occurs across the front windows of a school. In these cases, all 500 students in the affected classrooms could be at risk.

When examining the characteristics of victims several interesting trends are discovered. In some incidents, the offender takes the life of a family member before they commit their act at a school, but very often this occurs immediately prior to their arrival at the school. This does not generally allow the initial violence to be discovered prior to the school event occurring.

Unfortunately, in the vast majority of school violence incidents at least one person is going to be injured 75 percent of the time someone will die. In *traditional* school violence acts, random people will be injured most of the time, but in *gang-related* incidents their target most often will be the only one injured.

This is true in *associated* and *nonassociated* incidents, too. Those who have identified individual targets will most often injure or take the life of that individual, but no other. On the other hand, those who wish to do as much damage as possible to a certain group or institution will often hurt anyone they encounter as they carry out their act of violence.

CONCLUSION

In conclusion, it is hoped that this work will contribute to the exploration of the extremely complicated phenomenon of school violence in American K–12 schools. Most researchers insist on combining all school shootings/violence incidents into one type of act and therefore one type of actor. However, there is a great deal of variation in these incidents as seen in the evidence presented in this study. Public mass shootings, university environments, international incidents, and K–12 school shootings and violence are not the same. They have different catalysts, motivations, types of occurrence, and offenders. Hopefully, this work will demonstrate the importance of not generalizing views on violence causation and find the benefit of the unique nuances that can be found when examining in detail one type of offender committing their acts in one type of environment.

Finally, it is hoped that the work presented will assist others in the national debate about the impact of the American Gun Culture and the resulting interest in, and availability of, guns and weapons in the U.S. upon K–12 American school violence.

REFERENCES

Crews, G. A. 2016. *School Killers Speak: A Comprehensive Examination of Perpetrators, Events, and Characteristics of K-12 School Violence in America.* Huntington, WV: The Veritas Group.

Crews, G. A. 2020. "The Phenomena of School Violence in America." In *Social Dimensions of Crime*, edited by K. Bell and R. McNamarra, 3rd ed., 81–103. Raleigh, NC: Carolina Academic Press.

Crews, G. A., Crews, A. D., and Burton, C. E. 2013. "The Only Thing That Stops a Guy with a Bad Policy is a Guy with a Good Policy: An Examination of the NRA's "National School Shield" Proposal." *American Journal of Criminal Justice*, 38(2), 183–199.

Crews, G. A., and Crews, G. A. 2019. "The American k-12 School Violence Incident: A Brief Study. In *Handbook of Research on School Violence in American K-12 Education*, edited by G. A. Crews, 1–51. Hershey, PA: IGI Global.

Crews, G. A., and Crews, G. A. 2020. "Mother Knows Best: A Brief Examination of the 1982–2019 US Mass Shootings Data from Mother Jones' Investigation." In *Handbook of Research on Mass Shooting and Multiple Victim Violence*, edited by G. Crews, 41–55. Hershey, PA: IGI Global.

Crews, G. A., and Crews, G. A. 2021. "The American K-12 School Violence Incident: A Brief Study." In *Research Anthology on School Shootings, Peer Victimization, and Solutions for Building Safer Educational Institutions*, edited by All India Management Association, 207–256. Hershey, PA: IGI Global.

Haider-Markel, D. P., and Joslyn, M. R. 2001. "Gun Policy, Opinion, Tragedy, and Blame Attribution: The Conditional Influence of Issue Frames." *Journal of Politics*, 63(2), 520–543.

Hollander, P. 1991. *The Survival of the Adversary Culture: Social Criticism and Political Escapism in American Society*. New Brunswick, NJ: Transaction Publishers.

Khromina, S. 2007. "The Broken Path: Juvenile Violence and Delinquency in Light of Sociological Theories." *Human Architecture: Journal of the Sociology of Self-Knowledge*, 5(2), Article 9.

Kimmel, M. S., and Mahler, M. 2003. "Adolescent Masculinity, Homophobia, and Violence: Random School Shootings, 1982–2001." *American Behavioral Scientist*, 46(10), 1439–1458.

Lawrence, R. G., and Birkland, T. A. 2004. "Guns, Hollywood, and School Safety: Defining the School-Shooting Problem Across Public Arenas." *Social Science Quarterly*, 85(5), 1193–1207.

O'Toole, M. E. 1999. *The School Shooter: A Threat Assessment Perspective*. Critical Incident Response Group (CIRG). National Center for the Analysis of Violent Crime (NCAVC). FBI Academy, VA: Quantico.

Spencer, H. 1898. *The Principles of Sociology, in Three Volumes*. New York: D. Appleton and Company.

Takacs, S. 2009. "Monsters, Monsters Everywhere: Spooky TV and the Politics of Fear in Post-9/11 America." *Science Fiction Studies*, 36(1), 1–20.

Tetlack, P. E. 1984. Cognitive Style and Political Belief System in the British House of Commons. *Journal of Personality and Social Psychology*, 46(2), 365–375.

Chapter 8

A Conversation on Gun Culture Research Trends

Jim D. Taylor, Lisa Fisher, and Craig Hovey

Eds: You wrote *American Gun Culture* about a decade ago. How have you seen the conversation about guns in America change since then?

JT: Since the research of the first edition of my *American Gun Culture* book was published back in 2009, firearm conversations have changed or expanded on a few notable fronts. First—and I'm only leading off with this one because it would not be on everyone's radar—is the subtle movement in dining and hospitality industries relevant to fine dining and shooting experiences. I have seen more restaurant establishments offer some kind of "eat and shoot," or "dine and shoot" experience for their patrons. Some even boast something along the lines of "bringing a little Second Amendment flavor to your fine dining experience." While the volume of firearms and gun owners were no surprise to me a decade ago, the thought of a growing national restaurant trend in this area had honestly never crossed my mind until I started to get contacted by reporters about my opinion on it.

Sandy Hook also occurred after the release of my book. While school shootings and mass public shootings were discussed between Columbine and Sandy Hook, they had certainly taken a back burner during the years in between. Both the Sandy Hook shootings and the Century 16 Movie Theatre massacre in Aurora, CO, occurred in 2012. Since then, we did witness an uptick in school shootings, as well as mass public shootings outside of schools. Press coverage in these areas has remained heightened, as have efforts to bring forth stricter gun laws. Possibly most notable would be the passing of New York's SAFE (Secure Ammunition and Firearms Enforcement) Act, which was signed into effect January 15, 2013, on the heels of these highly publicized shootings and public outcries that followed. As a direct result of this type of reform, and others (such as pushes to ban ordinance like assault rifles and related bump stocks), we have seen runs on ammunition and firearms in a few waves. There is also a heightened sense of concern and paranoia among many gun owners, enthusiasts, and Second Amendment advocates that federal and state governments are overstepping their powers in their efforts to disarm the public.

In more recent developments, we have also seen more public as well as media attention given to the use of guns in law enforcement. The #BLM movement has ushered in increased scrutiny of all types of excessive and deadly force used by the police, including debates of when firearm use is appropriate, what type of ordinance should or should not be used, etc. I hope this helps to answer your questions. These are the areas where I have seen what I would consider to be the most notable change or changes in these conversations, or the direction of these conversations. Some are new topics, and some have just come back in focus, had renewed popularity, or just expanded a bit.

How do you believe the events and circumstances you described have impacted gun culture?

At the very least, these circumstances serve as strong anecdotal evidence of a shifting narrative in modern American gun culture. With the narrative, we have seen evidence of heightened polarization. For policy-minded reformers, especially those calling for tighter gun controls, they have seen the floodgates open for this type of national conversation. Historically fast-pace reforms have been called for and implemented, and media outlets have continued to quite visibly report and represent agendas favorable to gun control. Second Amendment advocates, gun collectors, and enthusiasts have certainly reported feeling more under fire (no pun intended). They have frequently responded by stockpiling more weapons and ammunition, in fear of what many believe to be a government overstepping its authority, failing to protect, and casually disregarding the Bill of Rights.

How does your focus on gun collectors and their stories shed new light on what we understand about U.S. gun culture?

You have to understand that my ethnography was a bit different. I have spoken to literally thousands of gun owners, collectors, and enthusiasts over the past twenty years. My talks with the self-described "collectors" treated their guns much like genealogists treat a "family tree." One-by-one, I had them bring out their most highly valued guns, and tell me in their own words, why they valued the guns so highly, and what the guns meant to them, individually, on a personal level. What I found that was of most value to me as a man of science, was that the story of the gun, in terms of the individual, lived inter-action with each separate gun in a person's collection deeply influenced the way they interpreted the specific gun and its broader meaning in their life. In short, not every gun of the same caliber is viewed or defined the same way by a gun owner. Some are viewed as home defense, some as collectibles, some as somewhat of a trusty sidekick, and some as part of a family heritage. That revelation is a game changer on some fronts. Just in knowing that not every gun in the same category will come to be viewed and used the same way calls into question the likely effectiveness of global policies on gun controls. You can't remove someone's lived history with any single piece of culture. Guns included. Our life experiences inform us. In every way.

It seems clear that there are profound benefits to the kind of ethno-graphic work you've done. What are the areas of research on gun culture that you find most promising and exciting?

Great question. My research began in what was a very thin, almost nonexis-tent niche. On the surface, a lot of the research could even be easily dismissed as esoteric. What I have seen, however, is how practical some of the applied applications of this body of work really can be. Take our understanding of firearm selection and use in the commission of violent crimes, for instance. For the purpose of use by criminal justice agencies and policy pushers on both sides of gun debates, there are real benefits in understanding cultural practices, ritual activities, and the associated emotions that influence ways in which gun owners come to define, relate to, and interact with firearms in society. The research has already revealed pretty conclusively that differ-ent types of social narratives and the histories of individual firearms have tremendous impact on the ways in which those guns will come to be used. In short, change the narrative, and change the way guns come to be viewed and used—especially relevant to masculinity and conflict resolution. There are two exciting and brilliant areas of research on these aspects of gun cul-ture that I have already seen extend far beyond what I have done. The first is Cukier and Sheptycki's (2012) research on "pistolization," transnational understandings and depictions of guns in relation to masculinity, masculine identity, and masculine power. Their work was quite revealing. Then, on the front of gun use and emotion, while I had only begun to skim the surface of this back around 2008 and 2009, The Max Planck Institute for Human Development in Berlin, Germany held a conference titled "Comparing Civil Gun Cultures: Do Emotions Make the Difference?" in 2014. Considering that I was only first starting to make these types of connections a few years prior, having an international conference dedicated to the topic of guns and emotion come together so quickly was a very good sign. While no research, no matter how exciting or promising, ever moves at the pace we would like to see, these are two exciting steps in the right direction, and I see it as a sign of significant progress. Especially, when we consider that gun culture dates back a few hundred years, and it took less than two decades for the research to make such significant leaps in these promising areas.

In what areas/other areas do you think gun culture scholarship is most needed in the coming years?

There has always been and remains glaring gaps in existing literature on both the decision-making process to take up firearms to use in the commission of violent crimes and suicide, and practical policy to implement. We need more information on this process and related policy that can be implemented to help get ahead of the curve of gun-related violence. We are saturated by guns. They are everywhere. However, the presence of firearms does not cause someone to use them in any particular way. So, we need more research asking violent criminals and also individuals with gun-related suicide ideation to tell us more about how and why they have come to view guns as the solution to their problems. The process is not generally random. It is not as if most violent criminals just wake up one day and spontaneously commit to taking up a gun and committing some heinous act of violence. There is a complex process in play that sort of programmed or conditioned them to view the gun as the solution to their problems and forms of conflict resolution. Narratives about guns and their use becomes part of our cultural scripts. We also need to more fully understand the process, so we can interrupt the sequence of events that leads to acts of violence—whether committed with guns or by some other means. This is why I have always seen great potential in the research on warrior narratives, and the way we could easily tweak a few social practices to avoid normalizing the associations made between gun use and violence. Even simple public service announcements and minor alterations of standardized school health curriculum to add messages about gun use, gun safety, firearm statistics, etc. It would effectively be a form of firearm-related hygiene, if you will. It is not a perfect solution, but we have reason to believe it would have some benefit, and the benefits would outweigh any associated cost or risk. Most owners of massive gun collections do not use their guns for criminal purposes. However, whenever gun availability runs high, and a climate of fear also persists, we tend to see heightened instances of gun violence. So, more research into fear and management of it is also a good fit and path for this body of research. On a related policy front, with real possibilities, I believe policy makers are underutilizing available research on the correlation of fear and acts of aggression and suicide. For instance, research on the amygdala hijack and policy that has been implemented by some states and courts shows tremendous potential for the reduction of gun and other forms of violence. Ohio Divorce Courts, for instance, require a completion of a course on the amygdala hijack when there are underage children involved. The course teaches practical methods for overriding and interrupting impulses of violence we sometimes have when we are overwhelmed with the types of emotions common to heated interpersonal exchanges (such as family quarrels). If courts are willing to implement this type of policy to curb violence, the same type of message can easy be promoted via various public service announcement outlets and standardized school curriculum. We are talking about the possibility of mass reduction of all kinds of violence and suicide, whether gun related or other. It's a worthwhile investment for research and policy alike. I see greater need for research in these than any other areas of gun culture scholarship.

Those are some really interesting ideas and directions in scholarship, which raise equally interesting questions about available data sources. Do you have any tips for researchers, especially when it comes to collecting data about some of the vulnerable populations you mentioned?

Yes. Some of it's not so tricky. It's just not getting done. Take the policy suggestions I mentioned involving the courts and the amygdala hijack course requirements. Those trainings are implemented with the intention of reducing domestic violence in cases involving divorces when underage children are a product of the marriage. However, the implications are much broader. The trainings teach techniques to interrupt all sorts of violence, by suggesting methods to distract ourselves and retreat from violent thoughts and emotions before they escalate into actual acts of violence. This would include interrupting the emotional and thought processes that could lead to gun violence. It would be relatively easy for interested researcher to begin by comparing rates of violence by county before and after the courts began to implement these programs. In terms of conducting research where violent offenders are asked specific questions about their gun-related crimes, and the process by which the gun (or guns) came to be selected would be easy enough to get approved by different prison officials (Ex. wardens, parole boards, prison counselors, the Federal Bureau of Prisons, etc.). In my experience, prison officials have been pretty reasonable and accommodating with members of the academic community. I don't recall any of my past students ever having much trouble getting their requests approved to conduct different types of interviews with inmate populations. It can take a little time, but there is always a well-defined process outlined and followed by these different facilities. If it is for book research, sometimes it is necessary to use the protocols posted for "media," but there's usually not as much red tape as you might think. If a researcher did not have a specific facility in mind, they could also start with a very polite and well-worded request to the State's Department of Corrections. Of course, with all of the current Covid-19 restrictions, gaining access for interviews with inmates is going to be a little tricky for the time being.

Any predictions on the direction federal gun laws are likely to trend in the next decade?

Without a crystal ball to know how the legislature will be stacked over the next ten years, or which types of high-profile shootings the media will latch onto in the future, I can't say for sure. I will say that if current trends continue, I would expect to see Federal measures similar to what was enacted as part of New York's SAFE Act. The SAFE Act was aimed at preventing criminals and those known to be dangerously mentally ill from buying guns. It also cracked down on illegal guns, pushed for tighter restrictions and monitoring of transactions at gun shows, and banned only the most dangerous types of assault weapons. I could see the Federal government adopting a similar approach, while not really attempting to rewrite or vacate the Second Amendment, but still protecting and preserving law-abiding citizens' right to bear arms and not overly-restrict or fetter our ability to buy, sell, keep, or use guns. This is the most likely path I see over the next several years if our history and current political climate serve as good indicators.

REFERENCE

Cukier, W., and Sheptycki, J. 2012. "Globalization of Gun Culture Transnational Reflections on Pistolization and Masculinity, Flows and Resistance." *International Journal of Law, Crime and Justice*, 40(1), 3–19.

Chapter 9

Understanding and Misunderstanding America's Gun Culture

David Yamane

Understanding America's Gun Culture is part of a renaissance of interest in the academic study of guns over the past decade. In addition to individual books and articles, this volume sits alongside several other recent edited volumes (Carlson et al. 2019; Obert et al. 2019) and special issues of journals (Metzl as editor for *Palgrave Communications* in 2019; Steidley and Yamane as editors for *Sociological Perspectives* and Dowd-Arrow, Burdette, and Hill as editors for *Sociological Inquiry,* both forthcoming in 2021). All of these works contribute something to our understanding of American gun culture, to be sure. At the same time, they share in common some of the limitations that I have previously identified (Yamane 2017) and that others have highlighted for decades (O'Connor and Lizotte 1978; Wright 1995). Specifically, there is an excessive focus on gun culture as deviant and connected to violent criminal behavior.

This limited view of gun culture begins with the editor's introduction and continues through their conversation with Jim D. Taylor in the chapter preceding this one. Nodding to the various ways in which guns are a normal part of life for many normal Americans, editors Hovey and Fisher pivot quickly to the issue of gun violence and connect this to the question of gun control (Introduction, 1-2). Of nine total chapters in this volume, two raise ethical questions about gun culture. Ryan concludes that Christianity offers a rival to the "theo-ethical vision" of American gun culture (chapter 2) and Stolick argues that advocacy for gun rights is inconsistent with the teachings and example of Christ (chapter 6). Three other chapters specifically connect criminal violence to gun culture. Kumar argues that mass shootings "are the symptoms of the damaging influence and power of the gun culture" (chapter 3, 55). Crews and Crews seek to address "the impact of the American Gun Culture . . . upon K–12 American school violence" (chapter 7, 151–152). And a chapter ostensibly about understanding youth gun culture in the Caribbean actually focuses on gang involvement and violence among youth, and the authors actually operationalize involvement in gun culture in part by whether respondents had close friends who carried a gun to school (chapter 4, 81). Even Taylor, whose 2009 book on *American Gun Culture* is one of the few that seeks to understand its normality, centers his conversation with the editors on the use of firearms "in the commission of violent crimes" (chapter 8, 171 and 172).

To be clear: focusing on deviance and criminal violence in connection with guns is not a problem in itself. It becomes a problem when this limited focus is not supplemented by other perspectives. Although I have previously made this argument as concerns sociology (Yamane 2017), this interdisciplinary volume highlights how a limited understanding of gun culture is endemic in the field of gun studies writ large.

In what follows, I begin by using philosopher Firmin DeBrabander's interpretation of the violent storming of the U.S. Capitol building as a contemporary example of a longstanding trend that associates gun culture with criminal violence. I then offer an alternative perspective on gun culture that begins with the assumption that guns are normal and normal people use guns, and therefore relativizes the predominant deviance and criminal violence foci. Next, I highlight the shift in the center of gravity of American gun culture toward self-defense, what I call "Gun Culture 2.0." Having outlined these ways of understanding gun culture, I turn my attention to one of the major ways in which gun culture is misunderstood: the conflation of legal gun culture with the violent criminal use of guns. I conclude by offering a personal reflection on studying gun culture that moves beyond the partial and partisan views too often found in the field of gun studies.

THE MISSING INSURRECTIONIST GUN OWNERS

In early January 2021, my work on this chapter was disrupted by a text message from a friend: "They are storming the capitol." It took me a moment to figure out who "they" were, but I soon made the connection. *They* were people attending the march for Trump rally in Washington, DC. Formally organized by Women For America First, the rally included a motley crew of people wanting to "Save America" by overturning Donald J. Trump's defeat by Joseph R. Biden in the November 2020 presidential election. Joining run-of-the mill members of "MAGA nation" in forcefully entering the U.S. Capitol building were followers of movements like Stop the Steal, the QAnon conspiracy, Proud Boys, Nick Fuentes's Groyper Army, Boogaloo Bois, Oath Keepers, and III%ers. As some, at least, were attempting to disrupt a meeting of Congress to certify Biden's Electoral College victory, many have called the event an insurrection.

As a citizen, I was horrified at what I was seeing on TV on January 6th. As a sociologist of guns, I knew it would be only a matter of time before gun culture would be implicated. Sure enough, on January 11th, philosopher Firmin DeBrabander (2021) pointed a finger in *The Atlantic* at the gun rights movement, especially the National Rifle Association (NRA), holding it responsible for promoting "insurrectionist fever dreams" (see also DeBrabander 2015). The following day, a reporter contacted me for comment on "a story about gun advertising and how the industry's marketing strategies have helped fuel the insurrectionist ideology we saw on display at the capitol on Wednesday." Even though few guns were in evidence, people I spoke with frequently referred to the "armed insurrection."

To be sure, some gun rights proponents argue strenuously that an armed citizenry is "a final, emergency bulwark against tyranny" (French 2018), and militia movements like the Oath Keepers and Threepers are very, very progun (Jackson 2020). But blaming gun rights advocates, the gun industry, or gun culture for the clumsy coup at the Capitol makes a causal connection that does not reflect the broader reality of guns and gun ownership in America. Tens of millions of gun-owning Americans hear the exhortations of the NRA and other (even more fervent) gun rights groups, are exposed to gun industry advertising, and engage in other social activities around guns. And yet were *not* inspired to force their way into the U.S. Capitol Building to "stop the steal."

While many focused on the hundreds of people rioting in DC, I am wondering about the gun owners who we might call "The Missing Insurrectionists." I am inspired in this thinking by sociologist Charles Kurzman's book, *The Missing Martyrs*. In it, Kurzman (2019) takes the question of Islamic terrorism and turns it on its head, asking, "Why are there so few Muslim terrorists?" After all, there are 1+ billion Muslims in the world and revolutionary Islamists who seek to convert them to terrorist violence. And yet, the book's description reads, "As easy as terrorism is to commit, few Muslims turn to violence." This could, with slight editing, be rewritten to state: "As easy as domestic terrorism is to commit, few gun owners turn to insurrectionist violence."

To be sure, some gun owners are violent or potentially violent insurrectionists, and some of those surely have been fed by aspects gun rights rhetoric and imagery. But these *some* are proportionately very few. Let us not forget: there are at least 60-million gun owners in the U.S. who possess 400 million or so guns. About 1-in-5 gun owners characterize themselves as political liberals, nearly 40 percent as political moderates, and less than 1-in-20 as very conservative (Yamane et al. 2020). As I write this in late January 2021, 125 individuals have been charged in federal court in the District of Columbia for crimes committed at the U.S. Capitol on January 6th. Of those, only two are charged with gun crimes. One for "Carrying or having readily accessible, on the grounds of the U.S. Capitol Building, a firearm and ammunition" and one for "Possession of an unregistered firearm (destructive device) and carrying a pistol without a license" (U.S. Department of Justice, n.d.). So, to rephrase Kurzman's question, "Why are there so *few* violent insurrectionist gun owners?" That seems to me a question that also needs to be asked and answered.

Questions like this, to be sure, are not new to me. Entering the field of guns studies, I was struck by how hard it is to find scholarship on the lawful use of firearms by legal gun owners (Yamane 2017). I also found it remarkable that scholars have been noting this oversight at routine intervals for the past forty years. Wright and Marston (1975, 106) sought to correct the record by observing that "the vast, overwhelming majority of the 90,000,000 or so privately owned weapons are not involved in accidental shootings or intentional deaths." The same is true of today's 400 million civilian firearms. O'Connor and Lizotte (1978, 428) concluded similarly that lawful activities "which involve large numbers of people for whom guns occupy a central but routine and legitimate place . . . have been generally ignored by researchers interested in gun ownership and violence" (see also Wright 1995). *Plus ça change, plus c'est la même chose.*

The excessive focus on the criminology and epidemiology of gun violence impedes our ability to understand the normality of the lawful ownership and use of guns in the U.S. Without understanding this, scholars cannot understand American gun culture. In fact, in focusing excessively on deviance and criminal violence (including political violence), they actually misunderstand it.

GUNS ARE NORMAL, NORMAL PEOPLE USE GUNS

The task of understanding American gun culture begins with understanding the lawful use of guns by legal gun owners. To the extent that there is something called "American gun culture," it centers on this. In "America as a Gun Culture," Richard Hofstadter (1970) remarked on—more accurately, he lamented—the uniqueness of the U.S. "as the only modern industrial urban nation that persists in maintaining a gun culture." In Hofstadter's account, America's gun culture is rooted in the reality of widespread, lawful possession of firearms by a large segment of the population.

This reality stretches back to the colonial, revolutionary, and early republican eras in the U.S. Historically, guns were tools necessary for self-preservation on the frontier (when the colonies themselves were a frontier) and symbols of citizenship (hence according the right of ownership largely to white men). As gun historian Clayton Cramer (2009, 236) observes, guns played a fundamental role

> [f]or the collective military purposes of each colony; for the defense of individual families and isolated settlements; as symbols of being a citizens with the duty to defend the society; and more than occasionally, to demonstrate that nothing has changed in the human condition since Cain slew Abel.

Thus, Cramer (2009, 236) concludes, "Gun ownership appears to have been the norm for freemen, and not terribly unusual for free women and at least male children, through the Colonial, Revolutionary, and early Republic periods." In this early history of the American nation, guns were more practical than symbolic for most people. They were tools of necessity for hunting, self-defense, and national defense.

Although gun culture has evolved since then, the reality that guns are a perfectly normal part of life for a large part of the U.S. population persists. A comprehensive survey released by the nonpartisan Pew Research Center (2017) highlights this in a number of ways. To begin with, a majority of the population currently lives with a gun in their house or had in the past, and a sizable minority—what I call the "gun curious"—have thought about or are actively considering acquiring a gun (Kelley and Ellison 2021; Warner 2020). Only about one-third of Americans say they do not and will never own guns (Yamane 2019b). A remarkable 7 out of 10 American adults have actually fired a gun at some point in their lives—that is nearly 180 million people. Viewed the other way around: A minority of American adults has never shot a gun.

Hofstadter recognized that guns as material objects are central to the construction of any gun culture. Without guns there is no gun culture. But in itself this is a trivial statement. What is crucial to explain is how people understand and use guns, as well as how guns themselves change over time, both responding to and facilitating different understandings and uses. Which is to say that studying gun culture *as culture* means examining the knowledge, beliefs, and recipes for doing things with guns, the many tools and products that are created, and the various practices that are centered on guns (Yamane 2019a).

For some Americans, there is a true fascination with guns—their history, their mechanical operation, what they can do, and what they stand for (Taylor 2009). These people are not unlike collectors or aficionados or obsessives in other areas of life like automobiles, trains, boats, or bicycles. Others have a more practical or pragmatic approach to guns—their usefulness as tools to accomplish certain tasks like hunting or recreation (Kohn 2004). But as I have argued elsewhere (Yamane 2017), the center of gravity of American gun culture is shifting away from the historic emphasis on hunting, recreational shooting, and collecting to the contemporary emphasis on armed self-defense. Following gun writer Michael Bane, I call this a shift from Gun Culture 1.0 to Gun Culture 2.0.

UNDERSTANDING GUN CULTURE 2.0

On March 13, 2020, President Donald Trump declared a national emergency concerning the novel coronavirus disease (COVID-19) outbreak in the U.S.. On March 15, Reuters photographer Patrick Fallon captured an image of dozens of people lined up on the sidewalk in front of Martin B. Retting, Inc. in Culver City, California. The diverse group was waiting for the historic gun store—established in 1928—to open. The following day, gun sales in the U.S. peaked at approximately 176,000, according to an analysis of data from the National Instant Criminal Background Check System (NICS) (Levine and McKnight 2020). (Caveat: NICS data is commonly used by scholars, advocates, and the media as a proxy for gun sales. These data, as Steidley (2020b) argues, come with many caveats and must be interpreted with due modesty.)

Gun sales were so robust in the first month of the COVID-19 pandemic that total sales for March 2020 (6.95 per 1,000 people in the U.S.) exceeded the previous record month, set in December 2012 following the Sandy Hook Elementary School massacre (Steidley 2020a). That event amplified existing concerns that the recently reelected President Barack Obama would seek strong gun control laws, including an "assault weapons" ban. With gun sales in April and May 2020 also exceeding the previous year's figures, it was clear that COVID-19 had supplanted President Barack Obama as the "Greatest Gun Salesman" in U.S. history (Depetris-Chauvin 2015). As it turns out, this was just the beginning of a gun-buying spree that spiked again in the summer.

As the reality of the coronavirus pandemic was settling in, nationwide protests were breaking out following the May 25 death of George Floyd at the hands of Minneapolis police officers. Some of these protests had violent elements, including looting and property destruction. Calls to "defund the police" spread. Although not as high as March's record, gun sales in June again exceeded 2 million (Steidley 2021). Fueled by the ongoing pandemic, protests for racial justice, and a contentious presidential election campaign, gun sales remained high through the end of the year. According to the National Shooting Sports Foundation (2021), the primary firearms industry trade group in the U.S., background checks for firearms sales in 2020 were 60 percent higher than in 2019.

Many find these exceptional figures shocking and appalling. But as someone who has spent the past ten years immersed in American gun culture, I found them remarkable for how clearly they reflect ongoing trends. My research shows that defensive ownership has supplanted hunting and recreational shooting as the core of American gun culture (Yamane et al. 2019, 2020). Thus, faced with social uncertainty and social unrest, it is not surprising that a broad swath of the American population would respond by buying guns. The great gun-buying spree of 2020 is best understood in the context of this new Version 2.0 of American's longstanding gun culture.

Over time, self-defense has moved from being a part of American gun culture to being its core element. Incubated in the social unrest and global uncertainty of the 1960s and 1970s, Gun Culture 2.0 was hatched in the 1980s and 1990s and has been maturing since then. This is evident in various types of data, including the growing percentage of gun owners who say they own guns for self-defense, the increasing proportion of handguns solid in the civilian market, the rise of the civilian defensive firearms training industry, the codification of castle doctrine and stand your ground laws, the liberalization of concealed carry laws, and the growing number of Americans who have permits to carry concealed weapons in public (Lott and Wang 2020; Pew Research Center 2017; Yamane 2021).

The liberalization of concealed carry laws since the 1970s has further normalized—both culturally and legally—gun carrying outside the home (Yamane 2021). A survey in 1978 asked, "Do you ever carry [your] handgun or pistol outside of the house with you for protection or not?" Twenty-nine percent of handgun owners responded "yes" (Wright, Rossi, and Daly 1983, 142–43). This has grown to 57 percent today, according to the Pew Research Center (2017). That is nearly 30 million people. Almost 20 million American adults, according to one recent count (Lott and Wang 2020), have permits to carry firearms concealed in public. And an increasing number of states (seventeen currently) allow legal firearms owners to carry concealed handguns in public without a permit (Yamane 2021).

Carlson (2015) calls this a "gun carry revolution," and she is right. And yet social scientists have been oddly silent about it (but see Anker 2019; Shapira and Simon 2018). This is perhaps because it is hard to use criminological or epidemiological perspectives to understand law-abiding gun owners engaging in a lawful action. In the best tradition of ethnography, Carlson acts as a critical observer attempting to understand this aspect of American gun culture from the inside out. As a result of her ethnographic immersion, Carlson recognizes something that is so simple that its profundity may go unrecognized. In the last paragraph of her book *Citizen-Protectors*, Carlson (2015, 178) writes: "Guns solve problems for the people who bear them." If we want to understand why 30 million Americans carry handguns outside their homes and 20 million have concealed carry permits, we need to understand that this behavior solves problems for the people who engage in it. So the question becomes, what problems are solved by carrying a gun?

The primary problems solved by carrying a gun, according to Carlson, have to do with identity. It's not so much about what carrying lethal weapons can *do* for people in any practical sense as what it *says* about them. The subtitle of Carlson's book—*The Everyday Politics of Guns in an Age of Decline*—speaks volumes here. In an age of decline, carrying a gun allows men to engage in everyday political acts that reassert their masculinity and help them to "reclaim a sense of dignity" (Carlson 2015, 24). In *Good Guys with Guns*, Stroud (2016) extends Carlson's gender analysis to understand how racialized discourses shape the contrast between "good guys" and "bad guys." In opposition to the socially privileged (middle-class, White) "good guys with guns" are socially disadvantaged (poor, Black) "bad guys" who threaten to victimize them. The third part of the gender–race–class trinity comes to the fore in Stroud's examination of the binary distinction between the self-reliance of the socially privileged and the dependence of the poor and minorities—and especially poor minorities—who are the criminal other against which they define themselves as "good guys." Choosing to get a concealed handgun license is part of a larger, class-based ethos of self-sufficiency that articulates with the ascendency of neoliberalism in the U.S.

Without arguing that Carlson or Stroud are entirely wrong, their emphases on ideological problems solved by gun carrying push practical problem-solving to the margins. But in the recent Pew Research Center survey cited earlier, 7 percent of all adult respondents said they had used a gun to defend themselves or their possessions, whether they fired the gun or not (Pew Research Center 2017). That is over 17 million adults in the U.S. Even on either side of the margin of error, that is a lot of people. Moreover, although no one yet knows exactly how many, we have good reason to believe that a significant part of the 2020 buying spree—reflecting defensive gun ownership demographics more generally (Azrael et al. 2017)—was new gun owners, women, racial and sexual minorities, and political liberals. That is, those least likely to turn to guns for identity purposes.

This suggests more effort needs to be made to understand how guns represent for people part of their solution for safely negotiating a contemporary world characterized by social uncertainty and unrest. A recent imperfect but suggestive study of firearm purchasing in 2020 inadvertently highlights this (Lyons et al. 2021). New gun owners who bought a firearm in response to COVID-19 are also more likely than gun nonowners to have stocked up on hand sanitizer (63.1 percent vs. 32.9 percent), first aid supplies (40.2 percent vs. 14.0 percent), home security products other than guns (24.6 percent vs. 1.8 percent), and pepper spray (13.4 percent vs. 1.8 percent).

Of course, this does not mean gun buying only solves practical, real-world security problems. In a May 2020 news story on the increase in gun sales in Appalachia (Keppler 2020), I said first-time buyers are often purchasing some peace of mind:

> I think the intended purpose of the purchase is physical security, and they are also attempting to buy some psychological security. . . . It's like the toilet paper. If they can't have anything else under control, they know they have that one thing under control.

Not surprisingly, new COVID-19 gun owners were also more likely to stock up on toilet paper (74.3 percent) than nongun owners (46.8 percent) during the early months of the pandemic (Lyons et al. 2021).

Similarly, I do not want to reduce the study of American gun culture to the individuals who own and use guns. I have previously offered a number of concrete steps forward for those who want to understand the new incarnation of America's historic gun culture (Yamane 2017). These include understanding how the social world of gun culture is shaped by broader social institutions including the legal system, economy, and technology. For example, the widespread practice of legally carrying a gun in public was facilitated by the movement for "shall issue" concealed carry laws (Yamane 2021). The growing practice of concealed carry that is facilitated by these laws also creates a number of new challenges for the individuals who do so, as well as for the broader social worlds (other people, spaces, places) in which they do so. These challenges are individually and collectively addressed through the developing culture of armed citizenship—both the "hardware" of material culture like guns, accessories, and other products (Yamane 2019a), as well as the "software" of ways of thinking, legal frameworks, and the development of relevant abilities.

In addition, greater attention to the wider social worlds in which gun owners participate is necessary. According to Stebbins (2001, 54), "Serious leisure participants typically become members of a vast social world, a complex mosaic of groups, events, networks, organizations, and social relationships." The same is true for participants in both recreational and self-defense gun culture. America is not just a "Gun Show Nation" (Burbick 2007), it is a nation of gun clubs, training classes, shooting events, network meetups, gun collectors, and shooters associations. These aspects of gun culture have not been adequately studied to date (but see Taylor 2009 and Kohn 2004).

Finally, I do not claim that there should be no study of crime and violence in connection with guns. But my argument here does suggest a certain approach. In the balance of this chapter, I will highlight the ways in which gun crime and violence should properly be understood in relation to American gun culture.

MISUNDERSTANDING GUN CULTURE IN RELATION TO CRIMINAL VIOLENCE

In July 2017, the Michael Bloomberg-funded, antigun violence news advocacy outlet, *The Trace*, ran a story about the work of photographer Garret O. Hansen (Sauer 2017). Hansen was introduced to American gun culture when he took a job as an assistant professor of photography at the University of Kentucky in Lexington. Once there he was surprised to find that "it was not uncommon for friends and colleagues, including those of a liberal tilt, to fire off a few rounds after work before grabbing a beer." As I did a few years earlier, Hansen found that target shooting at the range is normal for a large swath of the American population. Hansen himself tried shooting and subsequently thought to combine the shooting he had discovered (with guns) with the shooting he did professionally (with cameras). Among his series of works, which have been displayed in galleries and museums across the country, is "Silhouette." For the pieces in this collection, Hansen gathered the cardboard backings which are used to hold paper targets at gun ranges. In a darkroom, he made prints of the cardboard which he then turned into one-to-one replicas in mirrored Plexiglas. Hansen describes the experience of viewing the works when they are displayed: "As viewers approach the piece, they see their own reflections hollowed out by the countless bullets" (Hansen, n.d.).

For the final works in this series, "Memorial," Hansen uses twelve panels to depict the actual monthly gun homicides in Kentucky in 2016. As he reflects, "This work acknowledges and lays bare the heavy price of having a heavily armed civilian population" (Hansen, n.d.). So Hansen's work, and *The Trace*'s coverage of it, follows a very common narrative structure that moves from law-abiding citizens engaging in a lawful activity of having fun shooting at targets at a gun range to homicidal violence involving guns.

But this narrative from gun culture to gun violence assumes a connection that needs to be documented empirically. Exemplifying the slow progress being made in understanding guns in America, O'Connor and Lizotte (1978, 428) already problematized this narrative four decades ago in a series of questions:

[H]ow are legitimate uses of guns related to illegitimate uses of guns? . . . [H]unting, sport shooting, and gun collecting are socially ordered activities which place a strong emphasis on the safe and legitimate use of firearms. Are hunters and sport shooters involved in a socially organized activity also likely to use firearms in illegitimate ways? . . . Are there any links between legitimate, socially ordered, activities in which guns are central, and illegitimate, though probably socially ordered, activities in which guns are used?

These questions remain largely unanswered today. In fact, according to a more recent essay by Legault and Lizotte (2009, 469), "A vast majority of legal gun owners never experience the illegal use of guns firsthand." What we see, in fact, is that gun culture and criminal gun violence exist quite literally as different social worlds.

Many, including the editors of this volume (Introduction, 1-2), observe that the U.S. has the highest rate of gun violence in the developed world. A study by four authors from the Centers for Disease Control shows that the firearm homicide rate in the U.S. was 3.66 per 100,000 from 2010 to 2012 (Fowler et al. 2015). Among thirty-one high-income members of the Organization for Economic Co-operation and Development, the U.S. indeed has the highest per capita homicide rate. That is significant. But while aggregating data for the entire country helps us see some things, it blinds us from others. Most importantly as concerns exposure to homicidal violence, no one lives in "the United States," per se. We live in fifty different states. But, we do not just live in one of fifty states, we live in one of over 3,000 particular counties or county-equivalents. But, we don't just live in one of 3,000+ counties, we live in one of thousands of cities, towns, municipalities, unincorporated areas, and so on. My risk of being a victim of homicide in my home town of Winston-Salem is different from the risk in the next city over, Greensboro, or the state's capital, Raleigh. There are cities in gun rich parts of the U.S. that have extremely low homicide rates, like Henderson (Nevada) at 1.5 per 100,000, Lincoln (Nebraska) at 1.1, and Plano (Texas) at 0.4. If the entire country had Plano's homicide rate, the U.S. would rank #211 out of 218 countries in the world.

Moreover, even citywide averages can obscure the realities of relative risk of gun violence. We do not even live in particular cities, but in particular neighborhoods. *The Trace* explored the issue of relative risk in St. Louis, the U.S. city with one of the highest homicide rates in recent years. "The homicide rates in several neighborhoods in the city are so high," *The Trace* reports, that "they exceeded those in Honduras, the deadliest country in the world" (Team Trace 2017). At the same time, in other neighborhoods in St. Louis, "the risk is negligible." St. Louis is the murder capital of the U.S., but some parts are more dangerous than Honduras and some as safe as Switzerland.

The problem with averages is that no one lives in "The United States." As the CDC researchers observe, "firearm violence is not evenly distributed by geography or among the populations living in these communities.

Rather it is highly concentrated in specific "hot spot" locations and often occurs within high-risk social networks" (Fowler et al. 2015, 11). Andrew Papachristos, in my opinion the leading sociologist studying gun violence, utilizes the complex mathematical tools of network analysis to uncover patterns of gun violence in communities. Papachristos shows that gun violence, while tragic, is rarely random. Gun violence is concentrated among certain people and in certain places. In Boston, 50 percent of gun violence takes place on just 3 percent of streets. Moreover, like a blood-borne disease, gun violence travels within social networks. In Boston, 85 percent of gunshot injuries took place in a network of just 6 percent of the population (Papachristos et al. 2012). In Chicago, 41 percent of homicides take place in a network of just 4 percent of the population (Papachristos and Wildeman 2014).

Understanding the highly concentrated reality of criminal gun violence has very little to do with understanding American gun culture. With two exceptions. There are two zones of intersection between the legal culture of guns and criminal activity that involves guns. The first is when "good guys with guns" become "bad guys with guns." The second is a specific instance of the first, when legal gun owners provide guns to criminals in underground gun markets.

Although she focuses largely on the lawful use of firearms by legal gun owners, Carlson devotes a chapter of *Citizen-Protectors* to the case of Aaron, an African American father who Carlson characterizes as "a model gun carrier" (Carlson 2015, 143). Aaron entered a gas station in suburban Detroit as a "good guy with a gun" and left it as a "bad guy"—arrested for felonious assault and eventually pleading guilty to a lesser charge of brandishing for pulling his gun on an unarmed woman. Carlson argues that it was Aaron's *over*-commitment to the citizen-protector ideal promoted in Gun Culture 2.0 that led him to break the law. This problematizes the notion of a bright line distinguishing "good guys" from "bad guys." Indeed, like "talent," being a good guy with a gun or a bad guy with a gun is something we can only recognize after the fact. At the same time, Carlson (2015, 142) herself notes, "Gun carriers . . . are not more likely to commit crime than the general population. As a general rule, a gun carrier is *much* less likely to be arrested than the general population."

Clearly, more work needs to be done to understand the processes by which some legal gun owners choose to engage in criminal activities with their guns. One of those ways is when guns move from legal to illegal status through underground gun markets (Cook et al. 2007). Although the bulk of trafficking in black market guns is done by individuals who have criminal backgrounds, some legal gun owners contribute to the black market through personal gun sales outside the criminal background check system.

A CONCLUDING PERSONAL REFLECTION:
GETTING BEYOND THE PARTIAL AND PARTISAN

I am an old scholar, but relatively new to the study of guns. I got into the topic when I realized how common and how normal guns are to so many different people in the U.S.. I first noticed this in my adopted home state of North Carolina, where I moved in 2005. Riding with now wife on an interstate not far from Winston-Salem one afternoon, I looked out in a field and saw a wooden structure that seemed very out of place. I said, "Sandy, isn't that a weird spot for kids to build a fort?" She looked at me as if I were from another planet, which I sort of was, and said, "That is a deer stand." She also had to explain to me what they are used for. (For some reason, she married me anyway.) Soon enough, without looking very hard, I began to find guns all around me. Gun shows are held several times a year at the annex to the arena where Wake Forest University's basketball team plays its home games. Ground signs abound on heavily trafficked street corners advertising "concealed carry classes." Gun stores regularly buy billboard space on area highways to advertise their products and services. Talking about guns with the highly educated professionals I play tennis with widened my eyes still further. One owned several long guns that had been passed down from his grandfather. Another had two semiautomatic pistols in his basement that he used to shoot regularly. Some of the women I play tennis with own or carry firearms for self-defense. As for myself, I had never seen, held, or touched anything other than a BB gun until I was 42-years old. I did so only thanks to my wife, a North Carolina native and Coast Guard veteran who used to carry a Beretta M9 service pistol. She introduced me to her high school classmate who is a gun trainer for the North Carolina Highway Patrol. From these experiences spring the idea that guns are normal and normal people use guns.

These experiences with people outside the academy could not contrast more sharply with my experiences in the academy, especially with other sociologists. Take Jonathan Metzl, for example. Metzl is Frederick B. Rentschler II Professor of Sociology and Medicine, Health, and Society at Vanderbilt University, Director of its Center for Medicine, Health, and Society, and a leading sociologist studying guns. He was tapped by the Social Science Research Council to lead an initiative on "social science research pathways into understanding American gun violence, gun culture, and its discontents" (Metzl 2018); served as editor of a special issue of *Palgrave Communication* on "What Guns Mean: The Symbolic Lives of Firearms" (Metzl 2019a); and published a book about how the politics of racial resentment has fatal consequences for White Americans, including gun suicides (Metzl 2019b). Clearly, he is a thought leader in the field of gun studies. As is often the case, it was in the less formal setting of a professional meeting that Metzl's fundamental view was laid bare. At the annual meeting of the American Sociological Association in 2018, Metzl organized and presided over a panel on "Guns and Violence in Trump's America." In his opening statement, he reviewed various negative outcomes associated with guns then, as if grasping for words, with exasperation concluded, "Guns are bad." I tweeted from the session that he had just summarized the dominant social scientific approach to guns.

Metzl, of course, is not alone. When I tell my colleagues I am studying "gun culture," they frequently hear me saying "gun violence," since their primary association with guns is with violence. Or they will respond, "Good, more people need to be studying gun control." It falls too far outside their experience with and understanding of guns to think of them in any way other than negatively. Others who have approached gun culture as normal, like Kohn (2004) and Joslyn (2020), recount similar encounters with colleagues. And I do understand this, because for the first forty years of my life, and the first twenty years of my academic career, I shared this approach to guns. I have now come to see, however, that it is a profound *mis*understanding to approach the academic study of guns in such a partial and partisan way.

No individual scholar is responsible for covering the entirety of any field of study. But, we do have a problem when the collective effort of scholars working on a particular topic focuses so relentlessly on one part of the entire field. This is the case with the study of guns and gun culture in the human sciences broadly understood. In addition to being partial, the study of guns and gun culture is also too frequently partisan. Emphasizing deviance and criminal violence as inherent in gun culture or following from it necessarily leads to policy solutions focused on gun control. So much so that one wonders the extent to which the interest in gun control drives these approaches, rather than vice versa.

My approach to studying gun culture, which I encourage others to follow, is taken from the late Weberian sociologist Reinhard Bendix. The approach does not advocate a nonexistent Archimedean standpoint of objectivity. Rather, as Bendix (1984, 28) summarizes this position, "Social research is characterized by an interplay between identification and detachment, of subjectivity and objectivity."

My identification with guns came not until my 43rd year of life, when a combination of circumstances led me to learn to shoot a handgun under the guidance of my future wife and a trainer for the NC Highway Patrol. From there I had the opportunity to do more fun shooting: plinking with .22 handguns, trap and sporting clays with shotguns, and destroying plastic bottles with a .50-caliber rifle. I also came to identify with armed self-defense after a close encounter with a drug addict and criminal in the parking lot of my apartment complex. Thus, even before I began studying Gun Culture 2.0, I had already formulated certain answers to questions such as "What are guns for?" and "Why do people need X/Y/Z gun?" and "Why carry a gun?" I necessarily approach empirical questions about guns with these prescientific intuitions and experiences in mind. This "value-relevance" shapes my choice of phenomena to study.

Although I am personally connected with this subject matter—as I was with my previous four books on Catholicism, by the way—my scholarship is not partisan. I am neither progun nor antigun. I am protruth. In seeking to understand Gun Culture 2.0, I turn not to speculation or advocacy but to my disciplinary training as a professional sociologist which stresses the aspiration to detachment and objectivity in the analysis of empirical data. This was best summarized for me by Reinhard Bendix himself, who I had the good fortune to meet at UC-Berkeley when I was an undergraduate and he a distinguished faculty member. Not long before his death in 1991, Bendix referred me to a quote from the philosopher Baruch Spinoza's *Tractatus Politicus* (i, 4), which I will always remember as embodying the social scientific ideal to which I still aspire and which I commend to others studying American gun culture:

> *I have sedulously endeavored not to laugh at human actions, not to lament them, nor to detest them, but to understand them.*

REFERENCES

Anker, Elizabeth. 2019. "Mobile Sovereigns: Agency Panic and the Feeling of Gun Ownership." Pp. 21–42 in *The Lives of Guns*, edited by J. Obert, A. Poe, and A. Sarat. New York: Oxford University Press.

Azrael, Deborah, Lisa Hepburn, David Hemenway, and Matthew Miller. 2017. "The Stock and Flow of U.S. Firearms: Results from the 2015 National Firearms Survey." *RSF: The Russell Sage Foundation Journal of the Social Sciences* 3(5): 38–57.

Bendix, Reinhard. 1984. *Force, Fate, and Freedom: On Historical Sociology.* Berkeley: University of California Press.

Burbick, Joan. 2007. *Gun Show Nation: Gun Culture and American Democracy.* New York: New Press.

Carlson, Jennifer. 2015. *Citizen-Protectors: The Everyday Politics of Guns in an Age of Decline.* New York: Oxford University Press.

Carlson, Jennifer, Kristin Goss, and Harel Shapira. 2019. *Gun Studies: Interdisciplinary Approaches to Politics, Policy, and Practice.* New York: Routledge.

Cook, Philip J., Jens Ludwig, Sudhir Venkatesh, and Anthony A. Braga. 2007. "Underground Gun Markets." *The Economic Journal* 117(524): F588–F618.

Cramer, Clayton. 2009. *Armed America.*

DeBrabander, Firmin. 2015. *Do Guns Make Us Free?: Democracy and the Armed Society.* New Haven, CT; London: Yale University Press.

DeBrabander, Firmin. 2021. "The Gun-Rights Movement Fed America's Insurrectionist Fever Dreams." *The Atlantic.* https://www.theatlantic.com/ideas/a rchive/2021/01/nra-americas-insurrectionist-fever-dreams/617627/ on 26 January 2021.

Depetris-Chauvin, Emilio. 2015. "Fear of Obama: An Empirical Study of the Demand for Guns and the U.S. 2008 Presidential Election." *Journal of Public Economics* 130: 66–79.

Fowler, Katherine A., Linda L. Dahlberg, Tadesse Haileyesus, and Joseph L. Annest. 2015. "Firearm Injuries in the United States." *Preventive Medicine* 79 (October): 5–14.

French, David. 2018. "Assault Weapons Preserve the Purpose of the Second Amendment." *National Review* (February 21). https://www.nationalreview.com /2018/02/assault-weapons-preserve-the-purpose-of-the-second-amendment/ on 26 January 2021.

Hansen, Garret O. n.d. "HAIL Statement." https://www.garrettohansen.com/hail/stat ement on 27 January 2021.

Hofstadter, Richard. 1970. "America as a Gun Culture." *American Heritage* 21: 6 (October 1970). http://www.americanheritage.com/content/america-gun-culture on 23 March 2015.

Jackson, Sam. 2020. *Oath Keepers: Patriotism and the Edge of Violence in a Right-Wing Antigovernment Group.* New York: Columbia University Press.

Joslyn, Mark R. 2020. *The Gun Gap: The Influence of Gun Ownership on Political Behavior and Attitudes.* New York: Oxford University Press.

Kelley, Margaret, and Christopher Ellison. 2021. "Who Might Buy a Gun? Results from the Guns in American Life Survey." *Sociological Inquiry.*

Keppler, Nick. "Gun Sales Are Up Across Appalachia. Here's Why" (May 11). *YES! Magazine.* https://www.yesmagazine.org/democracy/2020/05/11/coronavirus-gun-sales-appalachia on 26 January 2021.

Kohn, Abigail A. 2004. *Shooters: Myths and Realities of America's Gun Cultures.* New York: Oxford University Press.

Kurzman, Charles. 2019. *The Missing Martyrs: Why Are There So Few Muslim Terrorists?*, 2nd edition. New York: Oxford University Press.

Legault, Richard L., and Alan J. Lizotte. 2009. "Caught in a Crossfire: Legal and Illegal Gun Ownership in America." In *Handbook on Crime and Deviance*, edited by Marvin D. Krohn, Alan J. Lizotte, and Gina Penly Hall, 469–491. New York: Springer.

Levine, Phillip B., and Robin McKnight. 2020. "Three Million More Guns: The Spring 2020 Spike in Firearm Sales." *Brookings* (July 13). https://www.brookings .edu/blog/up-front/2020/07/13/three-million-more-guns-the-spring-2020-spike-in-firearm-sales/ on 26 January 2021.

Lott, John R., and Rujun Wang. 2020. *Concealed Carry Permit Holders Across the United States: 2020. SSRN Scholarly Paper. ID 3703977.* Rochester, NY: Social Science Research Network.

Lyons, Vivian H., Miriam J. Haviland, Deborah Azrael, Avanti Adhia, M. Alex
   Bellenger, Alice Ellyson, Ali Rowhani-Rahbar, and Frederick P. Rivara. 2021.
   "Firearm Purchasing and Storage during the COVID-19 Pandemic." *Injury
   Prevention* 27(1): 87–92.
Metzl, Jonathan. 2018. "Social Science and the Future of Gun Research." *Items:
   Insights from the Social Sciences* (October 2). https://items.ssrc.org/understandin
   g-gun-violence/social-science-and-the-future-of-gun-research/ on 27 January
   2021.
Metzl, Jonathan M. 2019a. "What Guns Mean: The Symbolic Lives of Firearms."
   Palgrave Communications 5(1): 1–5.
Metzl, Jonathan M. 2019b. *Dying of Whiteness: How the Politics of Racial Resentment
   Is Killing America's Heartland.* New York: Basic Books.
National Shooting Sports Foundation. 2021. "Taking Stock of a Record-Setting 2020
   Firearm Year." (January 7). https://www.nssf.org/taking-stock-of-record-setting
   -2020-firearm-year/ on 26 January 2021.
Obert, Jonathan, Andrew Poe, and Austin Sarat. 2019. *The Lives of Guns.* New York:
   Oxford University Press.
O'Connor, James F., and Alan Lizotte. 1978: "The 'Southern Subculture of Violence'
   Thesis and Patterns of Gun Ownership." *Social Problems* 25(4) (April): 420–429.
Papachristos, Andrew V., Anthony A. Braga, and David M. Hureau. 2012. "Social
   Networks and the Risk of Gunshot Injury." *Journal of Urban Health* 89(6)
   (December): 992–1003.
Papachristos, Andrew V., and Christopher Wildeman. 2014. "Network Exposure and
   Homicide Victimization in an African American Community." *American Journal
   of Public Health* 104(1) (January): 143–150.
Pew Research Center. 2017. "America's Complex Relationship with Guns." http://
   www.pewsocialtrends.org/2017/06/22/ americas-complex-relationship-with-guns/
   on 30 August 2017.
Sauer, Patrick. 2017. "Bullets Travel at 1,700 Miles Per Hour. These Stunning Images
   Capture What Happens After Impact." *The Trace* (July 28). https://www.thetrace
   .org/2017/07/hail-garret-hansen-guns-fine-arts/.
Shapira, Harel, and Samantha J. Simon. 2018. "Learning to Need a Gun." *Qualitative
   Sociology* 41(1): 1–20.
Stebbins, R. A. 2001. "Serious Leisure." *Society* 28: 53–57.
Steidley, Trent. 2020a. "How Unprecedented Was the Gun Buying Spree of March
   2020" (April 19). https://guncurious.wordpress.com/2020/04/19/how-unprecedente
   d-was-the-gun-buying-spree-of-march-2020-by-trent-steidley/ on 26 January 2021.
Steidley, Trent. 2020b. "Are All Gun Sales Data the Same?" (December 20). https
   ://socsteidley.com/2020/12/20/are-all-gun-sales-data-are-the-same/ on 26 January
   2021.
Steidley, Trent. 2021. "Quick Compare: 2020 vs 2019 NICS Numbers." (January
   14). https://socsteidley.com/2021/01/14/quick-compare-2020-vs-2019-nics-num
   bers/ on 26 January 2021.
Stroud, Angela. 2016. *Good Guys with Guns: The Appeal and Consequences of
   Concealed Carry.* Chapel Hill, NC: University of North Carolina Press.

Taylor, Jimmy D. 2009. *American Gun Culture: Collectors, Shows, and the Story of the Gun.* El Paso, TX: LFB Scholarly Publishing.

Team Trace. 2017. "15 Census Tracts, 97 Fatal Shootings, and the Two Different Sides to American Gun Violence." https://www.thetrace.org/2017/03/gun-violence -deadliest-census-tracts/ on 30 August 2017.

United States Department of Justice. n.d. "Investigations Regarding Violence at the Capitol." https://www.justice.gov/opa/investigations-regarding-violence-capitol on 26 January 2021.

Warner, Tara D. 2020. "Fear, Anxiety, and Expectation: Gender Differences in Openness to Future Gun Ownership." *Violence and Gender* 7(1): 11–18.

Wright, James D. 1995. "Ten Essential Observations on Guns in America." *Society* 32 (April): 63–68.

Wright, James D., and Linda L. Marston. 1975: "The Ownership of the Means of Destruction: Weapons in the United States." *Social Problems* 23(1) (October): 93–107.

Wright, James D., Peter H. Rossi, and Kathleen Daly. 1983. *Under the Gun: Weapons, Crime, and Violence in America.* New Brunswick, NJ: Aldine Transaction.

Yamane, David. 2017. "The Sociology of U.S. Gun Culture." *Sociology Compass* 11(7). DOI: 10.1111/soc4.12497.

Yamane, David. 2019a. "'The First Rule of Gunfighting Is Have a Gun': Technologies of Concealed Carry in Gun Culture 2.0." Pp. 167–93 in *The Lives of Guns*, edited by J. Obert, A. Poe, and A. Sarat. New York: Oxford University Press.

Yamane, David. 2019b. "Who Are The Gun Curious?" https://guncurious.wordpress .com/2019/02/07/who-are-the-gun-curious/ on 26 January 2021.

Yamane, David. 2021. *Concealed Carry Revolution: Expanding the Right to Bear Arms in America.* Berkeley, CA: AnewPress.

Yamane, David, Jesse DeDeyne, and Alonso Octavio Aravena Méndez. 2020. "Who Are the Liberal Gun Owners?" *Sociological Inquiry.* Online, December 27.

Yamane, David, Paul Yamane, and Sebastian L. Ivory. 2020. "Targeted Advertising: Documenting the Emergence of Gun Culture 2.0 in Guns Magazine, 1955–2019." *Palgrave Communications* 6(1): 1–9.

Yamane, David, Sebastian L. Ivory, and Paul Yamane. 2019. "The Rise of Self-Defense in Gun Advertising: The American Rifleman, 1918–2017." Pp. 9–27 in *Gun Studies: Interdisciplinary Approaches to Politics, Policy, and Practice*, edited by Jennifer Carlson, Kristin Goss, and Harel Shapira. New York: Routledge.

Index

About the Contributors

Garrison Allen Crews is a research associate at The Veritas Group Consulting Firm in Port Isabel, Texas. In this role, he supervises and contributes to the development of primary research databases. Prior to this position, he was a research and teaching assistant in the Political Science Department at Marshall University, West Virginia. His presentations and publications deal with extreme cases of school violence, issues in higher education, the effect of media framing and misrepresentation on political agenda setting, gun violence in the U.S., and the use of fictional metaphor in understanding social and institutional values and mechanisms. His current research interests involve the examination of modern surveillance techniques and pervasiveness on the incidence and likelihood of deviant behavior.

Gordon Arthur Crews is chair and Keith A. Ferguson endowed professor in criminal justice at the University of Texas Rio Grande Valley. He is also president of the Veritas Group Consulting firm in Port Isabel, Texas. In addition to over thirty years of postsecondary education experience, Dr Crews has conducted POST certified law enforcement training in South Carolina, Rhode Island, Georgia, Ohio, and Alabama in the areas of proper police practice. He has also worked with the Turkish National Police and Ghana National Police on community policing initiatives. His publications include refereed journal articles and book chapters dealing with juvenile and school violence, Occult/Satanic involvement and youth, and various law enforcement and correctional issues.

Lisa Fisher (Ph.D., University of Cincinnati) is consulting director at a Washington, DC, IT and management consulting firm. Dr Fisher has more than twenty years of experience as an applied social psychological researcher, analyst, strategist, facilitator, writer, and editor in the fields of management consulting and higher education. She also has extensive experience designing, facilitating, and evaluating adult learning in a variety of contexts. She has authored numerous articles, chapters in edited volumes, and one book, all of which converge on applied social psychology in American society.

Carolyn Gentle-Genitty is the assistant vice president for University Academic Policy and the director of the University Transfer Office at Indiana University. She received her Ph.D. from Indiana University and her bachelor's and master's degree from Spalding University in Louisville KY. She brings extensive leadership and programmatic experience from over 20+ years in the field of youth development locally and internationally serving as executive director of a YMCA and chair of numerous volunteer, nonprofit, and governmental organizations. Gentle-Genitty also served as a youth consultant for Belize and UNICEF. She taught at the University of Belize for five years prior to IU. Her areas of interests within the academic setting include teaching and teaching effectiveness, theory application, online learning, millennial, and student engagement. In the realm of research, she focuses on exploring the school-to-prison pipeline trajectory, school competence, truancy, and social bonding. In the community, she explores and offers service in prison/jail/community reentry, cognitive tools for reentry, case management, adjunct/associate faculty mentoring, and the cradle to career initiative by the Talent Alliance. Dr Gentle-Genitty has engaged extensively locally, nationally, and internationally in assessment of youth-on-youth violence and school social bonding. She has done this for the last ten years using her Perception of School Social Bonding instrument and other assessment measurements.

Craig Hovey (Ph.D., University of Cambridge) is professor of religion at Ashland University in Ashland, Ohio. He is the author or editor of numerous books including coeditor of the *Cambridge Companion to Christian Political Theology* (Cambridge University Press, 2015) and *Sports and Violence: History, Theory, and Practice* (Cambridge Scholars, 2017).

Jangmin Kim is an assistant professor in the School of Social Work at Texas State University. He earned a Ph.D. in social work from Indiana University, IN. His research interests are broadly in macropractice with organizations and communities, with a specific emphasis on vulnerable children and youth. More specifically, contemporary lines of his research have worked in three distinctive, but not mutually exclusive areas: (1) collaborative governance and cross-system collaboration; (2) child welfare administration and service delivery, and (3) youth development and engagement in schools and communities. He has actively engaged in research projects that explore youth violence, school bonding, and school–community partnerships.

Binod Kumar is an independent consultant pursuing research and philanthropy in the areas of societal issues, violence, and nonviolence. His research interests are related to philosophy, history, and practice of nonviolence; specifically, as they emerged from the Indian civilization and their contemporary interpretation. After retirement from a full time position at the University of Dayton Research Institute in 2014, he joined and served the Human Rights Center of the University of Dayton till 2019. Dr Kumar was recipient of M.S. and Ph.D. in ceramic science and engineering from the Pennsylvania State University.

Corinne C. Renguette is an associate professor and the program director of technical communication in the Purdue School of Engineering and Technology at IUPUI. Dr Renguette designs and teaches face-to-face, hybrid, and online courses and training programs in technical communication and other related areas. She is also a co-coordinator for the Diversity Equity & Inclusion Track of the Assessment Institute. Her industry background supports her practical research approaches that focus on UX, inclusion across the curriculum in STEM education, and the assessment of educational materials, especially those that use innovative pedagogies and technologies, in both academic and workplace environments.

Mark Ryan is lecturer in Christian ethics at the University of Dayton. He teaches ethics to students at the University's School of Business Administration and theological ethics to students in the Masters of Theological Studies. He is author of *The Politics of Practical Reason: Why Theological Ethics Must Change Your Life* (Cascade Books, 2011) and a member of the Ekklesia Project.

Riley Satterwhite graduated from Wake Forest University in 2020 and is a J.D. Candidate at The George Washington University Law School. This chapter builds on her Honors Thesis in sociology.

Matt Stolick is professor of philosophy at The University of Findlay (Ohio), where he has taught for twenty years. He earned his B.A. from Westminster College (PA), M.A. and Ph.D. from University of Tennessee-Knoxville (1998). His specialization is applied ethics, health care ethics, sports ethics, and other areas of professional ethics. He is a regular contributor of the Ethics Perspective for the American Journal of Hospice and Palliative Medicine, regular member of the Association for Practical and Professional Ethics, and originated, organizes, and hosts the Annual Ohio Regional High School Ethics Bowl, entering its sixth year. He has published one book: *Otherwise Law-Abiding Citizens: A Scientific and Moral Assessment of Cannabis Use* (Lexington Books, 2009).

Jim D. Taylor (Ph.D., The Ohio State University) has been a professor of sociology and criminology for over twenty years. Dr Taylor is author of two editions of *American Gun Culture: Collectors, Shows and the Story of the Gun*, co-author of *Deviant Behavior* (Pearson), and author of other books and articles on social problems, self-injury, and teaching graduate statistics. Dr Taylor also works with at-risk dropout prevention and incarcerated student programs. He has three wonderful children and dabbles in songwriting as a hobby.

David Yamane is a professor of sociology at Wake Forest University in Winston-Salem, North Carolina. For the first twenty years of his academic career, he specialized in the sociology of religion, a field in which he authored, co-authored or edited six books and two major scholarly journals. In a departure from his previous work, Yamane became a student of guns in 2011. He is particularly interested in the new self-defense-oriented core of American gun culture that Michael Bane calls "Gun Culture 2.0." Yamane blogs at gunculture2point0.com and guncurious.com.

Paul Yamane graduated from Wake Forest University in 2016 with a degree in finance and dabbles in data analysis as a sidelight to his work in real estate investing.

www.ingramcontent.com/pod-product-compliance
Lightning Source LLC
Chambersburg PA
CBHW050651280326
41932CB00015B/2859